The Social Worker's Guide to the Social Sciences

The Key Concepts

The Social Worker's Guide to the Social Sciences

The Key Concepts

John Pierson and Martin Thomas

LEARNING
RESOURCES
CENTRE
HAVERING
COLLEGE

Mc Graw Hill

Open University Press

Open University Press
McGraw-Hill Education
McGraw-Hill House
Shoppenhangers Road
Maidenhead
Berkshire
England
SL6 2QL

email: enquiries@openup.co.uk
world wide web: www.openup.co.uk

and Two Penn Plaza, New York, NY 10121-2289, USA

First published 2013

A catalogue record of this book is available from the British Library

ISBN-13: 978-0-335-24571-0
ISBN-10: 0-335-24571-4
eISBN: 978-0-335-24572-7

Library of Congress Cataloging-in-Publication Data
CIP data applied for

Typeset by Aptara, Inc.
Printed and bound by CPI Group (UK) Ltd, Croydon, CR0 4YY

Fictitious names of companies, products, people, characters and/or data that may
be used herein (in case studies or in examples) are not intended to represent any
real individual, company, product or event.

The *McGraw-Hill* Companies

Dedication

We would like to dedicate this volume to our grandchildren.
For Martin: Amarachika, Georgia, and Benjamin
For John: Silas, Marguerite and Theodore

Praise for This Book

"This should be one of the first books you put in your bag in the morning. It explains, in clear language, the most important social science concepts, ideas and theories which social workers use in their practice. Students will find this an invaluable aid to understanding. Concise yet thorough, with full and accessible explanations, it is set out in a way that readily demonstrates the link between social science and social work. An exceptional, user friendly guide which you will use and re-use as a 'must have' reference text."
Martin Sheedy, Senior Lecturer and Programme Leader for the BA (Hons) Social Work at Liverpool John Moores University

"Keeping the 'social' alive in social work is both important and necessary, and this book aims to do just that. It provides students with an accessible and easy-to-use account of key ideas and concepts which shape the lives of social work users and those who work with them. It is set to be widely used and much appreciated by teachers and students alike."
Mark Drakeford, Professor of Social Policy and Applied Social Sciences at Cardiff University, and chair of the National Assembly for Wales' Health and Social Care Committee.

Acknowledgements

We wish to express our gratitude to David Jary, former dean of social sciences at Staffordshire University and esteemed colleague and friend, whose work and vision of higher education has always been an inspiration to us.

John Pierson would like to thank Claire Stockdale, Colleen Cloete and Linda Houlton of the Chester and Cheshire West Library based at the Bishop Heber High School for all their work in tracking down – and keeping track of – the many volumes I requested of them over the last year during the writing of this book. He would also like to thank Miriam Sharp Pierson for her preparation of the figures used in the volume.

Introduction

For over a century the social sciences have been central to social work thinking and practice because they address the big questions – the relationship between society and the individual, why and how society changes, why individuals behave as they do. Social work and the social sciences developed together at roughly the same point in the late nineteenth century. The founding of the London School of Economics in 1895, 'for the betterment of society', can be taken as the pivotal moment: it was the first university in Britain to teach sociology and the first to offer social work training when it linked up with the Charity Organization Society, one of the founders of casework, in the late 1890s.

From that point on the social sciences have provided the core of the curriculum in social work education. Yet today students undertaking qualifying programmes in social work and social care do not currently have access to a reference book that enables them to make sense of the terms, concepts, theories and discourses central to social sciences. Neither do they have to hand a volume that is a ready reference for research methods and epistemological debates specifically devised to address their concerns, priorities, needs and interests in relation to the social sciences.

This book addresses that deficit. It is essentially a study aid and primer providing an understanding of the social sciences for social workers, a guide through a diverse and complex ensemble of disciplines. Throughout, we have selected those concepts in social sciences that are most relevant to social work. Some of the subject matter we cover in our entries are:

- adult and child behaviour;
- bureaucracy and organization;
- 'place', community and neighbourhood;
- 'race', outsiders and ghettos;

- social exclusion, stigma and oppression;
- gender and sexual preference;
- poverty and inequality;
- the nature of risk;
- markets and capitalism;
- co-operation, partnership and collective action;
- statistical analysis and research methods.

Our book is a companion to the *Dictionary of Social Work*. The entries in the *Dictionary* were developed from the everyday concerns and working terminology of the social worker, offering orientation *within* the social work terminological universe, so to speak. This volume offers social work students and practitioners a briefing on the key concepts developed by social scientists *outside* social work but which students and practitioners not only draw on for their everyday work but use in their theories and conceptualization of social problems. The volume in effect should be regarded as an encyclopedia of the social sciences.

The key concepts are arranged alphabetically. The objective of each is to explain the concept in everyday language and point out its implications for social work. Each begins with an initial definition and then moves to a fuller explanation with references and suggestions for further reading where appropriate. The longer concepts in particular are written against a backdrop of what social workers do and the contexts of problems, methods and issues they encounter in their practice. Where we use terminology developed within the social sciences that may be unfamiliar to social workers, we have taken care to explain what those terms mean in everyday language.

Many entries are part of larger, ongoing debates, and are continued in related entries. The links to these other entries are identified in bold in the text. By following the links across the volume the reader can explore the major themes and questions that dominate both social work and the social sciences. Is human nature basically self-interested or willing to act for the well-being of others? Are we rational beings? Are people poor because of their personal habits or because of the social and economic conditions in which they live? Does society function as a system? What is the nature of co-operation and collective action? How much 'science' is in social science? These and many others are the kinds of 'big' question that this volume addresses. As the reader will discover, the book provides a range of explanations and presents different sides to specific debates, drawing on examples and approaches that we have developed over years of teaching. Ultimately, though, it is up to the readers to work through these and reach their own conclusions.

Martin Thomas
John Pierson

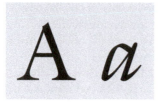

acculturation processes by which two cultural groups come together leading to the acquisition of new cultural forms and patterns by one or perhaps both groups. This can be an entirely comprehensive process where one group is effectively absorbed by another or it can operate at a very superficial level with just minor changes or adjustments in any group.

The process of acculturation can also operate with little physical contact between groups as in the influence of the US on the development of the English language internationally through major exposure of young people to American media. Acculturation can be a profound experience that poses difficulties for families of migrants as the children of migrants attend schools, adjusting to the new cultural context very quickly, whereas their parents who are, perhaps, refugees with poor English-language skills, are finding it difficult to secure work and participate in British institutions. This will pose very particular problems for women refugees who have migrated from very patriarchal societies and their place, their social locus, is deemed 'to be in the home'. (See also **assimilation, integration, multiculturalism, pluralism** and **socialization.**)

adaptation see **functionalism**

adolescence the period when a young person is growing into sexual maturity (puberty) but has not yet reached social maturity or emotional readiness for the responsibilities associated with adulthood as defined by society at large. The term was first used in 1904 by Stanley Hall in the US to denote what he at that time considered to be a new life stage. The idea of a period of life between childhood and adulthood seemed to fit the circumstances of young people who, as the economic base of the country was shifting from agriculture toward industry, were less able to move directly from childhood into employment than in the past. The spread of public education and other shifts in culture and society further worked together to define adolescence as a meaningful life period distinct from both childhood and adulthood. While characteristics of youth behaviour had been observed in the past – not least delinquency – adolescence was regarded now as a productive stage in its own right: a time when young people receive greater schooling, explore options and forge a sense of self.

For much of the twentieth century adolescence remained a relatively brief period essentially embracing the teenage years with all the hallmarks of adulthood in place by the early twenties. By their late teens only a very small fraction of young people remained in education and by their early twenties many had also left their family home, married, found work and set up home for themselves. The average age of marriage was 22 in 1958; in the US half of all women were married by the age of 20 with children arriving very shortly after that.

By contrast, the span of adolescence now has widened considerably and the social timetables for its beginning and end are more protracted and uncertain. It begins earlier, with the earlier onset of puberty, together with the increasing importance of peer relationships, access to adult media and new awareness about age-appropriate autonomy and inclusion in decision-making.

Its end is also extended. Entry into adulthood has become more ambiguous, occurring in gradual, complex and less uniform ways. When once gaining a foothold in the economy, acquiring skills or education, finding a partner and forming a family unit was a transition undertaken within a few short years, one both culturally scripted and structured by economic and social resources, this process has been dispersed over a greater number of years, often into the mid or late twenties. As a result young people are often left to make difficult choices with unclear consequences, a process that has been particularly hard on young people from lower income families. Changes in the economy place a premium on 'people skills' such as working effectively in teams and the manipulation of knowledge. This has been accompanied by the drying up of manufacturing careers that previously had offered secure employment and a reasonable wage for semi-skilled workers.

Changes in marriage and family patterns have also made the transition to adulthood more difficult: forming first households, finding sexual partners, delaying marriage and children (the average age of marriage now is 29) has brought greater freedom from familial obligations into the late twenties. Young adults now forming their first households are more likely to establish non-family situations, as single-person households or group living. There is also a well-documented trend of people in their mid- or late twenties returning to live with their parents. Such trends create ambiguity and uncertainty as to how to achieve the stability and income associated with adulthood.

Within this broad trend, however, researchers have noted a polarization in the transition to adulthood between those with working-class origins who leave school at the minimum age and become parents in their teens, behaviour that has become more problematic in the eyes of policy makers, and more stigmatized, and those from the middle classes who attend higher education and defer setting up a family and entry into the labour market for many years.

Sociologists and anthropologists have questioned the usefulness of the concept of adolescence by pointing to cultures outside the developed world where the transition to adulthood remains abrupt, characterized by specific rites of passage and without the problems associated with it in the West. There are those who argue that even in the developed countries the stresses of adolescence are overblown and that its association with social difficulties is symptomatic more of the way adults perceive young people than any conclusive research findings.

If negotiating the transition to adulthood that marks adolescence has become lengthier and more confused, the core of a more bio-logically determined definition of adolescence – the teenage years – remains a time of vulnerability and emotional turbulence. Key issues include peer pressure, adult expectations and stereotyping, emerging sexuality, the search for certainties and ideologies with which they can identify, the need to have a sphere of their own separate from school and family. Two factors – far higher rates of family breakdown than in the past and the power of the **social network** – have widened the generation gap and created social and cultural milieux in which teens are viewed with suspicion and perplexity. Perhaps of most concern are the surveys that report high levels of unhappiness among young people, notably the Unicef report in 2007 which placed Britain at the bottom of 21 affluent countries in terms of children's and young people's feelings of happiness and well-being.

Settersten, R., Furstenberg, F. and Rumbaut, R. (2005) *On the Frontier of Adulthood.* Chicago, IL: University of Chicago Press.

UNICEF (2007) *Child Poverty in Perspective: An Overview of Child Well-being in Rich Countries.* Florence: Innocenti Research Centre.

affirmative action see **positive action**

ageing and **ageism** ageing refers to the social constructions and meanings attributed to biological and chronological developments of human beings throughout their **life course**. The study of the social and psychological significance of age in society has focused upon a number of distinct issues including specific 'stages' of the life course such as childhood, **adolescence**, family life (from an adult perspective) and old age. In addition, social scientists have been particularly interested in **rites of passage** such as transitions from youth to adulthood (especially if the transition means leaving home and living independently) and issues about withdrawal from employment and retirement.

It seems clear that feelings and attitudes about children and people across the full age range are to some extent a reflection of their economic position, as either economically independent (an adult in work, earning a reasonable salary/wage) or economically dependent or vulnerable (a child or young person still in education or training, a person with significant disabilities or in poor health unable to work or an older person with a marginal income). However, such generalities are often contradicted by social circumstances and context depending upon many factors including wealth, social class, support networks and general levels of well-being. Ageism in general amounts to unjustified prejudicial and discriminatory behaviour in relation to any age group; although most attention in social research and policy development has focused upon older people.

(1) *Elders* – ageism in relation to elders is primarily about discriminatory behaviour towards older people underpinned by attitudes and beliefs that growing old is accompanied by loss of competence as well as intellectual and physical deterioration. In relation to older women, ageist attitudes are often combined with sexist prejudices figuring in phrases such as 'old hag' or 'old dear'. Caricatures of old women, interestingly, figure prominently in children's stories and folk tales such as *Snow White* and *Hansel and Gretel*. Ageing is thus frequently associated in the minds of many young people with the inevitability of decline and death, issues that younger people seek to distance themselves from by establishing another kind of 'lesser humanity' that is older people. Substantial differences exist in the attitudes to older people from one society to another, some clearly venerating and valuing them while others perceive them as economically unproductive and thus as a burden. One notable trend in the UK currently is the active involvement of elders in caring for grandchildren while their offspring work; a trend that clearly increases the functional usefulness of elders in helping extended families manage to maximize income generation. Anti-discriminatory practice includes countering ageist attitudes. Ageism is now included as a form of discrimination recognized by the Equality and Human Rights Commission in England and Wales, the Scottish Commission for Human Rights and the Equality Commission in Northern Ireland.

(2) *Children and young people* – the age at which it is legal for young people to undertake some adult roles such as leave school, work (both part time and full time), have consensual sex, vote, marry

and join the army (and be involved in combat) has varied widely within societies over time and between societies. Currently, it is legal for a 12-year-old girl to have sex in Columbia (14 for a boy) and 21 for both young women and young men to have sex in the Cameroons. It is currently legal for both genders to have sex in the UK at age 16 (both heterosexual and homosexual relations) and, in practice, for lower ages to be tolerated by social workers and the police if they are convinced that no one was coerced or exploited and that the age differential between the parties was not substantial. Voting age in the UK has been reduced from 21 to 18 in recent decades and there is a movement to give all 16-year-olds the vote too. Marriage with parental consent is legal at 16 for either gender in England and Wales and without parental consent in Scotland. This variation in conceptions of adulthood emphasizes different notions of 'age expectations' and thus the possibility of young people being regarded as behaving in an age-appropriate way or of straying from social expectations.

A very particular issue is that of how societies determine the age of criminal responsibility – the age at which it becomes possible to prosecute an offender in the criminal courts. In the UK, the age of criminal responsibility is set at 10 in England and Wales and 8 in Scotland; both figures are lower than in many European countries, prompting periodic debates mostly between those who advocate raising it and those who argue for retaining it as it is.

(3) *Adults* – ageist practices have long thought to have been evident in the world of employment with prescriptions about the number of years of relevant experience that have habitually been required for particular jobs or posts. Equal opportunities policies increasingly frame their job descriptions and person specifications in terms of the knowledge and skills required rather than the number of years of experience required because the latter does not necessarily imply the former. In essence, it has been argued that older men have been advantaged because they have been in a position to occupy senior posts to the detriment of both women and younger men who could well be able to undertake more senior jobs competently.

The notion of age appropriateness usually relates to ideas about how people with learning disabilities should dress, behave, take part in activities and be treated in ways suitable to their chronological age. This notion is often associated with normalization. In this context, the principle of age appropriateness suggests, for example, that adults with a learning disability should not play with children's toys, even if the toys might be apparently suited to their developmental level. The rationale for this approach is that such behaviour is at odds with social norms, is undignified and is unlikely to gain respect from other people. Concerns about age appropriateness also focus on the tendency for non-disabled people to treat adults with learning disabilities as if they were children. Similar concerns have been raised about this 'infantilization' of older people in some service settings and the importance of trying to sustain memory through interventions such as life story work and reminiscence therapy. Age appropriateness has also influenced the choice of toys and educational materials in relation to the play of both very young children and children of school age. Social workers have to make judgements in many contexts about age-related behaviour and skills in relation to, for example, whether a child is developmentally within any kind of 'normal range', or whether in relation to mental health problems regression to an earlier behavioural stage is indicative of problems. In relation to elders and people with a learning disability, avoiding any kind of infantilism is key to effective and anti-oppressive practice.

Bytheway, B. (1994) *Ageism: Rethinking Ageing*. Maidenhead: Open University Press.

Rogalski, H. (2010) *At What Age Can I?* Colchester: The Children's Legal Centre, University of Essex.

agency the power of individuals to act independently of social structures. If sociologists often have recourse to the phrase 'structural constraints' – meaning that social and economic factors are so dominant that they limit what individuals can do to effect change – the concept of agency embodies the power of individuals to move beyond those constraints to bring about change, whether in their own lives or in the social circumstances in which they find themselves. The term is intended to convey the volitional, purposive nature of human activity and its potential for individuals to act outside the powerful social and economic forces, such as discrimination or unemployment, that they face. It places emphasis on the human intention with the individual at the centre of analysis of social action, which, in turn, raises issues of moral choice and political action.

The conceptual dichotomy between the individual as actor versus the power of 'structure' over the individual is an important and continuing thread both within social science and in social work ethics, presented as a polarization between 'structure' and 'agency'. Among sociologists, Anthony Giddens has brought the two together, arguing that 'structure' must be seen as enabling as well as constraining. (See also **social structure**.)

aggression a hostile attitude generally underpinned by either fear
or anger designed to control, intimidate, harm and possibly injure.
Aggressive behaviour can be either instrumental or expressive or possibly both. Any predisposition to harm or physically injure would be
going beyond aggression into *violence*.

Some philosophers have been interested in what they consider to
be the essential aggressive characteristics of all human beings. The
English philosopher Hobbes spoke of the potential for life to be
'nasty, brutish and short' unless human aggression were somehow
curtailed in some reliable, secure and measured way. Hobbes felt
that each member of society needed to give up some of his 'personal
freedom' (especially the freedom to be aggressive and violent to
others for one's own selfish reasons) and in return the state would
guarantee certain *rights*. This is the important idea of a *social contract*
between individuals and the state that has been so influential historically in political thinking and in contemporary debates about what
rights and services should be guaranteed by governments and what
duties and obligations should be discharged by citizens. The rule of
law, especially punishments for offences against the person, is also an
expression of this social contract.

For psychologists, there are several strands of thinking that seek to
explain aggressive behaviour:

(1) *Ethologists* regard aggression as an instinctive reaction to an animal
    invading another's territory or attacking their offspring. There
    are clear connotations of aggression as an 'impulse to survive'
    in this explanation, developed through evolutionary processes.
    Fear-induced aggression as a result of someone, normally placid
    in temperament, being cornered or threatened is thought to be
    related to a wish to survive. In some studies varying levels of tes-
    tosterone in men have had some association with a predisposition
    to be aggressive, although it cannot be assumed that the individual
    has no choice but to obey the 'message from the testosterone'.

(2) The *frustration–aggression hypothesis* has it that aggression
    arises out of an individual's needs, wishes, goals or wants being
    restricted, unfulfilled or denied in some significant measure. The
    hypothesis has it that the aggression may be directed at a person
    considered to be the source of the frustration (say, a man harming
    his partner when he learns that she is intent on leaving him and he
    wishes her to stay); or on an entirely innocent party (an individual
    fails to secure a promotion he was hoping for, so he 'kicks the cat'
    on his return home). The latter has been labelled as 'displaced
    aggression'. Although many accept the frustration–aggression

hypothesis in broad terms, some have pointed to the fact that for some individuals sulking or social withdrawal rather than aggressive behaviour may be a personal response to frustration.

(3) *Social-learning* theorists locate aggressive behaviour in observations that individuals have made of others behaving aggressively and in subsequent 'imitations'. Imitated or copied behaviour will become reinforced if it has, in the eyes of the actor, been effective in securing the actor's objective(s). This kind of analysis has been found useful in understanding how young men, for example, learn aggressive behaviour in gangs where there is an emphasis upon being able to 'look after oneself', display a lack of fear in combat and embrace particular idea of manliness. Similarly the idea that domestic violence can be transmitted from one generation to another with a boy observing the abusive behaviour of his father has seemingly been a biographical feature of some aggressive/violent men.

There are overlapping possibilities in relation to these three different kinds of explanation. Clearly aggressive behaviour learned from one's social environment can also be enacted when the same person experiences frustration of any kind. Similarly, the survival impulse or instinct can also be activated with an aggressive person (where their aggression has been learned) should they be cornered by another gang or in combat should they be in the forces.

Finally, the social construction of gender and different cultural and sub-cultural influences on both attitudes and behaviour will have a bearing on whether aggression is more or less legitimated and considered to be more or less acceptable. Understanding the social determinants/influences on particular people's potential for aggressive behaviour is key to deconstructing interpersonal aggressive and violent behaviour that figures in the lives of individuals, families and groups as well as maybe helping social workers to estimate the level of risk they face personally when working with them. (See also **domestic violence**.)

alienation a person's feelings of estrangement or disaffection from any social group, community, culture, social institution or society and any social process. Such feelings can take the shape of unhappiness and a lack of satisfaction with work and life in general.

The term is associated especially with the work of Marx, particularly his early writings, where he clearly conceives of human nature as a social product and not something that is a priori and fixed. Here, Marx was concerned to explain the alienating effects of the capitalist mode of production on human relationships for both the oppressed (the proletariat or working class) and the oppressor (the bourgeoisie or ruling class). Within this paradigm, workers do not work to express

themselves or to be creative in any way; they most often are behaving
in an 'instrumental' manner to earn a living as 'wage slaves' and have
little control over work, usually acting in accordance with the wishes
(demands) of others (the bourgeoisie or their agents). Although
Marx's concerns were mostly about the oppressed he also acknowledged that to oppress others also somehow 'alienates' oppressors so
that their human potential also remains unfulfilled.

In a post-capitalist socialist society, Marx argued, a more humane
and creative system of social relations would be possible where workers
would not be exploited and where they had a measure of control over
both the means of production (because these would be communally
owned) and the products of their labour (only products that had
social benefits would be made/created). Thus the false consciousness
implied by the commodity-driven aspect of modern capitalism ('commodity fetishism') would disappear because consumerism would be
understood for what it was – namely an exploitative part of capitalism that rested upon the creation of false or spurious needs. Various
writers in the twentieth century have explored further the concept of
alienation and made potentially interesting connections with psychological insights. Marcuse, for example, argued that all societies
have to socialize their children and, in that regard, had inevitably to
'repress' or shape them in some degree. Here, clear connections
with psychoanalysis were evident in Marcuse's exposition as the child
moved from a personality with an ungoverned self-seeking *id* to a
social being with a social *ego* and a conscience in the form of a *super-
ego*. Marcuse argued that a creative repression was possible in a
genuinely socialist society that maximized the human potential of
all individuals. Investigating similar territory, Blauner, in his book
Alienation and Freedom (1964), tried to operationalize the concept
of alienation to potentially make possible empirical studies of people
in their various social settings, especially work. Blauner distinguished
between powerlessness, normlessness, meaninglessness, isolation and
self-estrangement as five discernible dimensions to alienation. His
thinking focused primarily upon employment, its organization and
contingent social relations. Although an interesting suggestive study
it has been criticized by some commentators because his analysis does
not actually root itself in a structural analysis of social relations around
the means of production but in a more modest analysis of employment-
related stress and associated matters.

Nevertheless, this analysis is potentially useful and relevant to social
work in two ways. First, in relation to service users the concept is helpful in understanding the social context of service users' lives and of the

pressures they experience outside the home (if our focus is upon work) that may have an impact upon their behaviour within the home. For example, a man who has a job where his opinions about the product of his labour do not count, the way the work is undertaken is beyond his control and he is not really valued by his employer may as a result feel fairly worthless. It is also possible that relationships between workers are conflictual because they are expected to compete with each other. Thus his self-regard may be minimal and this lowly self-image could affect his functioning, negatively, in his domestic environment. The ecological approach to social work should invite this kind of connection between the macro-environment and any individual's/family's functioning. In addition, low wages will probably mean that the man cannot consume as much as he would like and that, in this spurious game of commodity fetishism, he cannot perform as he would like or as he has been persuaded he ought.

In addition, the concept of alienation is also potentially useful in analysing the social work role. For example, social work has often been construed as an occupation trying to work in an anti-oppressive way with structural inequality; in effect, trying to find technical solutions to political problems. Yet clearly social workers have access to few resources to help service users themselves and in relation to influencing other agencies to provide resources their achievements are invariably modest. It is sometimes the case that social workers, in response to these kinds of insoluble pressure, resort to pathologizing the service users. Thus feelings of powerlessness often ensue. Moreover, working in (state) bureaucracies, social workers' room for manoeuvre is slim and any pretensions to professional autonomy quickly dissipate. Radical analyses of the social work role have also suggested that social work is often part of the state apparatus to control people living in poverty. It is, after all, a considerable political achievement to persuade poor people to be content with their poverty. The key task then is to try to develop a form of social work that is genuinely concerned to address structural inequality and to work in partnership with service users to this end.

Blauner, R. (1964) *Alienation and Freedom*. Chicago, IL: University of Chicago Press.

altruism the concern for the welfare of others rather than oneself; the opposite of self-centered or egoistic behaviour. Definitions of altruism usually include the intention to help others but it is possible to note that some behaviours benefit others rather than oneself, without necessarily having been explicitly intended to do so. The word was first coined in the mid-nineteenth century and was a widely discussed topic by Victorian social reformers as they tried to come to terms with balancing competitive self-interest in the market place with the voluntary responses to tackling the social deprivations that emerged in the capitalist, industrializing economy.

A mass of social science investigation of altruism suggests four possible sources:

(1) *Biological and genetic preservation* – sociobiologists such as Richard Dawkins and Edward Wilson believe that altruistic and moral behaviour is inborn in humans, in particular towards one's family and kin (especially parents protecting and nurturing children), with the function of preserving species within the context of evolution.

(2) *Cognitive development* – that development of a 'moral sense' and the capacity to empathize and place oneself in the position of another becomes more prominent as the young child matures.

(3) *Social learning* – learning to respond to the needs of others by observation and copying behaviour of role models; what sociologists broadly term **socialization**.

(4) *Reciprocal behaviour* – helping others is likely to encourage help for oneself in return.

With the exception of the second, the sources of altruism above can be said to derive from sources other than pure 'goodness of the heart' or freely chosen sacrifice of one's own interests to further the well-being of others. Yet those who engage in altruistic behaviours often prefer to think of themselves as acting in a selfless, virtuous manner. And psychologists have indeed proposed that there is such a thing as a personality trait for altruism, that is a predisposition to help others at some cost to themselves.

Any discussion of altruism raises a number of interesting questions concerning human conduct. How much of altruistic behaviour actually is wholly in the interest of the recipient and completely devoid of any kind of benefit for the person engaged in it? Are there psychic rewards or other hidden gains for the altruistic individual? How far do altruistic individuals actually engage in a calculation of personal benefit or mutual benefit beforehand? With such questions in mind it is possible to construct all human behaviour as **self-interested**, but to do this would lose any distinction between altruistic and egoistic behaviour. More commonly, social scientists have explored the mixture of altruistic and self-interested behaviour that seems a widely spread phenomenon.

There is intense debate now over whether the welfare state is itself a form of altruism toward anonymous strangers, supported by voters with altruistic motives. The donation of blood – freely given in Britain but receiving a payment in the US – is often cited in support. (See **gift relationship**.) That argument is countered by those on the political **right** who argue that the welfare state has been 'captured' by the public employees that staff it for their own benefit. Libertarians go further and criticize the concept of altruism itself. They argue that altruism demands that a person has no right to exist for her or his own sake; sacrifice for others is the only justification of existence and its highest moral duty. They point to the basic contradiction of altruism – that if it is good to sacrifice for others, is it not selfish and even immoral for others to accept the consequences of that sacrifice?

(See also **self-interest**.)

analysis of variance (ANOVA) a procedure used in statistics to determine whether the differences in the averages of data drawn from different **sample** groups are likely to be found in the whole population from which those groups are drawn. For example, take three groups of people with differing educational backgrounds for whom the average wage has been calculated. The analysis of variance then tests whether the differences in the average wage of each group are statistically significant by dividing the variability of the data into two types. One type, called *within-group variability*, is the variance within each group being investigated. The second type, called *between-group variability*, is the variability of the averages *between* the groups. If the between-group variability is large compared to the within-group variability of any one of the three sample groups it is likely that the average (or mean) wage for that group (see **measures of central tendency**) is not representative of the population as whole from which the sample group was taken.

Two assumptions underlie the use of variance analysis:

- each group must be a random sample drawn from a 'normal' population;
- the variance of the groups in the population are equal.

For social workers, statistical analysis such as ANOVA and the use of random samples and other techniques present a challenge because of their relative lack of familiarity with, or even use for, statistics. While social science never claims the same level of validity for its data as the natural sciences – human behaviour is too unpredictable and observer bias too often intrudes – it nevertheless is able to produce robust and useful findings across a range of user, practitioner and agency behaviours. While qualitative research has its own discipline and objectivity, it has come to dominate social work research, often drawing on small samples simply because these are easiest to come by. The method too often leads to what is referred to as *confirmation bias* in which the researcher goes looking for and finds what it is he or she wants to find. The habit of using different elements of statistical analysis, such as ANOVA, if nothing else, pushes social work research away from personal preferences and ideological confirmation and towards more rigorous forms of investigation.

(See also **research methods**.)

anomie a situation, condition or state without norms or lacking a measure of consensus about norms, to guide or frame social behaviour. Anomie can refer to an individual's lack of connection with his/her social group or society or to confusion and a lack of meaning in social interactions in society as a whole. Anomie as a concept was first developed by Émile Durkheim and has been used and developed by several other sociologists, notably Robert Merton.

Durkheim maintained that human beings, without the constraints of a consensual moral framework, would resort to self-seeking and unruly behaviour. He claimed that social change could be unsettling in its consequences. For example, pre-industrial or traditional societies were bound together by a considerable consensus about required behaviour, partly because there was comparatively little division of labour – a state which Durkheim dubbed 'mechanical solidarity'. Traditional societies might, for example, be organized around agriculture where many or even most people undertook roles that related to the growing of crops or raising of animals; in essence there was significant social **integration**. By contrast, industrial or modern societies are marked by very complex structures with considerable differentiation in roles and social institutions – a state of what Durkheim called 'organic solidarity'. This major change, with its emphasis upon individualism and competition, loosens the glue of a moral and normative consensus and creates potential for social conditions leading to anomie. He further claimed that anomie can arise out of social exclusion both because people are experiencing objectively difficult circumstances as with an economic slump or depression but also where times are comparatively good but where particular individuals, families or communities are not involved in the improved circumstances, but have in some sense been 'left behind'.

Durkheim had it that there were strong associations between anomic conditions and suicide; that a lack of social solidarity can lead to extreme feelings of being socially marginalized and not valued by one's membership and reference groups. Using the same broad framework, Robert Merton used the concept of anomie to analyse all social behaviour in terms of people's adherence to any society's general objectives, goals or aspirations (that is, broad culturally accepted or valued goals) as well as the culturally approved or legitimate means for achieving these goals. His now famous typology stipulates that a lot of social behaviour can be understood in terms of adherence to or rejection of culturally approved means and/or ends, as follows:

	Acceptance of culturally approved means	Acceptance of culturally approved ends
Conformity	+	+
Innovation	−	+
Ritualism	+	−
Retreatism	−	−
Rebellion	±	±

In the UK, it is probably safe to assume that the key message that young people receive from parents, teachers, politicians and the media is that it is intrinsically good to study hard in order to secure a good job, which, in turn, is likely to result in the possibility of leading a reasonably affluent lifestyle. A person who accepts this message will be, according to Merton's typology, a 'conformist'. A person who accepts the goal of a comfortable lifestyle but feels that their path to it is effectively blocked because of their comparatively poor economic situation might be tempted to steal to achieve those ends that might otherwise be denied him. In Merton's typology, the thief is an 'innovator'. The person who perhaps experiences trauma in childhood and who, as a result, becomes dislocated from family and friends and resorts to the use of drugs to manage anxiety is for Merton a 'retreatist', rejecting both the goals and means to achieve those goals that most of his contemporaries embrace. The 'ritualist' is someone who accepts the culturally approved goals but is unable to adopt the means because his social position prohibits meaningful progress in securing an affluent position. The 'ritualist' becomes stuck in habitual behaviour that is not productive. Merton himself cites the lowly bureaucrat as an example of a 'ritualist'. Last, Merton identifies the 'rebel' who would have us question either the socially approved means or culturally sanctioned goals or both in an attempt to establish an alternative vision or even a completely different society.

Durkheim and Merton have both been criticized for over-emphasizing the importance of consensus in society about both culturally approved means and ends and thus the significance of 'correct' socialization. These criticisms will be especially pertinent in, for example, grossly unequal societies or patriarchal societies. Societies characterized by multiculturalism will also offer differing narratives regarding what is important about how life is to be lived.

However, anomie is potentially a useful concept in analysing the behaviour of a variety of service users by asking questions about the social goals that they might regard as desirable or valuable and the, for them, defensible means by which such goals might be secured. When a youth justice worker questions a young offender about his criminal behaviour it is important for him to know how the young person thinks about social goals and the means he regards as legitimate to achieve a measure of success in his social group, set in a context of what is legal. Similarly the 'retreating' drug addict may well be experiencing both the problems of addiction and a disabling mental health problem that led to drug use. It is only by exploring the issues of service users' views about what they consider to be appropriate social goals and the acceptable means to achieve them that important evidence can be uncovered about whether there is a problem or whether we are simply having to confront a legitimate alternative view of how life is to be lived. (See also **norm.**)

anti-psychiatry a movement that opposed the theory and practice of psychiatry, influential in the 1960s and 1970s. It denied that there was such a thing as mental illness, concluding that the various psychiatric diagnoses had little or no scientific foundation. The mental and behavioural characteristics that attracted such diagnoses were better understood either as meaningful responses to the stresses of family life or essentially judgements passed by society at large on people who were found to be awkward and difficult to deal with.

Two of the movement's prominent spokesmen were R. D. Laing in Britain and Thomas Szasz in the US. Laing, based at the Tavistock Clinic from 1957, published *The Divided Self* (1960) when he was 28, drawing not only on psychoanalysis but on existentialists such as Jean-Paul Sartre and Samuel Beckett. Laing saw psychosis, particularly schizophrenia, as a system of thought possessing shape and sequence, which became understandable in terms of the person trying to produce rational strategies in threatening and confusing social environments. He wrote: 'I suggest, therefore, that sanity or psychosis is tested by the degree of conjunction or disjunction between two persons where the one is sane by common consent'. Psychiatry, with its pretence to objectivity, only widens the gap between those already deemed sane and 'the patient'.

In subsequent work, Laing highlighted the 'double bind' family in which family members collude to subject an 'elected' member to a pair of conflicting accusations or 'binds': whichever the victim chooses to try to deal with will be wrong because the other will not have been dealt with. The victim is unable to respond satisfactorily to both because they contradict one another. At the same time the family feels satisfied as it has discovered the sources of all its difficulties.

Thomas Szasz, a psychotherapist, developed parallel themes in his most important work, *The Myth of Mental Illness*, published in 1961. He saw that psychiatrists could not agree on criteria for diagnosing schizophrenia and concluded that it was not an illness at all but a means of exerting social control over those whose behaviour did not conform to accepted social norms. Essentially what is labelled mental illness involves 'problems in living', arising from failure to observe social rules and allotted roles. Szasz was strongly libertarian and criticized psychiatrists' power to involuntarily detain people in psychiatric hospital and to undertake invasive treatments such as electro-convulsive therapy and frontal lobe lobotomy. His view that privately contracted psychiatric care should replace state coercion under mental health legislation also fits with libertarian thinking. Szasz was among the first to offer a comprehensive critique of the 'medical model' and its approach to dealing with difficult behaviour; this was all the more notable at a time when medicine held unchallenged authority and public regard.

The ground rapidly shifted beneath the anti-psychiatry movement, however, beginning in the later 1960s. The introduction of specific drugs to control mood and curtail the florid symptoms of schizophrenia combining with the closure of large mental hospitals took much of the sting out of the charge of incarceration and patient abuse. Laing also sharply shifted gear. He fitted into the emerging zeitgeist of the later 1960s, becoming simultaneously more mystical and politically more radical. In his later work, having praised hallucinatory notions of reality, he began to celebrate the schizophrenic experience as both an indictment of the standards of conventional society and a pathway to transcendence. When Anthony Clare published his mainstream text *Psychiatry in Dissent* in 1976 he deftly combined the kernels of insight anti-psychiatry had formulated with an account of a more flexible, socially aware profession.

Anti-psychiatry was indeed a movement – it gained adherents and influence well beyond the writings of Laing and Szasz. Other sociologists extended its range. These included Thomas Scheff who developed **labelling theory** and Erving Goffman who studied 'total institutions' in his book *Asylums*. Both worked and published at the same time in the 1960s. Yet it was in the support groups, the advocacy organizations, the halfway houses and therapeutic communities that the broad premises of anti-psychiatry were adopted and modified to fit the real world. While in retrospect it is right to call attention to the exaggeration of the anti-psychiatry movement, it had an important impact on later developments in mental health. Not only did it offer one of the earliest critiques of 'the medical model', it alerted a wide swath of the concerned public to the repressiveness of standard psychiatric treatment. While the phrase 'mental illness' remained in use, the movement initiated progressive understanding that standard definitions of physical 'illness' do not capture the complexity of mental disorders. We are now more likely to say he or she 'suffers' from schizophrenia, rather than 'has schizophrenia', to use the phrase 'mental health problems' and to speak of 'mental health survivor', instead of 'patient'. We also now recognize that a psychiatric diagnosis has a social impact and countering social attitudes and discrimination are standard elements of the job description of social workers in mental health.

Clare, A. ([1975] 2011) *Psychiatry in Dissent*, 2nd edn. Abingdon: Routledge.

Laing, R.D. (1960) *The Divided Self: An Existential Study in Sanity and Madness.* Harmondsworth: Penguin Books.

Szasz, T. (1962) *The Myth of Mental Illness.* London: Secker & Warburg.

assimilation a way of theorizing relationships between any host society and immigrant or incoming groups whereby social groups become alike or similar or combine into an entirely new coherent social form. Assimilation is thought to be a more comprehensive process of 'coming together' than integration.

In sociological theory, there appear to be two variations on the theme of assimilation. The first suggests that it is the task of an incoming group to acquire the social characteristics of the host society and to merge with it. In this formulation of assimilation, there is also a corresponding expectation on the part of the host society that incomers must conform and enthusiastically embrace the 'new society's culture'; that the minority will abide by the expectations and wishes of the majority. The second formulation accepts that any incoming group will have an impact on the host society so that the 'assimilated whole' incorporates attributes of both or all groups. This second formulation has it that assimilation is a 'melting pot' so that the emergent society combines features of both the host society and the incoming group(s) into an entirely new social entity that may be different, perhaps markedly so, from any of the groups involved in the amalgamation. A good example of the latter is the profound influence of Asian food on the British menu, with chicken curry now matching roast beef and Yorkshire pudding as popular choices in both kitchen and restaurant.

account for development changes in the child. Recent research conducted by psychologists now suggests that attachment is a continuous process that passes through different phases, so that if there is disruption, even early on in the relationship between mother and child, this does not mean that attachment will not take place at all. Social workers have also learned to use the concept more flexibly, as one of many aspects they consider when forming a view of the strength of a relationship between a child and its parents. While it would seem that attachment theory would lead to a strong prediction regarding future behaviour this is simply not the case, because that behaviour is deeply and continuously affected by cognitive and social maturation.

Bowlby and Ainsworth developed their model as one of expectations and beliefs about oneself, other people and relationships rather than as predictive of particular behaviours. Even within parent–young child relationships not all interactions are driven by attachment considerations by any means and it is wrong to suggest that infant attachment is directly responsible for how the child adapts as he or she grows older.

Cassidy, J. and Shaver, P. (2008) *Handbook of Attachment: Theory, Research and Clinical Applications.* New York: Guilford Press.

attitude a relatively permanent disposition, regard or orientation towards a person, thing or social process. At a simple level, an attitude may concern a dislike of broccoli and a love of peas; at a more complex level, it may encompass a commitment to equal opportunity policies.

The formation, origins and maintenance of attitudes has been the focus of much research by psychologists, sociologists and political scientists. For example, psychologists have been preoccupied with issues concerning cognitive and emotional development especially in childhood and adolescence; sociologists have been especially interested in the relationship between social influences and attitudes as with the formation of gender identities or the development of ideas of social deference or rebellion; and political scientists have been preoccupied with issues around voting behaviour and general engagement in political institutions.

Many writers have found it useful to distinguish three aspects of attitude:

- a *cognitive dimension* – concerning both simple and complex formulations of ideas, concepts, theories and beliefs;
- an *affective dimension* – concerning especially emotions, sentiments and values;
- a *behavioural dimension* – concerning an inclination or tendency to act or behave in a particular way or an orientation implied by actual behaviour.

The relationship between these three dimensions of attitudes can be complex, leading to the possibility that they will reinforce one another or that there might be some inconsistencies in the expression of these various dimensions. For example, a committed, able and loving parent might be able to express attitudes that are very positive about their child, that will also display considerable emotional involvement with them and be able to demonstrate that their actual behaviour is entirely consistent with their emotional and cognitive engagement with their child. Social workers, by way of contrast, are often dismayed and perplexed by discrepancies between the expressed attitudes of some parents and their apparent emotional distance from their children and their inability to, say, play with them or to attend school activities where their children are involved or attend meetings with teachers who have concerns about their children.

In quite another context, youth justice workers are currently required to deconstruct offending behaviour with the young offenders they are supervising. Trying to determine the 'real' attitudes of offenders is often part of a wider remit to determine: the offenders' understanding of criminal behaviour, their acceptance of their personal responsibility for offences, their response to information about the impact of their offending behaviour upon victims and, finally, whether any apparent 'insights' are likely to lead to changes in behaviour. Similarly, men who abuse their partners often reveal inconsistencies in the cognitive, emotional and behavioural aspects of their attitudes. Such men typically express attitudes expressing affection while also displaying negative views of their partner's motivations and, often, behaving in a very controlling, bullying and sometimes violent manner towards them.

Thus, exploration of the possible inconsistencies between the cognitive, emotional and behavioural dimensions of attitudes is a potentially very useful diagnostic tool in understanding a range of human behaviour. A key skill is to be able to frame questions that will uncover evidence about these three dimensions of attitudes. It is certainly not uncommon for there to be discrepancies between expressed attitudes and actual behaviour. Although some claim that behaviour is the more accurate indicator of an attitude, it is entirely possible that social expectations about, for example, gender, age or workplace will distort what a person actually thinks. Similarly, expressed attitudes can also mask a person's real attitudes because they think their actual position on any issue will be regarded as socially unacceptable because they are not in accord with group norms. (See also **cognition, cognitive dissonance and scales** and **scaling**.)

attribution theory a process for making decisions, judgements or inferences about the motives, characters or behaviours of other people and/or the causes of particular events.

Individuals, in their attempts to interpret and understand people and the world at large, attribute particular character or personality traits to others (dispositional attribution) as well as to the causes of particular events (situational attribution). In everyday situations, we feel we have to decide whether someone's negative remarks about our work, for example, reflects genuinely unsatisfactory achievements/output on our part or whether the person dislikes us for other reasons. In relation to situational attribution, an individual may be predisposed to locate the cause of a car crash in snowy conditions rather than the unwise speed of the driver, thus attributing more or less blame to the driver.

Often individuals will, in effect, rationalize their own motives or account for their own behaviour by reference to the circumstances in which the behaviour occurred and, in relation to other people, attribute the other's behaviour or motives to character. However, much will depend upon who the person is and the nature of their relationship to the observer. Friends and family members may well enjoy more positive attributions than, say, complete strangers especially if the stranger appears to have a dress code that is unappealing to the observer or maybe is using foul language in a public place. Social class, gender and ethnicity, as well as other social identifiers, in relation to the observer, the observed and the situation may well also have an influence on attributions.

audit an examination, usually conducted annually although other intervals are possible, of the finances of an organization to determine whether funds are being acquired, banked (invested) and spent in a legal manner. Audits are investigations designed to discourage fraud and corruption and to encourage probity. They are usually undertaken by a body considered to be independent of the company, department or agency being studied. In the case of public bodies, audits were until recently carried out by the Audit Commission. The Commission now retains a small presence, with virtually all work contracted out to the private sector.

Audits have been a feature of the organization and management of public bodies for some considerable time. In the UK, auditors were appointed to examine expenditure underpinned by the Poor Law in localities in the first part of the nineteenth century. Rigorous examination of expenditure by public bodies (and also private organizations delivering goods and services to local and/or central government),

including local authorities and the National Health Service, is now
an established component of public accountability especially since
the 1982 Local Government Finance Act (consolidated by the 1998
Audit Commission Act) came into force. In sum, the annual accounts
of public bodies have to be published, and the auditors will normally
'sign off' the accounts if they are satisfied that they are 'accurate and
fair' and refuse to sign off any accounts they deem to be 'misleading'
in any way.

Audit, in its focus upon probity and a fundamental obligation to
determine that expenditure is in line with statutory guidance, has
conventionally been distinguished from activities associated with critical appraisals of economy and efficiency. But the remit of the Audit
Commission and, more recently, private sector agencies undertaking
work on behalf of the Commission has inevitably, perhaps, strayed
into issues associated with 'value for money', partly because it has
had at its disposal data on both expenditure and outputs for all public
bodies, encouraging evaluations of 'comparative value'. This territory,
however, has been hotly contested because it is essentially influenced
by matters political that have to take into account, among many other
issues, measures of deprivation and the visions of councillors and, in
addition, that judgements rarely consider the views of service users.
(See also **cost–benefit analysis** and **opportunity costs**.)

authority the right to determine how others should behave; the **power**
to control or judge others; a person, group or institution exercising
power that may or may not be a 'legitimate' authority.

Sociologists have been concerned with the different ways in which
power is *legitimated*. Here the central concern is how those who exercise power uphold their authority by reference to some right located
in tradition, law or some other social entity. The sociologist Weber
has been influential in his analysis of differing forms of legitimating
authority; namely:

* *Traditional authority* – this form of authority is effectively justified
  on the basis that 'we have always done it this way'; a reference to
  well-entrenched custom and practice.
* *Legal–rational authority* – here the emphasis is upon explicit rules
  or law with the person exerting authority in a manner that is consistent with said rules/laws. For example, this could be a person
  elected to a post or a person appointed to, say, a public position
  (for example, a teacher, social worker, or nurse) by a legally constituted public body.
* *Charismatic* – this form of authority rests entirely upon the personal qualities and characteristics of the individual. He or she

commands respect and inspires others to follow and emulate the
ideas and actions of the 'leader'.

Clearly, different forms of legitimating the authority of particular
institutions can change over time. With reference to charismatic
authority, for example, Weber asked the question: 'How does a movement develop after the inspiring and exceptional leader has died?'
and his response was that charisma becomes 'routinized'; that is,
institutions such as the Catholic church develop doctrine and ritual
to interpret and sustain the commitment to the original leader's teach-
ings. Similarly, traditional authority can acquire the trappings of legality if, say, the traditional rights of a monarch become reconfigured by
constitutional law.

Other writers have recognized different forms of authority that
include the authority of absolute power, as in totalitarian regimes or
situations of lawlessness, say in a civil war, although both may try to
render such power as respectable by reference to imposed rules and
regulations. Another form of authority resides in the idea of a profession, where the professional's authority rests upon his or her knowledge, skills and expertise.

In social work the different forms of authority that are commonly at
play include legal–rational or bureaucratic authority (located in legally
elected councillors for local government and ministers for central
government – as well as legally appointed social work professionals
and managers) and professional authority, although it is also possible
that exceptional practitioners might attract followers by virtue of their
personal, charismatic qualities. A common source of tension in social
work is where professional judgement is at odds with bureaucratic
authority because, perhaps, managers are not prepared to take the risks
that the practitioner feels should be taken in the interests, say, of a
child and his or her family. In statutory social work, bureaucratic hierarchies habitually carry more power than even the most experienced of
practitioners. (See also **bureaucracy, power and profession**.)

B b

behaviourism the theory that human and animal behaviour is largely shaped and modified by the consequences of that behaviour. These consequences are essentially either pleasurable and rewarding, in which case they encourage the behaviour to be repeated, or painful and dissatisfying, which discourages the behaviour from being repeated. The leading behavioural theorist, B.F. Skinner (1904–90), described this process as 'operant' behaviour – because it acts on the environment. Consequences that cause behaviours to increase he called 'reinforcers' and consequences that cause behaviour to decrease he called 'punishers'. Although he only studied animal behaviour Skinner believed he had discovered a universal law of 'operant conditioning' which he and others readily applied to human behaviour.

At the height of its influence in the middle of the twentieth century programmes based on behavioural theory were developed particularly in relation to young people and people with learning disability. Within these programmes, reinforcers could be physiological – for example, receiving food – or emotional such as a being complimented or approved of. Punishers could be in both forms too – an electric shock, for example, or through a telling off or verbal abuse. The notion of 'negative reinforcement' was also added to the behaviourists' repertoire, in which the removal of an unpleasant stimulus such as an enforced unpleasant activity will also encourage the behaviour that brought that removal about.

Many behavioural programmes with proclaimed 'therapeutic' ends were little more than institutional abuse. Gays, for example, were administered electric shocks in the 1950s and 1960s in an attempt to create aversion to their sexual preference. The 'pindown' regimes of some Staffordshire children's homes in the 1980s were loosely justified on behaviourist principles.

By the 1990s behaviourism, once so dominant, had lost much of its former influence in part because philosophically it denies that individuals are autonomous, able to reflect and choose courses of action outside the simplistic notions of reward and punishment. However, more sensitive programmes survived in relation to children with difficult and challenging behaviour, where assessments were based on an A-B-C chart noting the *antecedents* or 'triggers' in the child's environment that sets off the behaviour, the duration and intensity of the *behaviour* itself and the *consequences* of that behaviour. Often this is an exercise undertaken by the parents themselves in order for them to see how their own reactions to their child's difficult behaviour often encourages more of the same and how they might modify their own behaviour as a result.

bureaucracy a type of organization in which administration is hierarchically arranged with decisions made according to specified rules.

The word first emerged in France in the eighteenth century, combining 'bureau' (desk) with the Greek word for rule – literally the 'rule of the desk'. The investigation of bureaucracy was one of sociology's early triumphs, principally undertaken by Max Weber whose clarity in laying out what bureaucracy is and how it functions remains readable and relevant today. He noted that German industrial organizations derived enormous efficiency from their bureaucracies. In his work *Economy and Society* (1922), he brought together the essential features common to bureaucracies:

- power belongs to an office and not the office holder;
- a hierarchical division of labour with authority specified by the rules of the organization which are formally codified;
- powers are precisely delegated within the hierarchy, expressed in terms of duties, obligations and responsibilities specified in contracts;
- requires staff to be qualified, promotion is based on seniority or merit and staff are salaried with no personal gain to be derived from their decisions;
- communication, co-ordination and control are centralized in the organization.

Bureaucracies are 'goal rational', Weber argued, in the sense that as organizations they pursue their objectives in the most effective way open to them. He also identified authority, based on rational rules, as central to bureaucratic organizations. Officials within a bureaucracy are obedient to an identifiable body of rules and those rules are perceived to be rational. The legitimacy of those rules – acceptance of its decisions by the public – depends on how the rules were made and in particular that they are a product of public officials working in a systematic and impersonal way. People obey not the person but the office holder and respond to the demands of the office.

Weber wrote:

The individual bureaucrat cannot squirm out of the apparatus in which he is harnessed. In contrast to the honorific or avocational 'notable', the professional bureaucrat is chained to his activity by his entire material and ideal existence. In the great majority of cases, he is only a single cog in an ever-moving mechanism which prescribes to him an essentially fixed route of march. The official is entrusted with specialized tasks and normally the mechanism cannot be put into motion or arrested by him, but only from the very top. The individual bureaucrat is thus forged to the community of all the functionaries who are integrated into the mechanism. They have a common interest in seeing that the mechanism continues its function and that the societally exercised authority carries on.

(in Gert and Mills 228–9)

In everyday usage, 'bureaucracy' has taken on a negative connotation, for example when an organization's behaviour is described as 'bureaucratic', conjuring up manufactured excuses for delay or inaction, pointless restrictions, or seemingly arbitrary decisions. Some social scientists have theorized that this negative image is deserved under the concept of *public choice theory* which essentially holds that, far from having the public's interest at heart, bureaucrats make decisions according to their self-interest.

Social workers have a complicated relationship to bureaucracy. They are themselves bureaucrats working within large, hierarchical organizations. As such their experience reflects much of what Weber noted about bureaucracies. But they also have a certain level of individual discretion in decision-making – in fact they could not develop relationships with individual users or make decisions that fit those individuals if they did not. In this respect the qualities and skills of the individual social worker are extremely important and embody a certain level of authority attached to that individual social worker. In this respect, Weber's view that actions are rule bound and the office not the person carries the authority to act may not always apply.

Their discretion in decision-making and their aspiration to broaden or at least maintain use of that discretion has brought social workers, from time to time, into conflict with their own organizations. This was particularly acute in the period after the single social services departments were created within local authorities in the 1970s. While a flat organizational hierarchy is effective for social casework, it is not effective in co-ordinating the work of large departments with a vast array of responsibilities which requires centralized control relying on layers of middle management to effect that control. Specific pressures built up on social workers in the 1970s – location in area offices, with clients walking into the office on a regular basis, reduced administrative support, staff shortages and increasing statutory duties. Because of the degree of personalized decision-making social workers were also more liable to be singled out individually for errors of judgement. Against both the impersonality of the large organization and the sense of being individually vulnerable, the social work team offered some form of mutual support with members aware of the great responsibilities shouldered by each of them.

Gerth, H. and Mills, C.W. (eds) (1958) *From Max Weber*. Oxford: Oxford University Press.

Weber, M. ([1922]1992) *Economy and Society*. Los Angeles, CA: University of California Press.

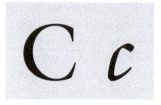

C c

capitalism a social and economic system based on the following:
(1) the ownership of the means for producing goods and services is private, in the hands of corporations, businesses and individuals, and not the state;
(2) profit is pursued by these firms and corporations through the mechanism of the **market** in which goods and services are bought and sold; and
(3) the labour of employees is bought through the labour market – wage labour.

The system acquires its name through the central role played by 'capital', that is the stored, accumulated value in plant, machinery, land, tools and other forms of production of goods and services.

The strengths and limitations of capitalism was the central focus of much social science from the eighteenth century onwards. The Scottish economist Adam Smith (1723–90) was among the first to analyse how the pursuit of individual self-interest in the market place was a distinctive feature. He argued that as individuals pursued their own self-interest, co-operation across society would increase. He was, however, by no means the apostle of unregulated free enterprise he is taken to be by enthusiasts in our own time but a moral philosopher as well who supported the idea that workmen should be allowed to form 'combinations' – the eighteenth-century word for trade unions.

The sociologist Max Weber (1864–1920) insisted that capitalism was characterized by a higher level of rationality and the most efficient economic system given the intricacies of industrial capitalism. He also took issue with those who identified capitalism with unscrupulous greed. At the same time he was ambivalent about the cultural impact of capitalism – fearing that it created people who were so caught up in the pursuit of money that they lost sight of deeper, more worthwhile goals in life.

Two economists from the mid-twentieth century remain particularly influential in our current discussions on capitalism. One is Friedrich Hayek (1899–1992), an Austrian, who also taught in the US and Britain (he eventually became a British citizen). Hayek argued that free markets are the foundation of liberty and that governments should not interfere with their workings; central planning behind the welfare state moreover was 'the road to serfdom', to quote the title of one of his books in the 1940s. The other is John Maynard Keynes (1883–1946) who argued during the severe economic depression of the 1930s that markets are not always self-correcting and that government intervention was required to ensure their stability and restore full employment. The opinions of both are still current in discussions about how to respond to the great recession of 2008 and the period of economic stagnation that has resulted from it.

Capitalism is now almost universally adopted as the preferred socio-economic system, but there are so many different varieties of capitalism that it is difficult to use the term as describing anything other than the general elements listed above. This has been particularly so since the early 1990s when the state socialism regimes of the former Soviet Union and its allies disappeared and with it what was considered, for better or for worse, an actual alternative economic system to capitalism.

Since then capitalism has remade itself in a more intensive form, less willing to compromise with sources of restraint on it. Various 'new' elements have contributed to this super-charged capitalist environment. In particular, bank debt creates the money by which production of goods or services is either created or liquidated. This is what gives capitalism its peculiar, even ruthless, dynamism: it can swiftly dissolve physical capital – factories, service organizations, labour forces – and just as swiftly reconstitute them elsewhere (or nowhere). Other features relatively new to capitalism over the last 30 years include:

- the weakening of state regulation – particularly in the bank sector which has seen the wall between investment banking and retail banking largely disappear;
- globalization - which has loosened the connection between communities and the economic process;
- the decline in trade unions' capacity to defend wages and working conditions;
- the social policy of governments such as the US, the UK and the EU that has introduced active market mechanisms into areas of social life where they had not previously operated.

The functions and consequences of twenty-first-century capitalism touch social work practice in myriad ways and raise a host of questions. Price and Simpson outline several areas in which capitalist society demands and reproduces social and economic outcomes that social workers have to deal with. They argue, for example, that consumption shapes our **identity** and social status. When once an individual's place within production – such as shop worker, foreman, middle manager –

determined one's social class, our class position is now more shaped by what we buy, and therefore our identity. Social workers work primarily with low-income families and the socially excluded who attempt to engage with the consumer society often at the cost of considerable debt.

Social workers also work with families grappling with what Price and Simpson call 'reproduction' – how society 'reproduces' itself along capitalist lines. Whether it is parents struggling to provide care for older relations or young people attempting to negotiate the transition to adulthood through the fast-changing requirements of the labour market, social workers are inserted into the lives of those struggling to meet the demands of an intensive, globalized market economy.

Price, V. and Simpson, G. (2007) *Transforming Society? Social Work and Sociology.* Bristol: The Policy Press.

caste see **social stratification**

causal modelling a family of techniques for creating models from statistics that aim to test relationships among underlying correlations in relation to specific social events, problems or behaviours. The aim is to discover whether or not any of the suggested correlations in fact bring about or cause the event or behaviour under investigation. The approach requires the researcher to formulate and test different theoretical models of possible causal relationships in order to find the one that best fits the data on hand about the event or problem. One widely used causal model is *path analysis*. A weakness of causal modelling is that the initial assumptions on which a particular model is based can be biased or partial, which then, despite apparent technical sophistication, produces skewed or biased conclusions. Nevertheless, in general causal modelling offers a more informed, more objective procedure than can be achieved by merely highlighting correlations with a particular problem or behaviour. (See also **causality**.)

causality the relationship between two or more actions or events with the second arising as a result of the first. Generally, a causal connection is claimed where two events either occur closely together in time, with one preceding the other, or take place together in a physical location. For a claim to have any validity it must also establish that the second event appears unlikely to have happened without the first even occurring. When a particular causal relationship is established and is seen to happen regularly it acquires a 'lawlike' relationship, a rough parallel to laws of nature where action and consequences are more readily identifiable and predictable. Distinctions may also be drawn between an 'immediate cause' of something and the underlying causes in which the first acts as a trigger for subsequent events or behaviour.

In the realm of social phenomena and human behaviour, causal relationships are often claimed to exist but are just as often difficult to establish with any objectivity. For example, what 'caused' the riots that swept through several English cities in the summer of 2011? While it can be said with certainty that *something* caused them, and even some agreement that the shooting of the young black man Mark Duggan was a trigger, there was no real agreement on what that something was. Straightforward criminality, response of disadvantaged youth to being locked out of the consumer society, absence of responsive policing, lack of parental control, collapse of social norms, the behaviour of some 150,000 troubled families – all were seriously advanced as reasons as to why the riots took place.

The English urban riots demonstrate just how difficult it is to establish cause and effect in areas that social workers have to deal with – human behaviour in individual, familial and social contexts. Talk of causation in these arenas is always about *multiple causation* – several or many different causes. But saying this, or simply 'all of the above', does not make the problem of cause any easier to establish. One difficulty is that correlation is not causation. In other words, just because there is a statistical association between one event or set of circumstances and another does not necessarily mean that there is a causal link between the two. In regard to the English urban riots for example, research did suggest that many of the main neighbourhoods and districts where rioting took place were in fact disadvantaged as defined by multiple indices of deprivation. There was therefore some correlation between disadvantage and rioting but can it be said that disadvantage caused the riots in any objective sense? (Those on the **left** might be tempted to say 'yes' while those on the **right** would be equally tempted to say 'no'.) There is confusion also around correlation versus causation in relation to risk factors in **child development**. For example, children are considered to be at greater risk of poor nutrition in 'workless' households – does that mean that 'worklessness' *causes* poor nutrition? From some viewpoints it might; contrariwise, if unemployment benefit were of a sufficient level a 'workless' household could afford more nutritious food. Which is cause and effect?

Clearly in social arenas the notion of 'cause' is complex and can be closely allied to political viewpoint. However, that does not mean that we have to abandon efforts to locate causes and causal chains. Social scientists have developed several ways to identify the relative importance of multiple causes of an event and to distinguish correlation from cause. These include multivariate analysis, **causal modelling**, logical frame analysis and theories of change, all of which require

systematic investigation into how various possible causes relate to a
particular social problem and generate some conclusions that, while
not as certain as in the natural sciences, nevertheless attain some level
of objective results.

census see **demography**

child development the broad term to describe the processes by which
children grow into adults, from a state of extreme dependence in
infancy to an independently functioning adulthood. This process of
maturation is thought to have several separate but interacting dimensions including physical changes in the body as well as behavioural,
emotional, cognitive and social adaptations and developments.

Conflicting views of childhood can be identified in Western thought
with one view perceiving children as self-centred and in need of discipline and an alternative 'romantic' view which has stressed its inno-
cence and purity. Cultural differences have also been identified, with
some cultures 'protecting' children from work and economic responsibilities and others minimizing the differences between the states of
childhood and adulthood and thus justifying, for example, child labour
and the early assumption of adult duties. In addition, sociologists have
noted ambiguities, within advanced industrial societies, in the state's
perception of children as being both the vulnerable yet treasured
offspring of their parents and a major call on, often limited, family
finances. The state's involvement in the lives of children and young
people also admits of both a humanitarian interest in their welfare and
a wish to prepare them for the world of competitive capitalism. Thus,
adulthood, in respect of the ability to live independently of parents in
capitalist societies, has clearly been increasingly delayed as the school-
leaving age has been consistently raised and young people are spending
longer periods in higher education.

Social workers have an interest in issues concerning children's
maturation given that they have responsibility for assessing whether
any child's development has been delayed or impaired unnecessarily
or that 'significant harm' has, or has not, been caused to the child.
In this context, judgements have to be made about what constitutes
'normal' or 'abnormal' development in relation to a particular child.
These judgements are often difficult given that all children will have
had experiences that are unique, reflecting the very individual innate
characteristics they were born with; characteristics that will then
interact with a social environment that will also have been singular. It
is now also understood that children's innate characteristics, their tem-
perament and emotional robustness will also actively affect the general
environment in which they develop and the responses of parents as

they deal with, say, a demanding baby as against one who is placid and sleeps a lot. Children born with multiple disabilities will also present significant challenges to even the most experienced and relaxed of parents.

Social workers, in their assessments of children, have come to rely on detailed descriptions of what are conceived of as discernible 'developmental stages'. Underpinning these very pragmatic frameworks used by social workers and health visitors is the work of many psychologists and physiologists who have researched key aspects of children's growth and development. Influential theorists have included Piaget with his theory of cognitive development. Piaget has it that children are born with senses, reflexes and instincts that he collectively calls *schema*. Schema predispose children to interact with their environment in particular ways; for example, experiments have been done which demonstrate that a very young baby of just a few months will respond to a picture of a cartoon face and not to another cartoon if the same ingredients of eyes, nose and mouth are jumbled up. However, schema are also capable of development into new schema as the child interacts with his or her environment; thus Piaget's four-stage theory of children's cognitive development:

- *Sensori-motor stage* (0–2 years) – at this stage the baby experiences the world very keenly through its senses; it does not have a sense of self neither is it able easily to distinguish itself from its immediate environment with which it interacts.
- *Pre-operational stage* (2–7 years) – in this stage children are extremely egocentric but they are increasingly able to conceive of objects that need not be present. Abstract thought is not possible at this stage; experience is strongly concrete and unique.
- *Concrete operational stage* (7–11 years) – here children begin to understand relationships between different concrete situations and objects partly by being able to start classifying them and partly by beginning to understand causal relationships. Abstract thought continues to elude most children.
- *Formal operational stage* (11+ years) – at this stage the ability to classify for most children becomes secure and the ability to undertake abstract cognitive functioning such as solving mathematical problems is achieved for most children. It is now possible to tackle problems that have not been encountered before by the application of 'reasoning' based upon generalized earlier experience.

Many critics of Piaget acknowledge that much of his research has validity but have taken the view that the movement between stages is often more fluid and that movement into the next stage can be partial. It also seems that many children, especially those with a significant learning disability, may not progress fully through all stages. Critics have also claimed that the methods used for assessing children can affect notions of progress and that it is crucial to avoid any assessment tools that might be easier, for example, for children from middle-class backgrounds to navigate than children from less privileged backgrounds.

Researchers have also focused upon other aspects of children's maturation including moral, social and emotional development. Piaget argued that moral development operates in parallel to intellectual development. Observing children at play with games involving, for example, marbles, he concluded that rules are only considered to be just or unjust in any abstract sense when children achieve the formal operational stage. Similarly, in relation to children's ideas of justice, they are more likely to focus on the consequences of acts when younger and more likely to think of the intentions of acts when older. These changes, as children grow, also echo social and emotional development as they become able to 'see things from another person's point of view' and are, for example, able to share things with others and work in co-operation with others to solve problems and achieve specified outcomes.

Where developmental delay is suspected, social workers, paediatricians, health visitors and workers in children and adolescent mental health services (CAMHS) teams often rely upon the detailed descriptions of 'normal maturation' to determine what can reasonably be expected of children at various ages. These detailed descriptions acknowledge that there will be sometimes significant differences in physical size, for example, given different ethnicities, disabilities and, to some extent, gender. Workers also acknowledge that some children seem to begin to use language with the hesitant use of a few words and others speak later but with a wider and more complex vocabulary. Much will depend upon their innate abilities, the stimulus provided by their parents and carers and the emotional climate of their environment. But most researchers now agree that a broad framework by which to assess the developmental progress of children and young people is now in place.

Sheridan, M.D., Sharma, A. and Cockerill, H. (2007) *From Birth to Five Years: Children's Developmental Progress.* London: Routledge.

child poverty the effects of poverty on the development and well-being of children.

Historically, the number of children in the UK affected by poverty has been among the highest in the developed world. In 1998–9 a record four and a half million children were living in households with less than half the average national income after housing costs were taken into account. This represented one in three children in poverty (up from one in 10 in 1979), twice the rate in France or the Netherlands and over five times that in Norway and Sweden. Despite the attempts of successive governments, the number of children living in poverty remains stubbornly high at just under four million children. The number of children living in households in which no one is working is just under two million – the highest proportion in Europe and fully two-thirds higher than in France or Germany.

Children brought up in poverty tend to:

- remain on low income throughout their lives;
- incur health penalties at every stage of their life cycle with tendencies to low birth weight and respiratory diseases in childhood, and obesity, heart disease and diabetes in later life;
- be more likely to have mental health problems;
- experience educational disadvantage where the accumulative effect of poverty on schooling widens the gap between the excluded child and his peers year on year.

Poverty also has a disruptive effect on parenting. When combined with changes in family structure and the physical concentration of numbers of people living in poverty, the range of choices available to parents in raising their children are limited. For example, low income has been shown to weaken the extent of parental supervision of children and engagement with their child's school. Parents in disadvantaged neighbourhoods may rely on erratic forms of discipline, moving between harsh forms of punishment, in an effort to keep their child safe, and disengagement as those efforts prove futile. Psychologists have long identified this inconsistency as contributing to anti-social behaviour. Families that sustain economic stress often cope also with social stress – social isolation, overcrowded households, children's difficult behaviour, drug abuse and psychiatric disorder.

While lone-parent families are often viewed as vulnerable, particularly in relation to poor supervision of their children, all the evidence suggests that it is not family structure that is critical but the level of income poverty that the family experiences. Jonathon Bradshaw's exhaustive study of child well-being across the developed world clearly shows that the number of children raised within lone-parent families in Sweden, for example, is as large as in the UK but levels of child well-being are far higher, largely because of the quality of services available and the higher levels of income lone-parent families receive (see Figure 1).

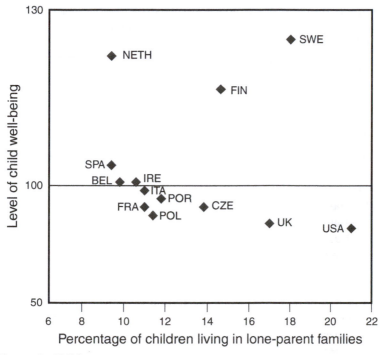

Figure 1 Child poverty

The financial costs of child poverty to society as a whole are also enormous: one recent estimate has calculated that the public spending required to deal with the fallout from child poverty is about £12 billion a year, much of which goes to social services, education and the criminal justice system.

citizenship legal, social and political status conferred by a state on individuals in which certain rights, duties and obligations are placed on both the state and the citizen. In effect, citizenship is legal membership in a nation state. It emerged as a concept in the seventeenth and eighteenth centuries with the consolidation of strong centralized state authorities in Europe and in the wake of the English, French and American revolutions, which called into question the limits of that authority in relation to individuals. Citizenship was underpinned by the idea that states should be founded on the will of the people, involving a contract of mutual rights and responsibilities. One of the most influential interpretations of citizenship has been that of T. H. Marshall, who broadly linked citizenship with the acquisition of rights over the last three or 400 years: legal rights, such as the right to property and freedom from arbitrary arrest; political rights, such as the right to assembly and to vote; and social rights, such as health care and welfare benefits. In Marshall's view, citizenship in our own time has come to include economic welfare and security for each citizen as well as the right to live life according to the standards prevailing in the society.

A number of factors have undermined Marshall's progressive concept of citizenship. Much of it was based on the presumed permanence of a thriving welfare state providing a range of entitlements and a safety net for the poorest. Financial limits placed on welfare spending and the widespread retrenchment of the welfare state have called into question the inevitability of this concept of citizenship. The political philosophy of the new right, which emphasizes responsibilities rather than rights and believes in the market as a way of allocating services, has also introduced new elements into discussions of citizenship.

Feminism contests such an understanding of citizenship and its gender neutrality, and challenges the inherently male precepts of citizenship. Feminists argue that such a concept is defined by male interests and concerns, and needs transformation to include the development of feminist political and social theory. It is being increasingly recognized that citizenship may also contain negative connotations to include restrictive citizenship, as defined within the UK immigration laws and restrictive practices within the European Union. There remains considerable debate (and sometimes conflict) regarding tests for citizenship – for example, should all British citizens be compelled to speak English, and what should constitute the grounds for citizenship in an increasingly diverse, multi-ethnic and multi-faith society?

civil rights see **rights**

civil society the sphere of public participation and social relations that is separate from the family, the economy and the state. While the term would seem to be the same as 'society', civil society denotes the particular sphere of engagement in which the activities of local associations, voluntary organizations, faith institutions, neighbourhood functions and community activities all take place. The term has been regularly used by social theorists since the later 1700s when it was contrasted with 'natural societies' (i.e. society in the state of nature) or despotic societies dominated by feudal or kingly hierarchies. Marxists, such as the Italian Antonio Gramsci in Italy (1891–1937) used the term to denote the area of social relations that was not explicitly under the direct control of government or part of industrial production. While Gramsci viewed civil society as dominated by ideas favourable to the advance of capitalism (see **ideology**), he argued that it nevertheless offered some space in which socialist and communist parties could take on conservative, right-wing ideas and pro-market assumptions with some hope of success – what he called 'the war of position'.

The concept of civil society has enjoyed something of a renaissance since the late 1980s particularly in the wake of the fall of the communist regimes of Eastern Europe which, once the authoritarian state regimes were dismantled, revealed a scarcity of self-organized social activity. Social theorists began to look again at the potential energies within civil society and how many facets of social life depend on its energy and vibrant nature. Successive governments in Britain have been active in cultivating civil society both as a source of social cohesion and as having the creativity and energy to tackle difficult social problems that government has neither the financing nor the expertise to solve. The coalition government's 'Big Society' is based wholly on the idea of a strengthened civil society.

clinical psychology see **psychopathology**

cognition the process of thinking involving the acquisition and use of language, conceiving, memory, problem-solving, judging and perception. Although the convention is to conceive of mental activities generally as having feeling and thinking dimensions (the cognitive and emotional), it is now understood that feelings can affect thinking and that thinking can similarly affect feelings. If a person has been through a stressful or even a traumatic experience then many social workers have acknowledged that clear thinking and thus decision-making may be impaired. In similar vein, a person who thinks clearly (perhaps to accept that they have a terminal illness or that a relationship is no longer viable) may become sad or depressed. In contrast to behaviourism, cognitive psychology is primarily concerned with the innate characteristics of thinking; although it is acknowledged that thinking can be affected by social, cultural, environmental and situational factors.

Cognitive development is a key concern for social workers (and teachers, psychologists and education social workers) as they try to assess whether children are maturing in an appropriate or acceptable way. Studies of child development indicate that children move through discernible stages where perceptions and thinking are very egocentric and concrete through to later stages where they are able to conceive of things that are not present and later still are able to think in abstract terms. Judgements and the ability to make moral decisions also emerge later as teenagers and young people can think in terms of general rules that can be applied to different contexts and problems. These kinds of understanding enable social workers to make decisions about whether a child has 'developmental delay', or a learning difficulty or perhaps some kind of behavioural problem such as attention deficit hyperactivity disorder (ADHD). Similar developmental paradigms are used with social workers dealing with offending behaviour where the focus might be upon a young person's notions of right and wrong and their sense of 'personal responsibility' for offences, especially where others have been harmed in some way. In yet other contexts, judgements need to be made about people with mental health problems or where there is a concern about 'mental capacity' in elders or with people with early onset dementia. Assessments with these groups of people focus upon memory, perceptions and the ability to act responsibly in relation to others. Significant 'failures' in any of these tests may mean that people's abilities to live independently are compromised or that they are potentially a danger to themselves and/or to others.

cognitive behaviour therapy   see behaviourism

cognitive dissonance   a strong and discomforting experience where an individual holds differing or competing thoughts or feelings about the same subject or closely related subjects. Usually if dissonance is recognized and experienced very explicitly there are likely to be attempts by the individual to reduce dissonance and to try to achieve congruence.

It is not uncommon for people with racist attitudes, for example, to have a positive attitude to a colleague who is perhaps hard working and a good team player. Dissonance in this context might be sustained by the racist arguing that the colleague is an exception to the rule. But if further close experience of ethnic minorities suggests that they are perfectly decent human beings then dissonance is likely to be experienced in a more discomforting way. In another context, it might be possible for a person with alcohol-related problems to claim that a few drinks make him feel 'a whole lot better' after a hard day at work when his GP is also telling him that some liver function tests have given some worrying results.

Social workers can be alert to evidence of 'dissonant thinking' especially where the competing thoughts or attitudes concern a problem that is the focus of the work or intervention being considered. In relation to alcohol-related problems, for example, social workers and counsellors have found the *cycle of change* (Prochaska, DiClementi and Narcross) approach useful. This perspective has it that before any work with a person with alcoholism can usefully be initiated, workers look to see whether the person has got beyond the pre-contemplation stage; that is, the person is acknowledging the difficulties their addiction is creating for them and is not rationalizing contrary attitudes.

Festinger, L. (1957) *A Theory of Cognitive Dissonance*. Palo Alto, CA: Stanford University Press.

Prochaska, J., DiClementi, C. and Norcross, J. (1992) In search of how people change, *American Psychologist*, 47(9): 1102–14.

commodification the process by which public goods, services and human labour, generally available at low cost or no cost, are converted into commodities or products that are bought and sold at a price through the **market**. An historical example of commodification is the widespread transfer of common land in the eighteenth century, which was open to use by all in a particular village, into private ownership where it then could be bought and sold at a price. Commodification can also be a relative phenomenon: social care for instance, although always paid for, has been increasingly commodified – hours are divided into 15-minute segments and each quarter of an hour paid for at market rates.

The term originated within **Marxism** where it referred to the goods, services and human labour that were produced for the market, where they were exchanged for money instead of being valued for what they are intrinsically and used directly by those who produced them. Thus Marxist theory distinguished between *use value* and *exchange value*. Chickens raised on small farms to provide eggs for the farming family is an example of use value while the surplus taken to market for sale by that family is an example of exchange value. Commodification in this sense is widely found within studies of developing countries where subsistence economies were once based on small farmers consuming ('using') what they themselves produced but were then transformed at the point when such farmers began to take their produce to market to be sold.

The term now has a more general application and often simply refers to humans becoming commodities through the labour market. For example, children in certain countries are pressed into work often as young as 8 or 9 (as they were in Britain at the start of the Industrial Revolution); in that sense their labour power – even their childhood – is commodified. As a further example it can also be said that caring responsibilities have been commodified – for example, mothers of very young children are compelled to enter the labour market and then to pay for the care of their children when at work. Esping-Anderson has noted how some welfare states *decommodify* individuals – for example lone parents – by providing financial support so they do not have to enter the labour market in order to survive. This then is the reverse of commodification where children can be looked after in arrangements that are *not* determined or influenced by the labour market.

Esping-Anderson, G. (1990) *The Three Worlds of Welfare Capitalism*. Oxford: The Polity Press.

communism see **left, left wing**

communitarianism a perspective in social theory that argues that individuals are not the wholly autonomous, rational beings that liberalism and particularly rational choice theorists maintain. Rather, individuals and their beliefs and choices of action are the product of heritage, tradition and community that brings with them ties of obligations to the other members of the same tradition and community.

Communitarian thinking came to prominence in the early 1990s as a philosophical reaction to the heavy emphasis on free market economics of the Thatcher and Reagan administrations in the 1980s, on the one hand, and the insistence on expanding individual 'rights', on the part of some on the **left**, on the other. Both of these orientations, communitarians argue, undermine what holds society together and in effect would reduce us all to isolated rights-bearing agents without the strength of social and community ties to support us.

Communitarian writing, particularly in the 1990s, was dominated by a social psychologist, Amitai Etzioni, who together with other like-minded theorists put forward several key points:

- individuals have responsibilities and duties, which are socially determined; they have been lost sight of in the constant barrage of 'rights talk' – maintaining, arguing for and justifying individual rights seems to drown out all discussion of socially determined obligations;
- individuals have too much freedom – this has led to a loss of sense of what is moral and to moral confusion;
- there is a 'parenting deficit', arising from two parents typically at work and/or marriage breakdown; the result is lack of moral guidance for children and young people within the family home;
- communities legitimately identify the common good and the informal social norms needed to maintain it; individual members of a community are expected to uphold both.

The communitarians of the 1990s were criticized for placing undue emphasis on the weakened family as a source of social problems and in this sense echoed some of the themes embedded in notions of the **underclass**. Nevertheless, communitarianism was explicitly embraced by the Clinton administration in the US and by the Blair government in Britain. Both adopted the notion that citizens were obliged to recognize their responsibilities and both loosely based their approach to welfare reform partly on communitarian grounds to demonstrate that they were centrist in politics and had left behind the older radical thinking of their political parties.

Criticism of communitarianism came from two different directions. One tackled the notion of a 'parenting deficit' which seemed to be pointing to working mothers as the source of the problem and wanting to restore the conventional household roles of the 1950s as a solution. The other called attention to the potentially repressive nature of communities and argued that the autonomous, empowered individual provides the better basis for a free society. This debate between communitarians arguing for the power of communities, on one side, and liberal political theorists arguing for the autonomy of the individual, on the other, raised interesting questions in practice and in theory. For example, how should the individual respond if the community in which she or he lives shows hatred for Muslims, adopts restrictions on abortions or does not tolerate gays or lesbians? And, just as importantly, what is the social philosophy that grounds this kind of decision?

Other communitarian-leaning social theorists, such as Michael Sandel, focused more on how the **market** undermines community and asked in a less dogmatic way than Etzioni what kinds of obligations do individuals owe to their society or community (if any)? How far are these a product of their commitments and social obligations?

Although now used less frequently, in retrospect, communitarianism highlighted themes that were later investigated through the concept of **social capital**. It also helped revive interest in the concept of **civil society** and community-based solutions that the Labour government (1997–2010) and the subsequent coalition government adopted.

Sandel, M. (2012) *What Money can't Buy: The Moral Limits of Markets.* London: Allen Lane.

community a set of social relationships that operate within certain boundaries or locations. Communities are usually assumed to be geographical, based within a neighbourhood or part of a city or town, but sociologists and social geographers have found the same elements of reciprocity and mutuality that underpin geographical communities in faith groups and other 'communities of interest' which form around common interests or social objectives.

Sociologists first began to explore the concept of community in the later nineteenth century and were aware from the beginning that relationships they perceived as the foundation of community were already under severe threat from a rapidly industrializing economy. Communal ties of all kinds and community life based on tradition, faith and extended families were being eroded in the onrush of capitalist development. Agricultural workers left rural areas in huge numbers, disrupting community and family in the countryside, and what had been family cottage industries such as handloom weaving were abruptly destroyed as weaving and cloth manufacturing began to be produced in steam-powered factories.

In this sense 'community' stood in contrast to the word 'society', which was used to describe the new social structure that emerged during the Industrial Revolution from the early 1800s on, with a vastly expanded middle class and a large working class who lived often in impoverished urban districts dominated by factory enterprises and whose lives were controlled by a harsh labour market dominated by employers. Thus it emerged that 'community' came to stand for familiarity with a locality, face-to-face relationships and shared values, while 'society' embodied the pursuit of self-interest that prevailed in capitalist society of the nineteenth century.

The late nineteenth-century German sociologist Ferdinand Tönnies captured this difference between 'community' and 'society' in the words *Gemeinschaft* and *Gesellschaft* (which provided him with the title of his book). They are, said Tönnies, the two principal types of human association. *Gemeinschaft* is based on a common set of beliefs about appropriate behaviour and responsibilities and is characterized by strong personal relationships and kinship. Social control is exercised internally through the high degree of bonding and loyalty that the individual feels toward a collective unit larger than herself or himself.

Gesellschaft can be translated as society (or 'civil society'), an association in which the pursuit of individual **self-interest** is dominant and in which shared beliefs about behaviour and roles are conspicuously absent. Rather than family ties or obligations to the community being dominant, what holds *Gesellschaft* together is the division of labour, the bureaucratization of administration and corporate life and the pursuit of self-interest through the market economy. Within *Gesellschaft*, relationships are impersonal, fleeting, contractural and competitive, often characterized by anonymity and **alienation**. We can see in his work the threats that industrialization and market economies posed for the idea of community with its supposed built-in sources of mutual support.

In the middle of the twentieth century sociologists began to analyse more systematically what 'community' is. Many of the classic studies of community arise from that time, partly as a reaction to wider trends of mass consumer society. In Britain, studies tended to document the shared burdens and pleasures of living in close-knit terraced streets and to show how people pulled together in the face of adversity and in responding to the rhythms of the industrial age: the factory whistle, chapel on Sunday, wakes and informal support networks among extended families and friends. Wilmott and Young in their classic work on the east end of London (1964) documented the changes in family life that urban communal life demanded. Overall, they concluded that the social links and family connections brought people together in patterns that changed only slowly over time – which allowed people to develop a sense of belonging.

The second half of the twentieth century witnessed a reaction against such studies and their tendency to overlook just how difficult and hard edged life in urban neighbourhoods could be. These studies questioned how much of a sense of togetherness really existed in neighbourhoods. Did all groups living in a particular area really share the same values? Did women hold the same dominant patriarchal values that allocated to them a relatively confined role of looking after the home and raising the children while husband, as sole breadwinner, went out to work? Did religious dissenters or newly arrived immigrants of different ethnic origins and different faiths actually feel part of 'the community'?

Generally, among those commentators and analysts who looked closely at the concept of community toward the end of the twentieth century, the answer to all of these was 'no'. Such questions pushed analysis of community in the opposite direction, with some authorities arguing that there is no such thing as 'the community', at least in the sense of a single community occupying the same geographical space. The notion of 'community' obscures the values and perspectives of a dominant group, allowing them to appear to represent the views of all groups and people within that geographical area. Rather, this critique runs, if the concept is to be used at all, it has to be acknowledged that there are many communities within any given geographical space each based on different values, different ways of looking at life, and different definitions of well-being. These communities may be formed according to faith, ethnicity, language, culture or more particularly around disability, sexual orientation and age.

Another group of critics argued that, whatever may have been the case in the past, in contemporary Britain, the very fabric of community is weakening. The diversity and mobility of resident populations, the thinning of social networks, the demise of the extended family, the decline in volunteerism have undermined all community orientations, making any policy and practice based on a community focus difficult to sustain. This critique is largely associated with post-modernist thinkers and sociologists who argue that an age of **individualization** is upon us in which all social connections are suffering.

Much of the foregoing critique of the concept of community is valid and has had a major impact on how we now view communities. It is no longer possible to think that a geographical area will hold a single community; any locality is going to be made up of many different kinds of community – some may have a geographical basis, others are based on common interests, such as culture, or on unifying institutions, such as churches or mosques. In the final analysis, there is widespread agreement among scholars that we should be careful not to romanticize the notion of community or endow communities with powers and allegiances that do not exist.

Robert Sampson has developed the idea of a community of 'limited liability'. He acknowledges that for many of our deeply personal relationships as well as work we are far less tied in the developed world to the geographical community in which we live. Nevertheless, he argues, the concept of community remains essential as a site for the realization of some common values such as public safety, norms of civility and mutual trust, voluntary associations and collective socialization of young children. Geographical communities are also the place where the inequalities in economic resources and social–structural resources are located and sharply evident. Such resources, particularly income, housing stock and educational attainment, are distributed unequally across spatial areas.

We now have compelling evidence that shows that where a person lives profoundly affects her life chances and opportunities. The differences between communities, in terms of institutional resources, patterns of social organization and networks, levels of community safety, quality of physical environment and levels of trust, either support or undermine individual capacities such as aspiration and resilience. Communities that work well are ones in which there is social diversity, a range of resources, good-quality services such as schools, a range of enterprises and shops, reasonable levels of employment. But they also have more indefinable qualities – trust between people, a concern for public spaces and how they are used, informal social controls (see **social capital**). Such communities and neighbourhoods add substantially to the quality of life for those who live in them and provide improved levels of health and well-being.

Young, M. and Willmott, P. (1969) *Family and Kinship in East London*. London: Penguin Books.

Sampson, R. (1999) What 'community' supplies, in R.F. Ferguson (ed.) *Urban Problems and Community Development*. Washington, DC: Brookings Institution.

community development purposive action aiming to expand the capacity of a geographical community to respond to social problems. This can include building community organizations and local networks that can pool skills, provide training and transmit awareness of political and economic power in order for those problems to be addressed.

Community development work has a long association with working for groups that are disadvantaged and contending with discrimination. It does this by:

- seeking to create links and liaisons between groups and individuals within a locality, around issues of common concern on a basis of mutual respect, while recognizing diversity and differences;
- promoting the development of alliances and the recognition of collective action by encouraging people to reflect and act together in order to achieve common goals and influence decision-makers;
- acknowledging the specific experience and contribution of all individuals in communities, to enable people to enhance their capacity to play a role in shaping and determining the society of which they are part;
- recognizing that the unequal distribution of power is both a personal and political issue, and that community work has a responsibility for linking the personal learning which empowers people, through to the collective learning and action for change which empowers communities. Community practice is important because it generates the skills in working with people collectively and sees strengths where others would see needs and deficits. This is quite simply because in seeking to mobilize and empower local groups, train their leaders and build local organizations, community practitioners must start with assets and local capacities.

The Brazilian Paulo Freire (1921–97) has framed community development as an educative process. He argued that perceptions of powerlessness erode hope and create a 'culture of silence' in which poor people seem to accept the harshness of their lives and settle for explanations of individual failure rather than as collectively experienced oppression. He thought that all human beings are capable of critically engaging with their world once they begin to question the contradictions that shape their lives through a process of what he called 'conscientization' – the process of becoming aware of contradictions, whether political, cultural or socio-economic. The community development worker seeks then to draw out from people's experiences what they regard as the most pressing problems and to 'problematize' them, that is look at their complexity and their relationship to forces well beyond the power of the individual to change on his or her own. Education cannot be neutral in Freire's view – either it serves the *reproduction* of the dominant order or provides space for *production* in which citizens learn to think for themselves. He called the latter 'critical pedagogy' which always includes dialogue – a mutual and reciprocal form of discussion that embodies respect and acknowledges the importance of relationship. Without this community development would only begin to recreate another system which would impose its own values, assumptions and perceptions.

When social workers look at the wide range of approaches and interventions in communities and neighbourhoods it is useful to distinguish between those that are *community based* and those that are of *community level*. Both provide services to people and community but they work in different ways. Community-level interventions aim at the community as a whole and intend to change that community as their first priority and not necessarily to help specific families or people in need. This approach is based on the conviction that social problems, especially those created by disadvantage, are best dealt with by developing the capacity and the strengths of the community as a whole rather than by identifying individuals with problems and providing services to them. The aim is to improve levels of well-being across the whole community for all who live there.

Community-based interventions seek to do the opposite. They aim to meet the needs of specific individuals and families through services and supports delivered locally. Services are typically available through common access points, such as local schools or health clinics, local 'hubs' or offices, drop-in centres or through detached or 'floating' formats. Many programmes seek to do both: build community capacity and provide family services. Sure Start children's centre were an example: they had the objective of raising the standards of parenting across the neighbourhoods in which they were based while at the same time providing services to individual families such as child care, speech therapy or support for mothers with post-natal depression. In practice, it can be difficult to pinpoint where the community-based service ends and the community-level activities begin.

Ledwith, M. (2010) *Community Development,* 2nd edition. Bristol: The Policy Press.

compensatory education programmes and policies designed to help disadvantaged children overcome the negative effects of social deprivation, within their families and communities, upon their performance in schools and their low levels of participation in further and higher education.

There have been wide-ranging initiatives in many countries, notably in the US and the UK, beginning with Headstart in the US in the 1960s and later in the UK Education Priority Areas (Plowden Report), culminating recently with the UK's ambitious Sure Start programme. Policy analysts and government have concluded that the achievements of the Sure Start programme have generally been disappointing, resulting in a significant reduction in funding. Research has been more equivocal, suggesting that some features of Sure Start programmes have been successful and that the key strategic issue is to identify which projects have worked well, which need recasting and which need to be abandoned. Among many complex issues the notion of 'additionality' has been key; this concerns whether Sure Start programmes have been genuinely additional to existing provision within any locality or whether local authorities have closed pre-school projects of their own because Sure Start was opening up in their localities. The other major issue seems to have been whether it has been possible to create a genuine partnership with parents so that any gains for pre-school children achieved by Sure Start staff are subsequently sustained by parents. In this regard, some Sure Start programmes have been singularly more successful than others.

Other kinds of initiative concerned with compensatory education have included targeted projects concerned with the following, for example:

- *Teenage parents who are still of compulsory school age.* Some projects concerned to encourage teenage mothers to remain in full-time education despite having the responsibility of early parenthood (mostly small, dedicated projects) have been remarkably successful if they have been properly resourced with crèches for their children and others kinds of sympathetic support.
- *Looked-after children and young people.* Looked-after children have had consistently poor educational outcomes, a finding that should not be surprising given the continued instability in the care experience for many. Multiple moves of residence usually involving multiple moves of schools, communities and resultant fractured relationships with siblings and families of origin all undermine attempts to create stability – a fundamental requirement for educational success. Initiatives such as the creation of posts of teachers who will have the responsibility to support looked-after children are considered useful but insufficient in themselves to compensate for chaotic lives.
- *Disabled children.* Higher expectations of children with disabilities, the increasing integration of disabled children in mainstream schools and various grants to pay for support technologies as well as educational assessments of learning disabilities have improved the outcomes for disabled children and young people but most commentators have it that there are still many residual disadvantages to address.
- *Young people post-compulsory education.* Their participation in further and higher education in general as well as the problem of NEETs (those 'not in education, employment or training') continue to be sites of major underachievement. It has been accepted by

many commentators that economic factors underpinning family poverty have a major part to play in young people staying on in full-time education after the age of 16. Similarly, many perceive the programmes designed for NEETs as essentially diversionary, leading few young people to employment opportunities of any substance. Some have usefully pointed to changes in the economy as critical in this regard, with fewer unskilled jobs available in advanced industrial societies where many of the driving forces are technological.

Other kinds of persistent educational disadvantage in relation to identified groups, such as, for example, Afro-Caribbean boys and the children of traveller communities, have enjoyed really superficial attention and little in the way of serious new initiatives concerned to address their very particular problems. In sum, initiatives concerned with compensatory education seem to date to be at best partial solutions to intractable problems rooted in structural disadvantage, and in this respect education as currently programmed really cannot hope to be the principal means to achieve significant measures of social mobility.

conditioning see **behaviourism**

conservativism see **right, right wing**

cost–benefit analysis an evaluation of whether the cost of a project, service or policy will realize or is likely to realize certain specified social benefits or outcomes. Such an analysis will attempt to identify and quantify the 'inputs' (usually money) dedicated to the project, policy or service(s) as well as the 'outputs' or effects of the project, policy or service(s) in terms of social benefits; although it may also be possible and desirable to estimate the monetary value of the social benefits. In many or most instances, this will be a challenging and complex task because cost–benefit analyses (CBAs) can pose considerable methodological problems.

First, in relation to costs (or 'inputs'), politicians and researchers may initially focus on money as the obvious unit of analysis. But it is entirely possible that any project could insist upon, say, the involvement of residents in the delivery of new community services. Such involvement could be seen as both an output (if residents responded to the call to become involved and did so with enthusiasm) and, subsequently, an input as the residents become an additional resource in actually delivering services or using services more constructively. Second, it is often difficult to estimate the value of social benefits. For example, how might the benefits of saving lives by investing in traffic management systems be calculated? Third, how might the benefits of social investments be estimated for a project that is modest in scale but might be started immediately in comparison with a more ambitious project that could only be started later because of current resource constraints?

A related activity that involves both costs and benefits is to try to estimate the real costs of any social problem. For example, the multifaceted problem of **domestic violence** has been deconstructed to reveal that if a woman should feel it necessary to leave a violent partner and move home and relocate to another community, there is the potential for consequences that are costly to the public purse. It is possible that she would need rehousing, perhaps after spending some time in a refuge; claim benefits because she cannot sustain her employment; need legal advice; benefit from counselling to work through traumatic experiences; involve the police and the justice system because she has been assaulted; refer to social services if there are safeguarding issues and to medical services if she had been injured.

Similarly, sustained critiques of the care system have consistently argued for significantly enhanced funding to support specialist fostering schemes, improved residential provision and other kinds of dedicated resource to support children and young people in care for much longer. Researchers have argued that it makes little sense to ask our most vulnerable people to live independently at, say, aged 16 or 17 when the average age for young people to 'fly the nest' is around 25 and rising. Given that care leavers figure prominently in 'downstream problems' such as entering prisons, becoming homeless, using services concerned with addictions and psychiatric and counselling services, the total costs of the care system 'failures' clearly need to be articulated on a much larger canvas.

Cost–benefit analyses can be seen as making relevant information available to key decision-makers so that they might make informed decisions. Analysts have to demonstrate 'relevance' of social indicators to a problem or service where any new investment is being considered and attempt to estimate likely outcomes. Since these kinds of model cannot be confined to the laboratory and will always be subject to the broader influences of, for example, wider economic circumstances, there will always be an element of the unpredictable. But overall, cost–benefit analyses do promise a more considered and rational approach to social policies than that of the committed partisan. By implication, they also often require different organizations and departments with differing but overlapping responsibilities to think about how they might most usefully collaborate to address a problem meaningfully.

criminology broadly, the study of behaviour considered to be criminal and the general context of such behaviour including the study of offenders; the causes of crime; preventions, remedies and treatments; and the experiences of victims and interventions to support them.

- *The social construction of crime* – what is considered a crime in any society is something of a variable, in that what has sometimes been considered a crime may later not be regarded as criminal (for example, homosexual relations were considered to be a crime in the UK until 1967; to deny the existence of God has historically been grounds for a death sentence in many societies and has later been regarded as a legitimate point of view). There are also examples of acts that were regarded as of no interest to the justice system, but are now regarded as crimes – for example, *domestic violence* and *hate crimes*. The general seriousness attached to particular acts has also often changed significantly. For example, sheep stealing was an offence in the nineteenth century in the UK that might have led either to hanging or deportation to the colonies. In contemporary Britain, there is probably growing support for the idea of decriminalizing drug-taking; to reconfigure our thinking about the issue to redesignate addicts as people with a health problem and, at a stroke, to reduce what addicts consider they have to do, reluctantly perhaps, namely to commit offences or maybe prostitute themselves to raise money to buy drugs.

- *Theories about the causes of criminal behaviour* – early attempts to make sense of criminality, construed as a *positivist perspective*, included Lombroso's atavistic criminals – physical types regarded as throwbacks to a more primitive humanity (he actually measured the skulls of prison inmates) – now considered wholly spurious; a much later explanation about chromosome malformation has also been discredited and Sheldon's theory of physical types (endomorphs, ectomorphs and mesomorphs – the last, built like a front row rugby player, is thought to be predisposed to criminal behaviour) is similarly regarded as without foundation. *Social structural or social pathological explanations* all emphasize the negative aspects of capitalist societies with regard to grossly unequal wealth, life chances and the degradation of working-class life. But capitalism is also interested in workers as consumers and, in this regard, it needs to convey the idea that workers too can access the 'good life', although it knows that many will not. This paradigm was developed by Merton in his development of the concept of **anomie**, suggesting that criminal activity is undertaken by individuals who wish to secure the social ends (goals) of the society of which they are a part, but recognizing that, from their lowly position, they cannot realistically hope to achieve those ends legitimately – but are prepared to *innovate* (steal or commit other criminal acts) to try. Using this broad framework, other theorists have sought to understand the mechanisms by which criminals learn how to act criminally. Some have concentrated on cultural aspects of communities that encourage criminality or transmit criminality from one generation to the next including notions of *sub-cultures* or neighbourhoods and *peer group* influence or *gangs*. Later *critical criminologists* held that the criminal justice system in general could best be understood as a system of class domination especially with regard to policing strategies. The key issue here is the idea that certain communities will be policed more rigorously than others; that, as a result, more offences will be 'uncovered' thus justifying the continuation of intensive policing. *Labels* will thus be attached to these communities and to the individuals within them. It is also argued that workers in the justice system work in a manner which is consistent with this paradigm. Youth justice workers and probation officers in preparing pre-sentence reports do not write of the ravages of capitalism in relation to a particular community, but rather of the offender's attitude to the offences and the effects of his offences on victims, his family circumstances, his employment/ school record and other immediate micro issues. The National Standards for Youth Justice Services set by the Youth Justice Board and the very influential book by McGuire and Priestley (1995) are indicative of locating the problem almost exclusively in the individual offender, his immediate family and his *micro*-social environment. Critical criminology also points to the very real problems that are generated by punitive regimes in prisons and young offenders' institutions, of racist practices in the justice system with regard to over-zealous policing (including *institutional racism*) and disproportionate sentencing but also deaths in police custody and widespread sexism.

The *feminist* critique of critical criminology has developed in the UK since the 1970s. The key strands have included:

- the comparatively little attention given to crimes against women by the criminal justice system including sexual violence and **domestic violence**, the low conviction rates for those prosecuted and thus low reporting rates of these kinds of offence to the police;
- the relatively harsh treatment meted out by the justice system to women offenders in comparison with the sentences awarded to men for comparable offences. The key notion here was held to be that women offenders strayed from conventional notions of womanhood and were additionally punished for doing so. This paradigm seemed to include women who killed abusive partners, even

when they had experienced abuse over many years and their actions in killing their partners could be construed as self-defence;

- the lack of attention given by the police to the needs of women working in the sex industry; and the failure of the police to protect them or take them seriously in relation to violence including sexual violence. Indeed, many prostitutes have claimed that the police are a major source of oppression in their collusion with violent men.

The training of probation officers was dissociated from social work education a couple of decades ago in the UK, with the professional probation paradigm relocating from a quasi-social work role to being *'officers of the court'*. The establishment of the Youth Justice Board for juvenile offenders has also entailed a similar paradigm shift. It is indicative that, for example, most transactions between probation officers and youth offending team (YOT) workers and their clients now take place in the office. The whole focus of their work is to try to encourage offenders not to offend again but the clear emphasis is upon locating the offenders' problems in their failure to take personal responsibility for their actions and on the need for them to do so. All strands of opinion researching the justice system as well as most practitioners would argue that encouraging offenders not to offend and to become more responsible citizens are key objectives, but such a paradigm completely overlooks any structural factors that often underpin offending behaviour. (See also **punishment**.)

McGuire, J. and Priestley, P. (1995) *What Works: Reducing Reoffending*. Chichester: Wiley.

critical theory investigating the ideological assumptions that underpin the way society, culture, institutions and policy function as a whole. In practice, critical theory calls for searching questions to be asked of social programmes, to expose interests or objectives that those who create such programmes would prefer to keep hidden.

Critical theory originated in Germany and came to prominence after the Second World War. It combined some elements of **Marxism** and psychoanalysis to investigate the contradictions of Western capitalist societies. In particular it sought to show how new modes of mass culture would undermine the political consciousness of the working class and make any kind of socialism more difficult to achieve. In this respect it was significantly more pessimistic than traditional Marxism in its view of the direction society would take, emphasizing instead the way a narrow and dehumanizing 'technical rationality' in the social organization of capitalism deformed if not obliterated completely the ideals of freedom of thought and meaningful exploration of the good society. One of the chief tasks of critical theory was to combat this trend.

The most notable critical theorist of the second half of the twentieth century is Jürgen Habermas who has developed a more optimistic
approach. He argues that in a thriving **public sphere**, where people
have access to information, opinion and debate, critical theory works
by searching out internal contradictions and gaps in the systems of
thought expressed. The task of critical theory, Habermas argues, is
to push these contradictions to the point where a different consensus
can emerge. Habermas acknowledges that he is portraying an ideal:
that humans fundamentally draw on language and symbols to engage
in free communication, undistorted by social inequalities, external
oppression or internal repression. He balances this ideal by looking at
how contemporary society distorts this process of deliberation and free
exchange of opinion.

Social work students are often urged to engage in 'critical analysis' –
whether of their own practice or of specific policies or institutions. In
this sense critical theory is only loosely applied, prompting the student
to examine all sides of an issue as deeply and rigorously as possible.
At this level, it also asks the student to explain the deeper ideological
motivations that may lie behind a specific form of practice or policy.

Critical theory has been explicitly embraced by some social work
theorists, for example Jan Fook. She has developed a framework of
critical **post-modernism** which she largely applies to social work
practice itself. Language is important because it constructs substantial
outcomes. Holding fluid rather than fixed notions of identity is also
useful for practitioners. Most importantly, she holds that social work
cannot be locked into rigidities and orthodox thinking. Neither is
there one thing called social work – rather it is a way of acting that can
engage anywhere and at any level.

Fook, J. (2002) *Social Work: Critical Theory and Practice*. London:
Sage Publications.

culture the totality of ideas, tools, and the creative arts produced
within a given society, community or group. Culture embraces the
varieties and intricacies of human science, technologies, language, art,
music, literature and dance.

Social workers encounter aspects of culture in different contexts – for
example, in the very loose use of the word in relation to 'changing the
culture of the agency'. Culture in this sense refers to 'the way things
are done around here' – the values, ethos and perspectives of the
organization or profession. More importantly, social workers encounter differing understandings of culture in relation to ethnicity and
religion particularly as these are found in local communities of which
service users are members. Culture in this sense covers the totality of

community or group life embracing religion, language, food preparation (especially meat), child-rearing practices, dress codes, relationships to parents, and gender roles. It can also cover the smallest aspects of behaviour such as the degree of acceptable eye contact. In marginalized groups that are based on physical impairment or sexuality, culture may also embrace ways of communicating, a shared sense of the adversities faced by members in daily life, and the promotion of positive values and resilience within the group.

While black social workers and educationists in the US and Britain initially promoted culturally sensitive practice in relation to black families, the notion that social workers should be culturally competent has widened under the pressure of large-scale global mobility and demographic changes, together with the now widely recognized inadequacy of the 'melting pot' model of cultural **assimilation**. Models of cultural competence for practitioners now embrace cultures outside ethnicity such as that of deaf, lesbian, gay and disability groups.

The British Association of Social Workers' Code of Ethics states that social workers should recognize and respect ethnic and cultural diversity, and the further diversity *within* ethnic and cultural groups, and promote policies, procedures and practices that are consistent with this objective (BASW 2009). (See also **multiculturalism**.) The code requires them to undertake a critique of the culture within which they themselves were brought up, to identify its stereotyping actions and the values that it privileges as well as those it discounts.

The pursuit of cultural competence broadened social work's concern with the disadvantaged and marginalized. Standard casework for example had leaned heavily on psychodynamic judgements based on generic notions of individual developmental stages using labels such as 'immature', 'lacking ego strength' or 'overly dependent' to describe behaviour that originated in completely different cultural contexts. Equally, Eurocentric biases in social work practice had established a deficit-oriented view of human behaviour that paid no attention to customary behaviours of non-European cultures.

Criticisms of the concept of cultural competence make the point that it targets change at the level of social workers' personal beliefs and agency practices, but does not go far enough to change agency, systems and institutionalized oppressions. It has also been criticized for creating a 'multicultural umbrella' in which the most historically enduring and violent oppression – racism – is fundamentally lost sight of. 'Culture' in the view of such critics is seen as promoting a bland discussion of 'difference' that has largely replaced 'race' in relation to marginalized groups.

Other critics of the cultural competence model ask whether it is possible for social workers to be educated for cultural competence. Can they actually be expected to become culturally competent across the range of user cultures they encounter? According to Ben Ari and Strier, to do so 'assumes that there is a well-defined and measurable "cultural knowledge" that people can learn in order to handle cultural differences in competent ways' (2009: 2162). This they argue is a commodified conception of cultural knowledge and a dangerous reduction that 'totalizes' the Other (that is, it equates the identity of the user from a minority group with a ready-made construct of the user's home culture) in order to subordinate him or her to institutional purposes.

Ben-Ari, A. and Strier, R. (2009) Rethinking cultural competence: what can we learn from Levinas?, *British Journal of Social Work*, 40: 2155–67.

culture of poverty the idea that poverty arises not only from socio-economic causes such as low wages or racism but from lifestyle choices and moral failings that entrench poverty in a neighbourhood or family. In general, the concept of the culture of poverty has been promoted by social theorists on the political **right** who often argue that over-generous welfare states have created a dependency on state benefits that they see as part of that culture (see also **underclass**). Social theorists on the **left** have also worked on the cultural and behavioural dimensions of poverty but do so within a different context. While arguing that economic causes are central they have explored what it means to live in areas where there are high concentrations of people on low incomes – for example the impact on family life and community safety (see also **neighbourhood**).

Oscar Lewis, an American anthropologist who investigated impoverished families in Mexico and Puerto Rico in the 1960s, is generally credited with first using the phrase 'culture of poverty'. In his ethnographic studies, Lewis used the word 'culture' to denote a way of living and coping, rather than in the more general understanding of the word. Within the culture of poverty. Lewis noted the frequent violence, lack of a sense of history and a neglect to plan for the future that dominated lives there. Because people saw no way out of their poverty they made decisions based on small, short-term gains. He wrote: 'the low aspiration level helps to reduce frustration, [and] the legitimization of short-range hedonism makes possible spontaneity and enjoyment', but added that 'there is a great deal of pathos, suffering and emptiness among those who live in the culture of poverty. It does not provide much support or long range satisfaction and its encouragement of mistrust tends to magnify helplessness and isolation.'

Economists investigating developing countries also helped define 'culture of poverty' when they were surprised that the communities they investigated did not seem to be interested in greater prosperity or in new opportunities for greater affluence. This went wholly against their understanding that rational behaviour is self-interested and always prefers gains to loss. They were mystified to observe poor people only doing enough work to survive. They attributed the apathy to cultural 'inertia' – a form of irrationality and attachment to the past. This was linked to personal characteristics with key words such as 'apathetic', 'feckless', 'lazy', 'childlike'. Thus what began as a cultural theory was linked to individual psychology, with the implication that the problem of poverty was located in irrational behaviour that was beyond the reach of **cost–benefit analysis**.

The debates around the 'culture of poverty' are important for social work because they address issues of the relationship between inequality and behaviour that social workers need to think through. Are people poor because their cultural norms devalue saving and striving to get ahead – or are they poor because of economic constraints they have to contend with, constraints that are beyond the power of culture to change? Do particular communities seem to have low aspirations for themselves and their families and fail to show the necessary energy and commitment to find and hold a job? And if they do is that a means of coping or is it that they actively choose to be without work and rely on benefits?

For social workers, these are live questions in relation to the actual individuals and neighbourhoods they work with. For example, does an emphasis on 'culture of poverty' in relation to Muslim communities explain or mask the reality that Pakistani and Bangladeshi neighbourhoods experience the highest level of poverty in the UK? The same kind of question can be asked of specific families. Social workers operate on the terrain of 'non-ideal theory' – not from the principles and ideals of a perfectly just society but from the social world and human behaviour as it is. They begin with empirical investigation of users' circumstances – an assessment – and reach conclusions on the basis of that investigation. In this process, questions about aspiration, capacity, drive and resilience are never far from the surface.

D d

data pieces of information, facts, measurements or statistics gathered for purposes of analysis and research.

Data are collected from a wide variety of sources using a range of methods such as surveys, interviews, observations, participant observations and documents of many kinds. The efficacy of the data will reflect both the research design and the rigour of the research instruments. There are now many data banks, managed by either government agencies such as the Office for National Statistics in the UK (among many databases, this office keeps data on the census conducted every 10 years) or academic initiatives such as the Economic and Social Research Council Data Archive or the joint American/ European International Federation of Data Organizations for the Social Sciences. Although there are different areas of interest and priorities in these data banks, most are happy to share data for purposes of secondary analysis by the academic community in general. (See also **demography**, **research design** and **research methods**.)

death and dying the permanent end of life in a person and the process for approaching that end.

- *The social construction of death and dying* – for the atheist, or the person convinced that the end of life is the end of them as an individual, death is a transition into non-existence; for the religious, death offers the possibility of an afterlife (in a heaven or, perhaps, the other place) or a rebirth or variations on that theme. Although sociologists are not in the business of siding with either the religious or the non-believer, they are interested in the 'social consequences of belief' in the arrangements that people and their social groups make to deal with death and dying. Sociologists, in effect, ask the questions: What do the dying do when they are dying and why? What do people around them do and why? Who are the key players in this context and what are their roles?
- *The management of dying* – the now familiar debate claiming that getting pregnant and giving birth to children have been unnecessarily 'medicalized' with the development of contraception technologies, conception technologies, childbirth technologies and foetal

technologies all governed by doctors has more recently led to another debate about medicalizing the process of dying. Although having children and dying have clearly benefited from medicine with significant reductions in both infant mortality and the birth of damaged children, on the one hand, and the management of pain, on the other, both developments, it is argued by some, have increased medical control of these issues at the expense of women and the dying respectively. However, in practice, in relation to dying, the doctor–patient relationship is capable of differing expression. Glaser and Strauss's (1965) study identified different *awareness contexts*:

(1) *Closed awareness* – the patient does not know that s/he is dying and is kept in ignorance of the serious nature of his or her condition.

(2) *Suspected awareness* – the patient has a feeling or suspects that s/he is dying.

(3) *Mutual pretence awareness* – both parties are, in fact, aware that the patient is dying but behave as if the patient does not know.

(4) *Open awareness* – both patient and medical staff are fully aware of the realities and are open in their acknowledgement of approaching death.

Underpinning the variations in the behaviour of medical staff is probably a notion that, just as there is a **sick role**, there is also a *dying role* that is, perhaps, covertly expected of those terminally ill. Here there is an expectation that patients will face their death with dignity and composure, that they should continue playing their family roles effectively, relate to medical staff in a calm and co-operative manner and that they should seek to avoid any embarrassing or undignified behaviour. This, in a sense, identifies the key elements of a '*good death*'.

- *Individual responses to dying* – Kübler-Ross (1973) has been an influential thinker in relation to her analysis of how people respond when they learn they have a terminal illness. The five stages that she identified seem to involve an initial denial (there must be some kind of mistake or maybe the tests were not conclusive); second, a stage of being very angry and/or a feeling that this 'sentence' is wholly unjust (why do I have to die? – I have always tried to lead a healthy life); a third stage might include some attempts at bargaining or negotiating, although implying some kind of acceptance (if I can only see another Christmas or survive long enough to see my first grandchild); fourth, a depressive stage of withdrawal, of having reclusive inclinations; and, finally, a kind of acceptance that might entail preparation for death or dealing with important issues, having accepted the inevitable. Although Kübler–Ross later acknowledged that not everyone proceeds through the five stages of coming to terms with imminent death, she claimed that many people do or that they experience at least some of these stages, although not necessarily in the order specified. Later she claimed that these stages might also be useful in understanding personal responses to **loss** in a more general sense – including the imminent loss of the person dying.

Given the inevitability of death, individuals who know that they are dying and social workers involved with them and their families, may try to work towards bringing about a 'good death'. What constitutes a good death is of course a matter for debate. Many people seem to be preoccupied not just with death itself but also about the process of dying. A life ending without a lot of pain is one clear objective; thus palliative care, sometimes in a hospice setting, has become a key feature of direct work with dying people with a clear focus upon the management of pain and the enhancement of a feeling of well-being as circumstances allow. Other aspects of a satisfactory death might include trying to deal with problems that are of significance to the dying person such as unresolved problems in close relationships or dealing with issues related to economic matters for dependants.

It is known that some people when they have an incurable disease where there is great pain, or their dependence on others is likely to be substantial, consider euthanasia or they issue other instructions to caring and medical staff such as 'do not resuscitate' (DNR order) or a living will that makes clear that doctors should not continue with their efforts if there is little chance of recovery. They take the view that they have a right to die when and in a manner of their choosing. Some others oppose this view, claiming that life and its cessation is a matter for God. In this context, there may be a counselling role for social workers to ensure that people are making informed decisions free from any external coercion.

Attitudes to suicide too are similarly wide ranging because it can seem to embrace extreme social solidarity as with suicide bombers or a way out of an unbearably difficult and painful life, although most faiths seem to discourage it if not explicitly disapprove of it. In addition, there is currently a growing interest in the possibility and legality of *assisted suicide* for those unable to take their own lives because of their condition. The social work task here is likely to be about supporting the people who are close to the person who has ended his or her own life or helping with the emotional distress of those whose attempts to end their lives has failed. Social work with the dying is a significant specialism within interdisciplinary palliative care teams that might operate in hospitals, hospices or in outreach services where people opt to stay in their own homes. (See also **sick role, social constructionism**.)

Earle S., Komaromy, C. and Battholomew, C. (eds) (2009) *Death and Dying: A Reader.* London, Maidenhead: Sage Publications and Open University Press.

Kübler-Ross, E. (1973) *On Death and Dying.* London: Tavistock/ Routledge.

demography the statistical study of the social characteristics of human populations. Key social characteristics in demographic studies include the size of any social group such as nations, regions and communities in relation to social classes (and occupational groups), gender, ethnicity, marital status, age structures, peoples speaking particular languages, membership of religious groups and more generally variations to these populations because of changes in fertility (birth rates), mortality and migration (both immigration and emigration).

The UK government makes projections of population every two years. In addition, various statistical analyses are made of UK populations by the Office for National Statistics. Very detailed analyses are made with the national census every 10 years; the last was completed in 2011. Other very useful sources of demographic studies are *Social Trends*, the *Family Expenditure Survey* and the *General Lifestyle Survey* (replacing the former *General Household Survey*). All of these publications are published annually and are, moreover, available online.

The number of people living in the UK has increased from 55.9 million in 1971 to over 61 million in 2011and the number of people aged 65 and over is expected to exceed the number aged under 16 by 2021, if not earlier. Another key ingredient in this mix is the proportion of people of working age. This is currently a shifting part of the population as government revises the age for retirement upwards before the state pension can be accessed; although this is somewhat tempered as larger proportions of young people are in full-time education or training before becoming economically active. The UK, however, clearly has an ageing population, a cause for concern as government seeks to plan both health and social care services to deal with greater numbers of vulnerable elders with health problems and acquired disabilities.

The nature of the ageing population does vary according to ethnicity and region. Migrant peoples tend to be younger in general than host societies and some often have larger families than UK white people. This provides the explanation for the relatively small proportions, currently, of people from ethnic minorities over the age of 65 and the relatively large numbers of ethnic minorities with children under the age of 16. Ethnic minorities also tend to live in large urban centres thus providing a different/skewed age profile from that which is evident in small towns and rural areas in the UK.

Population data are a fruitful source of information about the age at which women have children (it has been rising for many years); the incidence of marriage, divorce and separation as well as cohabiting relationships; and related to these familial characteristics the number of children born outside marriage. Both marriages and cohabiting relationships have become more unstable over recent decades, with cohabitation the more precarious. The composition of households has changed significantly as a result of these multiple changes with a consequential increase in the proportion of single-person households, single parenthood (never married or cohabited, divorced, separated, widowed) and various family forms including a marked increase in step-families which might include the children of combinations of former relationships.

This kind of population data analysis can assist social work organizations in anticipating the likely increase in the incidence of problems requiring intervention. For example, it is known that an ageing population does bring greater dependence of some elders; that single-parent families also figure more prominently on social workers' case files if only because they are more likely to experience poverty; and that step-families are known to experience additional problems because of, perhaps, intra-family stress from a variety of causes.

The analyses of local communities and neighbourhoods with regard to population statistics could also underpin effective community social work in making the case for advice services, nursery and child care provision and specialist accommodation such as sheltered housing and day centres. Such analyses could also reveal the pattern of usage of particular services, for example whether a particular ethnic minority was accessing advice services, or what proportion and what kinds of young people (in relation to age, locality, ethnicity and gender) were using dedicated youth services. The incidence of unemployment and occupational status in a community will also provide a very effective mapping of structural disadvantage – the key indicator of social stress with clear consequences for social work support.

deschooling attempts to reconfigure the relationship between educational systems and society to make them less institutionalized and less concerned with shaping a workforce ready to function in an unthinking way in competitive, industrialized societies.

The deschooling movement was very popular in the US and the UK in the 1970s. Schools were regarded critically as agencies of social control and increasingly lacking any concern for the development of rounded and creative human beings prepared to live co-operatively. Echoes of the deschooling movement are still to be found in concerns about the educational system continuing to 'dance to the tunes of employers' in the growing emphasis given in contemporary societies to vocationally relevant courses as well as generic skills useful in the world of work. Critics of the deschooling movement argue that many skills that are useful for work are also useful 'life skills' and that the contemporary curriculum is much wider than it used to be. However, there is widespread agreement that there are still major problems to confront, not least the very large numbers of boys emerging from the educational system with few skills, little motivation and their curiosity dimmed. For these boys, 'employability' might be considered an advance on their currently depressed status.

disability disability is a form of social oppression, discrimination, disadvantage and social exclusion based upon physical and/or mental impairment. The 'social construction' of disability entails recognizing the failures of societies, both historically and in modern times, to create an environment to enable people with impairments to participate fully in social, political, economic and family life. Impairment, however, refers to a level of 'functioning', in relation to any physical, mental and sensory characteristic or trait that is construed as outside medically defined norms. Such a definition includes people with mental health problems who experience mental distress as well as those with an intellectual impairment (people with a learning disability).

In some societies, impairments have been associated with witchcraft or bizarre notions about the impaired person having led an irresponsible life in a previous existence. Many societies have been indifferent or even hostile to some impaired people by institutionalizing them. In the UK, the phrase 'subnormality hospital' was widely used until just a few decades ago – places in which to 'warehouse' large numbers of people. Other societies have tried to 'eradicate' impaired people, as with the Nazis, who took the view that some people with impairments were not only subnormal but also 'subhuman'. Current, more hopeful debates about responses to people with impairments seem to be preoccupied with three key themes:

(1) *The medical model* – the medical paradigm has been dominant in thinking about people with impairments for some time. Here the notion of physical illness and, later, mental illness, diagnosed, treated and managed by doctors and often requiring medication

typifies the core aspects of the medical model. In this paradigm the individual is dependent upon the doctor, the expert, to cure, control or ameliorate an impairment.

(2) *The social model* – active pressure groups in many Western societies have sought to challenge the medical model, arguing that it is society that 'disables' by excluding people with impairments from mainstream activities. They point to key problems such as access to public buildings and transport, often segregated education and marginal or token employment opportunities and major difficulties in trying to sustain independent living. Despite a more enlightened environment, most people with impairments hesitate to admit as much when applying for jobs, despite being offered the chance to reveal an impairment on most application forms informed by a supposed commitment to equal opportunities.

(3) *Psychological effects* – the campaigns that have tried to convince governments that the social model ought to guide policy development, have also now acknowledged that there can be problems of adjustment to impairments, especially those that are not present at birth and may be 'acquired' because of trauma (for example, in combat or from accidents), illness or ageing. In this sense, an individual might experience loss of function that may constrain activity or social involvement and may possibly be life limiting. In these circumstances, there may well be significant personal issues for an individual to face as well as, perhaps, disabling responses from 'society at large'.

Data about people with impairments in the UK are at best approximate. Although invited to do so, most social services departments do not have reliable figures on the numbers of children with impairments on their patch or of adults with impairments. This lack of reliable data inhibits the planning of services except in the most rough and ready fashion. It is generally understood that with an ageing population larger numbers of elders will live longer, often with chronic health problems, and that modern medicine will mean that more children with impairments and significant health problems will survive birth and live where earlier they would not have done so.

The extent to which people with impairments can access mainstream activities, even with significantly more resources, is still being debated. There are many who argue, for example, that 'special schools' catering for the very particular needs of children and young people with significant and/or multiple impairments is a more 'needs-led' response allowing for economies of scale in the use of dedicated resources. Similarly, there are also cogent arguments about the need for workshops

for people with impairments because the kinds of work they are
capable of is increasingly hard to find in mainstream employment –
employment that has become ever more technical and devoid of routine
tasks. Many would accept that greater inclusion is possible, with both
of these scenarios above, but that in relation to education maybe the
most that could be hoped for would be to locate a special school or
special unit on a campus with mainstream provision and to encourage
as much contact as possible between the able-bodied and impaired
children and young people. Similar arrangements are also possible in
relation to employment and perhaps to a more rigorous use of initiatives such as the 'Access to Work' programme available at most job
centres, where it is possible for people with disabilities to be assisted in
a variety of ways to be able to demonstrate what they are capable of to
prospective employers.

Despite the rhetoric of anti-oppressive practice, even many social
work organizations do not have a very good track record of supporting social workers with impairments. Managerialism, in this context,
with everyday pressures to allocate work at all costs, has meant that
few if any concessions are allowed to impaired social workers (unpublished research by Castle).

Oliver, M., Sapey, B. and Thomas, P. (2012) *Social Work with
Disabled People*. Basingstoke: Palgrave Macmillan.

Castle, R. (2006) Disabled social workers: contributions and difficulties. Unpublished PhD thesis, Staffordshire University.

discourse an argument, exposition of themes or a set of ideas that
might be written or spoken, or both. In social sciences and in the
analysis of literature, a discourse entails an analysis of, for example, any
policies, statements, theories and generalized arguments that reflect
some underlying and shared themes, assumptions, principles and
concepts. It is entirely possible that discourses are relatively incoherent
and confusing, reflecting some of the contradictions and inconsistencies that are implicit in arguments, statements, policies and beliefs.
Nevertheless, discourses can be very persuasive among social groups
and have significant repercussions for inter-group relations.

According to **post-modernism**, the formation of a discourse as
a specific set of concepts and references that creates a 'narrative' or
way of thinking about a subject also creates its own centre of power
that defines and shapes the knowledge of those who use that discourse.
Language as discourse can be oppressive either by ignoring certain ideas
completely or by 'privileging' other ideas that have a built-in power bias
in favour of one group or another. Michel Foucault's conception of
discourse is broad – he began by investigating 'disciplinary institutions'

such as psychiatric regimes and prison and then extended these to include language per se. **Power**, he came to conclude, is embedded in everyday sources and everyday life. It is impossible to escape its 'gaze' for society is drenched in power. While Foucault explicitly denied he was a post-modernist his emphasis on discourse fitted well into post-modernist thinking particularly because power is to be found everywhere, an inescapable function of modern society.

Discourses invariably reflect and define the power relations between different groups. Foucault's close scrutiny of these power relations led him to conclude that there is an intimate relationship between discourses (or systems of knowledge) that codify techniques and practices for the exercise of social control within these particular contexts. For example, where relationships between ethnic groups have become '*racialized*' then it is likely that a racist discourse will underpin the relatively powerful position of one group over the relatively powerless position of the other. Such a discourse will often entail a **social construction** of the idea of a '*race*': that individuals believe that members of this 'racial group' have common characteristics that underlie particular behaviour – in effect, that biology causes specified behaviours and that the behaviours are inferior to that of behaviours that obtain with '*superior races*'.

Foucault also identified sexuality as a landscape for competing discourses on, for example, homosexuality. His analysis of nineteenth-century literature, psychiatric practices and law created homosexuality as a perverse orientation that in turn justified explicit social control. The emergence of *queer theory* in the twentieth century brought about an entirely different and challenging discourse that not only claimed 'normality' for gays and lesbians but also rejected any simple binary divide for sexuality in general. In social work, there are rich opportunities to deconstruct discourses in many areas of social work practice. For example, the discourse put together by men who are violent, abusive and controlling with their partners (**domestic violence**) has it that men are naturally aggressive and outward going; that their sexual drive is appreciably stronger than that of women; that women are attracted to strong men and wish to be dominated; that men are natural leaders and so on. Qualitative research methods, using content analyses of reported speech, can be very revealing of how service users perceive their world and of their place within it and of the discourses that underpin their predisposition to behave in a particular way. (See also **ideology**.)

Foucault, M. (1977) *Discipline and Punishment*. London: Allen Lane.

discrimination actions, processes, policies and practices by which unjustified unequal treatment is frequently associated with ethnic minorities, gender, disability, sexual orientation, age, cultural group, religious affiliation or health status. The convention is to distinguish between *direct discrimination* and *indirect discrimination*. Direct discrimination includes abuse, harassment, segregationist practices (black people being required to sit on the back of a bus in apartheid South Africa or the US) and over-zealous policing. Other examples include prohibiting disabled people from using particular buildings or effectively being disbarred from accessing public transport; prohibiting people with HIV/Aids or Catholics/Protestants (the latter in Northern Ireland) applying for jobs; or preventing women from, say, joining a golf club. Indirect discrimination refers to situations or conditions which are applied equally but are likely to have unequal implications for particular social groups. For example, a requirement that all applicants to join the police force must be at least six feet tall will, by implication, exclude applicants from ethnic groups that are invariably shorter in height; or a requirement that applicants for senior management posts must have had, say, 10 years' experience of middle management is likely to exclude many more female applicants because women habitually take out time to have and raise children.

Institutional policies and practices can also sometimes lead to discriminatory outcomes, although individual employees within organizations may not be, say, explicitly racist. The Macpherson Report (1999) made it clear that the failure to support black victims, recognize the racist nature of many offences, employ police officers from ethnic minority backgrounds in significant numbers or give due attention to crimes committed against ethnic minorities all constituted *institutional racism*.

In broad terms, successive governments in the UK have incrementally recognized the many groups that are vulnerable to discrimination. The Human Rights and Equalities Commission, a body established to deal with all forms of discrimination, has a very wide brief. However, social policies to deal effectively with discrimination are still the subject of wide debate and dispute. In the UK, it is illegal to positively discriminate, although **positive action** is permissible. Positive action includes measures such as targeted advertising in the press or in particular communities, dedicated training to give particular groups of people (usually women and/or ethnic minorities) the opportunity to compete on 'more equal terms' with white men and various forms of support to enable people with impairments to be able to take on particular jobs. It is also permissible for decisions to be made to appoint women or people from ethnic minorities to, say, management positions if they meet the person specifications for the post *and* women or ethnic minorities are *under-represented* at this level within the organization. In addition, it is possible to make some jobs only available to a woman (or a man) or to people from ethnic minorities if they are offering a personal service. Thus it would be regarded as reasonable to appoint a woman to a post in a rape crisis centre or a Muslim to a post preparing food for people from Islamic backgrounds. Finally, few organizations routinely monitor the profiles of their workforces; to do so is but a useful prelude to trying to implement an effective equal opportunities policy.

Sociologists have also tried to provide explanations about the persistence of discriminatory practices and of stratification based upon differentiated social groups. The most enduring explanation stems from Marx's writings, which locate discrimination, especially forms of discrimination about ethnic groups, in the ruling class's ability to divide the working class to prevent them becoming a cohesive resistant force. (See also **disability**, **ethnocentrism**, **positive action** and **prejudice**.)

domestic violence a term that usually refers to the physical, sexual and emotional *abuse* of women by their male partners or ex-partners. Such abuse on the part of the man can include social isolation, intimidating, bullying and belittling behaviours as well as economic deprivation.

The term and its definition are controversial. One view argues that the term 'domestic' implies a cosiness that detracts from the seriousness of the violence and prefer the term 'partner abuse'; terms such as 'marital violence', 'spouse abuse' and 'battered wives' imply that the couple must be married when many are not. It has also been pointed out that the terms 'battered wives' and 'battered women' divert attention from the key issue, which is one of violent behaviour by current male partners or ex-partners. Others have used the term 'family violence', which appears to group many different kinds of relationship violence, including child abuse, elder abuse and sibling abuse. Violence can clearly occur between any two or more members of families or cohabiting people. It can also refer to violence between couples who are lesbian or gay and to relationships where the abuser is a woman and the victim a man. Relatively recent research has established that *date violence* also characterizes a significant proportion of relationships even in the early stages.

Attitude studies have indicated that a high proportion of boys and young men feel it is reasonable to 'physically chastise' their girlfriends. However, convention seems to have established that the term 'domestic violence' is restricted to those who are, or have been, in a close, sexual, cohabiting relationship where the abuser is a man and the abused a woman. The term includes violence in cohabiting relationships that have only recently been established and relationships that have lasted many decades as well as relationships that have been terminated and where the couple no longer cohabit. In this respect, violence in the relationships of elders who have been together for a long time should properly be characterized as domestic violence rather than elder abuse. Similarly, domestic violence is not confined to the home but may occur in many locations, including public places. Given the complexities of all these issues, it is clear that the term is by no means watertight and that it lacks clarity at the 'edges'.

Attempts to understand domestic violence have been wide ranging. At first commentators emphasized pathological aspects of men's behaviour, arguing that domestic violence is perpetrated by damaged individuals or those whose personalities are warped. Pathologies of this kind were thought initially to be rare. Such explanations have been undermined by compelling evidence that domestic violence is widespread, found in many societies and among all ethnic groups and social classes. In the same vein, others have suggested that there are continuities between the attitudes and values of non-violent and violent men.

Biology has been thought of as offering another plausible explanation. Men, it has been argued, are predisposed biologically to be aggressive. In this context, high levels of testosterone in men have been held responsible for their violent behaviour. Critics of this theory have pointed out that any 'natural' drive does not compel a man to be violent. Any predisposition to behave in a particular way can be diverted, modified or even denied. There are, after all, many people who have sexual instincts but do not choose to express them. To further undermine this theoretical perspective, others have pointed to studies that have found no discernible differences in the levels of testosterone in violent men compared to non-violent men.

Other theorists have focused on accounts given by many women that appear to associate violent events with alcohol. Many men, it is alleged, are violent only when under the influence of alcohol, as if the man could somehow be 'other than himself'. This theory has been criticized on the grounds that although some men are violent in a generalized way after taking alcohol, most men 'under the influence' confine their violence to their partners or ex-partners or possibly other family members lacking power.

Social stress is another alleged cause of domestic violence. Theorists who favour this kind of explanation have tried to link structural inequality with an increased propensity for men to be violent. Thus,

unemployment, poverty, poor housing and, in general, few life chances
are thought to be instrumental in creating social stress, which is more
likely to be expressed in violence to women. Others have argued that
the evidence is equivocal. First, middle-class women are to be found
in refuges although, in absolute terms, in lower numbers. Second,
because of their comparative wealth, more middle-class women are
likely to have more options when trying to leave an abusive relationship. Third, analyses of accounts of violent relationships by survivors
and by their children have revealed that domestic violence is widespread in all social strata.

Some have perceived domestic violence as a problem caused by
family dysfunction. These theorists perceive families as social systems
that have structure, reciprocal relationships, boundaries, and that seek
to maintain some kind of equilibrium. Any family's equilibrium can
be affected if the structure, reciprocal relationships or boundaries are
disturbed. Violence in this context is regarded as evidence of something
fundamentally wrong with any of these features of the system. Thus, if
the established roles and responsibilities that brought about equilibrium
are challenged or changed, then families can develop negative relationships. Critics of this approach point out that families are not systems in
which power is distributed evenly between members. Usually it is the
man who is the dominant actor, and it is the abuse of power on the part
of the man that explains the unhappiness within families rather than a
'neutral' system that has somehow become unbalanced.

Feminists have provided persuasive critiques of the perspectives
outlined above. They believe that the issue of domestic violence is
best understood by analysing the patriarchal relationships that seem to
characterize most societies. Domestic violence, they argue, is part of a
generalized oppression of women. Men occupy most of the significant
positions of power in economic, religious, political and social institutions. This dominant position is maintained through men's control of
ideas or, more broadly, of ideology, reinforced by violence or its threat.
Women are in effect covertly persuaded to adopt attitudes and values
that are instrumental in their own oppression. Thus, pornography, the
perception of women as sexual objects, child-bearers and carers, and
as having primarily domestic roles with few claims on resources (both
within society and within families) are all indicative of a pattern of
inequality and a consistently subservient position for women. Feminists
acknowledge that there are stresses within society, within communities
and families, and that these stresses can be severe for individual men
and women too. In this sense, women are not being idealized. The
key question for feminists is 'why do men feel that it is reasonable to

use violence?' For them, the answer is that a patriarchal culture legitimates unequal power and the use of force to maintain such inequality. Records of the police, health and social welfare agencies, organizations dealing with victims/survivors and the British Crime Survey have consistently found that domestic violence is the most common form of interpersonal violence. Although estimates from these diverse sources vary, it is now generally accepted that domestic violence is a very significant social problem and that there is compelling evidence that domestic violence is connected to child abuse. First, children living in households where a woman is being abused can be directly abused emotionally. Second, abusers of women are often intentional abusers of children. Current social work practice is much more explicit about the need to intervene in families where there are children and domestic violence is also present. (See also **aggression**.)

Harne, L. and Radford, J. (2008) *Tackling Domestic Violence: Theories, Policies and Practice*. Maidenhead: McGraw-Hill.

E e

emotion a short-term inner state of feeling among which are happiness, sadness, joy, disgust, anger, hatred, embarrassment and other affective states.

Antonio Damasio distinguishes between *background emotions, primary emotions* and *social emotions*. Background emotions are not especially prominent in an individual's behaviour but are nonetheless important – the energy, enthusiasm, sense of malaise or excitement, edginess or calmness that can be detected at times before words are even exchanged, particularly through body language. Primary emotions are more prominent and quickly come to mind – fear, anger, disgust, surprise, sadness, happiness. They are easily observed in human beings across cultures and in non-human species as well and are also quite consistent across cultures and species. The social emotions include sympathy, embarrassment, shame, guilt, pride, jealousy, envy, gratitude, admiration, indignation and contempt.

Emotions are grounded in even more fundamental pain and pleasure behaviours which, in turn, arise from basic inborn reflexes and can be triggered by situations that awaken those responses such as fear or anxiety. But they can also be triggered by having become associated with earlier experiences – for example, an individual experiencing extreme discomfort when entering a building because he or she had had a powerful negative emotion in a similar building some years before.

Damasio, A. (2004) *Looking for Spinoza*. London: Vintage.

emotional intelligence the ability to observe and respond to one's own and other people's emotions. In particular, there is the ability to discriminate between different emotions and to use that information to guide thinking, behaviour and practice. There are four broad areas of competence within emotional intelligence:

- the ability to distinguish, evaluate and express emotions accurately and appropriately;
- the ability to draw on emotions as a means for greater understanding;
- the ability to understand emotional messages;
- the ability to regulate one's own emotions to promote growth and well-being.

The concept of emotional intelligence is popularly associated with the work of the American psychologist Daniel Goleman, who developed a number of scales to try to determine an individual's emotional intelligence quotient.

Goleman, D. (1996) *Emotional Intelligence: Why it Can Matter More than IQ.* London: Bloomsbury.

empathy the capacity to enter into another person's (or group's) feelings and emotions and/or to experience circumstances from the other person's point of view. As such, empathy is a step beyond sympathy for another person or group. Antonio Damasio in *Looking for Spinoza* (2004) gives the example of being told about a horrible accident in which someone is badly injured. For a time it is possible to feel the twinge of pain that mirrors the pain that the person has suffered. This capacity he calls the 'as-if-body-loop' mechanism in which the brain simulates certain emotional body states, an internal simulation that consists of a rapid modification of ongoing body maps. He notes that those with damage to the right cerebral hemisphere – the area of the brain that generates the capacity to simulate the emotional state of another person – have a low capacity for empathy.

Social workers have historically relied on their capacity for empathy, for 'understanding' the point of view of service users. It is striking, however, given the numerous references to empathy in discussion of social work values, how little it has been researched as a discrete element in social work practice and the kinds of decisions that should flow from it. On the whole, it is regarded as an undifferentiated good, that need not be investigated further. (See also **attachment**.)

Damasio, A. (2004) *Looking for Spinoza.* London: Vintage.

epidemiology the study of the incidence and distribution of illnesses (morbidity), conditions (for example, teenaged pregnancy) and of deaths (mortality) in any population. In addition, epidemiologists are interested to explain:

(1) any patterns and variations in the rates of illnesses and deaths in any population, social group or geographical locality in relation to gender, social class, lifestyle, diet and patterns of consumption, occupational group, place of residence, ethnicity and age as well as mapping changes over time in any society;

(2) changes in the incidence of illnesses and deaths as a result of health strategies such as immunization or health education programmes;

(3) variations in morbidity and mortality rates as a result of public health interventions such as, for example, improved sanitation or the quality of water or reductions in pollution.

In relation to morbidity, it is usual to distinguish between the *prevalence rate* and the *incidence rate*; the former charts the number of people experiencing a particular illness or condition at a particular time. The prevalence rate is especially important in understanding how epidemics develop. The incidence rate collects annual data on the incidence of an illness or condition. In the UK, all deaths have to be registered whereas the incidence of illnesses and conditions is collected less rigorously by a number of diverse agencies.

Reductions in both morbidity and mortality rates usually have implications for *life expectancy* and thus for the planning of services including social work services since there is an association between ageing and acquired infirmity, proportions of GDP to be allocated to pension funds and so on. Crucially, epidemiologists are able to comment upon a number of closely related issues such as:

- the causal connection between poverty, lifestyle and both morbidity and mortality rates, in essence health inequalities (see the Black Report 1980, which was able to establish that there was a 'class gradient' in relation to both morbidity and mortality);
- access to health services and differential use of them (again there are social class gradations to the use of health services as well as gender and other dimensions such as the withdrawal of people with mental health problems from using services).

Graham, H. (ed.) (2001) *Understanding Health Inequalities.* Buckingham: Open University Press.

equality of opportunity measures designed to confront **discrimination** in relation to the employment of staff and the delivery of services; and attempts to maximize **life chances** for all people within any society, especially those negatively affected by structural inequality.

Equal opportunities policies are usually prefaced by a guiding statement of principle. Such statements usually indicate which groups are recognized by the organization as experiencing discrimination within the wider society. Thus **gender**, 'race', marital status, **disability** and religious commitments are invariably found in such statements. Age, ex-offenders, social class or social status and sexual orientation or preference are mentioned less often, especially the last. In the case of public bodies and agencies, there is less discretion given in the way policies are formulated and statements are implemented, especially given the statutory duties imposed on them by anti-discrimination legislation such as the 2009 Equality Act.

In relation to *employment practices*, some social welfare employers operate procedures that are more rigorous than they once were. Thus, job descriptions, person specifications, interview schedules

and formal decision-making procedures have been adopted as good
practice by many organizations. The willingness of organizations to
adopt additional procedures to address revealed discrimination within
their organization is much more limited. Monitoring of applications,
the effectiveness of targeted advertising, appointments, promotions and
uptake of training opportunities are indicators of organizations' willingness to identify problems and to take **positive action** to address them.

All organizations ought to be able to present annual reports in
which they can specify progress made in relation to agreed policy
targets. For example, a report should be able to indicate how many
employees with disabilities are currently part of the workforce, what
efforts have been made over the past year to increase the numbers of
disabled workers (if, indeed, this had been an acknowledged problem in the previous year), an evaluation of those efforts and finally an
action plan for the forthcoming year. The organization's plan should
include all groups experiencing discrimination.

With reference to *service delivery*, the performance of different companies including social welfare organizations' has been very uneven. A
full and comprehensive equal opportunities policy should contain an
analysis of anti-discriminatory measures needed with all user groups.
Thus with older people, as a user group, the needs of black, poor and
disabled elders should all be separately identified, as should those who
have a religious affiliation or are gay or lesbian. Where little is known
about a particular group's needs, plans should be devised to collect
critical information. Also, action plans need to be drawn up to address
particular policy objectives. An example will serve to illustrate this
sequence. It may be noted, as a result of monitoring processes, that
no black elders use social service day care facilities, and it is not known
why this is so. A plan to consult black community organizations is
devised. Offers are made to arrange visits to day care centres for individuals, families and community groups. Critical information leaflets
are translated into the appropriate languages, and efforts are made to
highlight the services with other key social welfare personnel such as
doctors and other support health workers.

Such a process shows the link between reviews of policies, monitoring and planning. Sometimes, however, it is possible to have policies in
place, but an organization may make little progress in relation to anti-
discriminatory practice. Researchers have sought to understand this
problem by looking at the organization's culture or climate. Where
people are actually involved and committed to policies they are more
likely to work in practice. In this respect, it is likely that a commitment
to equal opportunities in relation to service delivery will enhance an

organization's commitment to equal opportunities in employment practices. An organization that actually employs disabled people, has women in senior positions and has black people at all levels is more likely to deliver services that promote equal opportunities.

Successive governments have identified the promotion of social mobility as a clear objective with trying to enhance equality of opportunity through improved educational standards as a key feature of such efforts. Differing conceptions of **compensatory education** have emerged from governments of varying hues with initiatives such as Sure Start (Labour governments after 1997) and current efforts by later governments to improve the quality of teaching in schools and to establish new kinds of school (for example, academies). Both Conservative and Labour governments take the view that education can reduce inequality, although they disagree about whether education by itself is enough. Most Labour Party policies seem to imply that additional measures such as income redistribution, access to decent housing and the promotion of healthy lifestyles are also needed.

ethical codes of practice bodies of guiding principles or value statements for professional organizations to set the standard for good practice in relation to service delivery, relationships with clients or service users, and professional relationships including relationships with other occupations and the 'world at large'. Codes should also be seen as binding on research, evaluation and any consultative processes.

The British Association of Social Workers has produced a code of ethics that has become influential within the profession, regardless of whether practitioners are members of the association or not. The code has been drawn up to be consistent with the *Ethics of Social Work: Principles and Standards*, devised for the International Federation of Social Workers in 1994. The British statement has been revised several times, most recently in 2002. The 1948 United Nations Universal Declaration of Human Rights has also been influential in the drafting of the British code. The British version has much in common with that produced by the Australian Association of Social Workers and emphasizes the importance of five basic values, namely, 'human dignity and worth', 'social justice', 'service to humanity', 'integrity' and, finally, 'competence'.

Each of these guiding principles is discussed further in the material supporting the code with some acknowledgements, here and there, about potential problems of using them in practice. For example, the statement on 'human dignity and worth' has it that all human beings have intrinsic value and that everyone has a right to 'well-being, self-fulfilment and to as much control over their own lives as is consistent with the rights of others'. The commitment to 'social justice' brings with it some strong statements about a 'fair and equitable distribution of resources', 'fair access to public services', 'equal treatment and protection under the law' and 'advocating strategies for overcoming structural disadvantage'. The last is interesting given that there is evidence to suggest that social workers on the whole are not involved in explicit political activity either through political parties or pressure groups and that the gains made by social workers on behalf of service users tend to be essentially modest.

With regard to the principle of 'service to humanity', the commitment to contribute 'to the creation of a fairer society' is repeated along with the view that the fundamental goals of social work are to, first, 'meet personal and social needs' and, second, to enable people to meet their potential. The commitment to integrity is every bit as demanding. The code states that 'integrity comprises honesty, reliability, openness and impartiality' and that it has a primary place in underpinning social work practice. Finally, social workers need to be competent and this umbrella statement brings with it a need to continue personal development, use supervision appropriately, take proper steps to deal with personal ill health and stress among many other exhortations to work to a high standard.

The General Social Care Council was wound up in 2012 and social workers joined health professionals in a new regulatory body, the Health and Care Professions Council (HCPC). The HCPC has taken an inclusive view that standards of conduct, performance and ethics 'apply to all registrants including those involved in direct practice, management, education, research and roles in industry'. The key duties prescribed by the HCPC comprise fourteen standards:

(1) You must act in the best interests of service users.
(2) You must respect the confidentiality of service users.
(3) You must keep high standards of personal conduct.
(4) You must provide (to us and any other relevant regulators) any important information about your conduct and competence.
(5) You must keep your professional knowledge and skills up to date.
(6) You must act within the limits of your knowledge, skills and experience and, if necessary, refer the matter to another practitioner.
(7) You must communicate properly and effectively with service users and other practitioners.
(8) You must effectively supervise tasks that you have asked other people to carry out.
(9) You must get informed consent to provide care or services (so far as possible).

(10) You must keep accurate records.

(11) You must deal fairly and safely with the risks of infection.

(12) You must limit your work or stop practicing if your performance or judgment is affected by your health.

(13) You must behave with honesty and integrity and make sure that your behavior does not damage the public's confidence in you or your profession.

(14) You must make sure that any advertising you do is accurate.

While consistent with earlier codes of conduct (their commitment to the 'Plain English Campaign' is welcome) they offer little guidance to practitioners who find themselves in situations where there is evident conflict between service users or when statutory authority demands that practitioners take a particular course of action whether or not consent has been obtained. The notes about respecting confidentiality are similarly unhelpful in not recognizing that confidentiality may have to be breached where the welfare of a child or vulnerable adult is at stake.

Health and Care Professions Council (2012) *Standards of Conduct, Performance and Ethics.* London: HCPC.

ethics the beliefs, principles and moral values that guide individuals in a society, culture or organization in their actions and behaviour toward others.

The study of ethics has preoccupied philosophers and political theorists for at least 2500 years primarily in the attempt to secure a firm foundation for defining what is ethical. Immanuel Kant focused on the rightness or wrongness of intentions and the motives for behaviour. His thinking underscored the need to identify what acts were morally required and which were immoral and forbidden. Kant's position and those who followed him is broadly called *deontology*, (*deon* – duty, *ology* – science or study), since humans have the duty to follow certain moral principles or imperatives. The deontological school of thought argued, and still argues, that consequences of an act do not provide a reliable guide as to whether that act is moral or not: after all, good consequences can arise by accident and bad consequences from well-meaning actions. This sense of duty is not based on compulsion but on freedom and respect for others.

Some twentieth-century philosophers, notably John Rawls, have adopted elements of the idea of moral duty, arguing that human behaviour should be governed by those principles that would be unanimously agreed by free persons who held the same degree of knowledge and information. The morality of right and wrong are regarded as duties we owe to one another out of our mutual respect for free persons.

Critics of the deontological school of thought argued that ethical principles, as a set of imperatives, means they cannot change. Neither can a conflict between ethical principles be resolved within such a framework. Such critics tended to coalesce around the *consequentialist* school of ethics – that the consequences of an act establish whether that act was moral or not. Chief among these were the utilitarians who still loom large in the debate around ethics: they reasoned that actions are right to the degree that they promote the greatest sum of 'utility' or happiness, by which they meant well-being. Utilitarians – they do not call themselves that any longer – in our own time maintain that the optimum well-being is reached when individual preferences and rationally informed desires are met. Such a philosophy under different names (see **rational choice theory**) remains a dominant force in economics and even in public policy where actions and laws are justified to the extent that they deliver the best consequences, effectively maximizing the public good and public well-being.

Many social scientists, sociologists and psychologists among them, have moved beyond the debate between deontologists and utilitarians. They largely admit the difficulty in finding a hard foundation for defining what is ethical particularly in the face of the new complexities presented by modern health technologies and in the competing moral principles among religious faiths. This has encouraged a sense of moral relativism – the view that since there is no single foundation for ethical behaviour one set of principles cannot be judged as 'more ethical' than the others. Developments in medical technology have generated possibilities for disagreement – around the use of stem cells, the unborn embryo or foetus, genetic manipulation, the so-called 'persistent vegetative state', to name a few. The result is ethical scepticism with the work of social science focused on being purely descriptive, telling us how people behave in different cultures or the different options when faced with various medical conditions with no basis for judging between them.

Ethical relativism has sparked its own reaction with a search again for basic propositions for behaviour and conduct that enjoy wide consensus. While relativism arises on the back of difficult health issues or socially explosive debates such as abortion, few would dissent that it is wrong to murder or to abduct a child or steal. Just because such things are done, even at times by governments, does not mean that ethical codes cannot be constructed on such fundamentals. Neither does the fact that there may be serious disagreement over particular values mean that there are no fundamental principles for conduct that characterize us as humans.

Ethicists currently are looking more at *the process* for establishing ethical conduct and making ethical decisions. One such principle is that of participation in decisions. While traditional moral codes emphasized obedience to the commandments of superior authority within hierarchical cultures we now expect to be listened to and our consent freely given to decisions that affect us. Old forms of professional paternalism no longer hold legitimacy while informed consent, whether in relation to medical decisions about us or in launching a war, is now required.

The tensions surrounding ethics and moral values affect social work profoundly. As Chris Clark has said, social work sits directly on top of the fault lines of controversy around social values. Roles within families, changing family structures, beliefs about sexuality, the conflict between religious commandments have upended all the older certainties and, as Clark says, it often falls to social work to mediate compromises across the fault lines. As well as being uncomfortable for practitioners he adds, 'this is not a role that is ever likely to win full-hearted popular support. Those who become involved in social work interventions will usually only be partially satisfied, at best' (Clark 2000: 2). But social work cannot evade adopting specific values since any intervention is going to reflect certain ethical values whether the practitioner likes it or.

To equip social workers for this choppy environment Clark draws out four basic principles to guide social work ethics:

(1) *Respect.* Combine the Kantian notion of respect for the person as a free-choosing, autonomous individual who can make their own decisions, and the utilitarian emphasis on reducing pain and maximizing well-being which sometimes requires the social worker to exercise respect by constraining the individual's choices (as in self-detrimental actions).

(2) *Justice.* This embraces the principle of due process, which requires decisions about another person to be taken according to rules and procedures that carry acknowledged authority and standing. Deprivation of liberty, or other severely invasive actions in an individual's private sphere, should only take place if due process is followed. Moreover, since the essentials of a decent life are not reliably delivered by the free market in an unequal society, 'deliberately crafted institutions and policies are necessary to ensure the meeting of human needs and the fulfilment of elementary social justice' (Clark 2000: 159).

(3) *Citizenship.* To ensure that users as citizens have the full range of social and welfare rights to which they are entitled. For the narrower range of targeted rights, this involves the use of professional discretion in deciding who should receive services and at what

level. It also entails engaging in public dialogue about the intent of proposed or current policies. Social workers should be prepared more than they are to articulate and support the development of obligations and responsibilities on behalf of the community and to foster community life and **social capital**. Accustomed to acting only on behalf of the individual they are often reluctant to act as agents for developing the welfare of the community in general.

(4) *Discipline*. Social workers should master the knowledge, theory and research in relevant academic subjects but also be in command of the practice knowledge, of practical wisdom that distinguishes the professional from the mere specialist.

(See also **ethical codes of practice**.)

Clark, C. (2000) *Social Work Ethics Politics, Principles and Practice*. Basingstoke: Palgrave.

ethnic group and **ethnic monitoring** a group of people sharing an identity that might include their own traditions, language, culture, norms, mores, beliefs (including religious beliefs) and national or sub-cultural forms. The term ethnicity is now preferred to that of the now discredited term 'race' because the latter has often been defined in biological terms where biology is thought to underpin both behaviour and relative value; that is, to claim that one 'race' is superior to another. In addition, supposed 'races' are not biologically distinct but overlap in virtually all characteristics with other 'races'.

Membership of ethnic groups seems to be rooted in an awareness of discernible differences relative to other groups. Ethnic boundaries can be drawn very rigidly or rather more loosely depending upon 'ethnic markers'. Such social processes can involve active exclusion of other groups or a willingness to be more open and perhaps inclusive. In times of conflict or friction ethnic identities can be emphasized and become more marked; in times of stability and economic well-being ethnic boundaries often become weaker. Much will depend upon whether any society has a significant commitment to integration or pluralism.

Ethnic monitoring is the process for measuring and recording the involvement of different ethnic groups in all aspects of social functioning. It can be instrumental in understanding key issues such as equality of opportunity and social justice generally. Such monitoring has revealed that, for example, Afro-Caribbean men are over-represented in the criminal justice system and as in-patients in psychiatric hospitals; that Afro-Caribbean women are the most active economically (in both full-time and part-time employment); and that ethnic minorities in general in the UK are significantly under-represented in senior managerial positions in large public and private sector organizations.

Ethnic monitoring is therefore very important in monitoring any changes in the representation of all ethnic groups in either social problems or in broad social institutions as a result of perhaps new policies designed to address discriminatory policies and practices. Ethnic monitoring is crucial in determining whether social work organizations are embracing equality of opportunity in both employment practices and service delivery. It is generally recognized that it is unlikely that a social work organization can deliver anti-oppressive services if it is not an equal opportunities employer.

ethnocentrism a belief that one's own cultural group or society is superior to others and that any formal comparative framework will find in favour of one's own culture or society. The concept has been extended to include personality types that display similar attributes.

Ethnocentrism was originally devised by the American sociologist Sumner to identify a belief that societies, other than one's own, were likely to be considered inferior in terms of their culture, collective morality and even 'race' or ethnicity. Sumner thought it also meant a failure to acknowledge that there could be no one correct way of organizing social life. In this context, trying to avoid ethnocentric thinking became a key facet of anthropology, inviting the notion that all societies could only be understood in terms of their own assumptions, values and cultural goals and that comparative frameworks could not reliably be developed or applied. Such relativistic thinking was later discarded to be able to allow comparisons to be made about, for example, moral standards, the place of women in different societies, the raising of children and the issue of human rights.

The work of Adorno and his colleagues (1950) in the book *The Authoritarian Personality* (Oxford: HarperCollins) was, to begin with, a study of anti-Semitism but was later broadened out to include negative attitudes towards all 'ethnic and cultural strangers'. The authors were able to reveal that hostility, suspicion and antagonism towards any 'out-group' (such as the Jews) was likely to be part of a wider authoritarian construct involving dogmatic and inflexible views on most things especially politics, economics, ethnic minorities, other nationalities and homosexuals. A further key component was the likelihood that authoritarian personalities would be anti-democratic, thus establishing a clear connection between personality type and right wing or even fascist belief systems.

ethnography research techniques similar to participant observation involving an 'immersion' in another society or community for a significant period of time enabling the researcher to comprehend in a 'sympathetic' manner the key features of what is being studied both structurally and culturally.

Ethnography is closely associated with the work of social anthropologists. One key issue has always been whether the 'observer affects the observed' and thereby the researcher is in danger of recording distortions of the society or social group. Proponents of ethnographic methods hold that researchers should only begin their study after a period of familiarization and that after this introductory period is over, societies or social groups tend to become accustomed to the outsider and to discount or ignore them. In addition, it is also possible to include other methods including, where available, the analysis of documents, diaries and other artefacts. A key research skill in this context is the ability to accurately record what is observed and, later, to be able to 'interpret' what has been observed. Examples of studies that have used ethnographic methods include Mead's studies *Coming of Age in Samoa* (1920) and *Growing Up in New Guinea* (1930) and Rosser and Harris's study *Family and Social Change* (1965) – a study of family structures in South Wales.

eugenics the supposed science of improving the population by control of inherited qualities. Eugenics was developed in the mid- and late nineteenth centuries well before the twentieth century discovery of genes and DNA as the mechanism for passing on physical characteristics through heredity. Its founders nevertheless believed they could point to scientific evidence – such as structure of the skull and racialized characteristics – to establish their main conclusion: that certain 'races', countries and social classes were superior in culture and accomplishment and that policies should be designed to further their dominance and to reduce as far as possible the population in inferior 'races' or classes. Twentieth-century science including the mapping of the human genome has established that the eugenicists' notion of scientific proof of the superiority of races was completely bogus.

Eugenics as then conceived was widely supported across the political spectrum until roughly the 1930s. There was both a positive and negative element to the policies that the eugenics movement advocated. The positive element involved deciding who should have increased offspring and to offer rewards for increasing the birth rate, while the negative element involved determining which groups should *not* increase and should be subject to sterilization, segregation and obligatory medical tests before marriage.

Some sections of social work supported eugenics objectives, for example, the Central Association of Mental Welfare which advocated voluntary sterilization of women with learning disability and the segregation of learning disabled people (then called 'mental defectives') in colonies. Other countries saw even more extreme policies put in place.

Some southern American states carried out compulsory sterilization, as did Sweden, in the 1930s; in Germany, the National Socialist government at the same time began a covert but widespread programme of euthanasia of both physically and learning disabled children.

Recent discoveries, particularly the mapping of the human genome, *in vitro* fertilization, stem cell research, cloning, genetic screening and gene therapy have raised some of the issues that the eugenics movement had previously touched on. This 'new genetics' is distinguished from the past in the sense that it is driven by would-be consumers in search of their own or their offspring's health care. The values this time around, it is argued, are based on personal empowerment, increased choice and health benefits. There are also at work a fast forming market in both provision of genetic information and gene manipulation with new groups such as researchers, private entrepreneurs, medical practitioners, genetic counsellors, parents and patients all making claims in the market place. Genetic screening and pre-natal testing, for example, allows the detection of genes connected with major impairments and allows would-be parents to choose healthy babies. This potential – built on real, not bogus science – raises an old question in the minds of some: is it desirable to prevent the births of certain foetuses?

The rapid development of genetic technology has converged with digital technology to shape the way we think about bodies, 'self' and society. New forms of surveillance have emerged in which people are genetically 'profiled' according to the level of risk to security and health that they are prone to as a result of their genes. Biological information can then be translated into categories and forms that can be easily read, interpreted and passed on to all kinds of organizations. Particular data can be obtained on an individual before an event such as a job application. Thus surveillance of individuals no longer has to rely on 'external' mechanisms such as cameras; rather individuals participate in their own surveillance. Although individuals are genetically unique, an individual's risk of various kinds (health, addiction, physical capacity) is profiled and determined by membership of a family, social group or attitudinal group.

evaluation a process of assessing the merit, benefit or significance of a policy, project or service (interventions). Such assessments might include measurements of the extent to which any intervention is meeting its objectives as well as capturing any unintended consequence(s) of the intervention.

Evaluations in social work often rely upon quasi-scientific quantitative methods such as measurements using performance indicators, attitudinal research and audits or qualitative methods including case studies which may, for example, capture the impact of an intervention upon individuals, families and groups. Formative evaluations can also be undertaken while the intervention(s) are still in process, making it possible to make changes or modifications to increase the likelihood of specified objectives being met. Summative evaluations are undertaken when any intervention has been completed and it is possible to draw reasonably accurate conclusions as to its effectiveness.

Evaluation reports are usually written with the objectives set by the agency paying for the research in mind, whether it be a statutory source such as a government department or a major voluntary source of research funding such as the Joseph Rowntree Foundation. But it can be really important to take into account the interests and perspectives of other stakeholders, such as service users. The commitment to partnership in social work practice is mirrored in academic circles by an increasing commitment to emancipatory research which consults with service users at every stage of evaluations from research design to both formative and summative reports. Emancipatory evaluations offer the opportunity for formative 'findings' to amend the way the interventions are delivered in the later stages of the study.

Other stakeholders in evaluations include providers of other services that might be affected if the new intervention is adopted. This raises issues about the scope and range of evaluative research if it is possible that apparent improvements in one service, based upon an evaluation, lead to changes in service delivery that have a negative impact on another service. For example, the contingent fields of health and social care, prone to this kind of inter-service rivalry, would be especially concerned about narrowly conceived research designs.

The most effective social work evaluations mirror the most stringent research designs and the meticulous applications of social research methods. However, experimental design – where randomly chosen groups of service users are provided with different interventions, or one group experiences the intervention and the other group does not – is rarely possible in social work research because such research is very expensive and there can be ethical constraints in the selection of service users. More often social work research has to rely upon other methods; for example, quasi-experimental design – where it is possible to study longitudinally, say, a large number of care leavers, estimate key outcomes by the time they reach the age of 30 against some specified aspects of social functioning (for example, employment, personal relations, mental health) and then attribute any positive or negative outcomes to services they did or did not enjoy earlier in their lives. In addition, detailed case studies can provide useful material to suggest possibly fruitful areas of research as a prelude to quasi-experimental research and quantitative data collected through questionnaires and surveys. Whatever research methods are used, validity, reliability and representative nature of findings are more likely to be achieved if qualitative material corroborates quantitative data collected through wider samples of service users' experience.

exploitation having sufficient command over resources, including human labour, to permit the extraction or appropriation of those resources without paying the cost equal to the extent of the resource extracted.

In **Marxism**, exploitation is central to its *labour theory of value*, which holds that workers produce *surplus value*, that is the difference between what workers receive in wages – low because of competition among workers for jobs – and the value of what they produce. The capitalist is able to appropriate that extra value in the form of profit. Others have noted that extracting profit out of other people's work extends beyond social class to include housework, caring for others, clerical work and other low-paid or no-paid 'menial' work. Exploitation can also occur with regard to natural resources that are privatized with the value in minerals, water, fuel extracted by owners who do not meet the costs of sustaining and replenishing those resources.

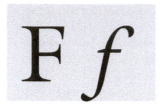

family and **kinship** a primary social group, related by ties of kinship (or comparable close ties) that includes two or more generations, where the care of children is undertaken. The children may be the natural offspring of one or more of the adults within the family, be adopted or fostered or be cared for as a private arrangement. Those undertaking the caring role in relation to any children can be the natural parent, another adult within the family or indeed another older child or sibling. Many sociologists have agreed that the family serves several important functions, notably: reproduction; the care and socialization of children; the management of sexual relations; and a primary unit for financing/paying for these activities – in essence, an important unit for the consumption of goods and services. Clearly families are not the only social entities that can fulfil any of these functions because it is possible for sexual relationships to be conducted outside families (even conducted by married people), for children to be conceived outside families and for children to be cared for, as just one alternative, by the state. Nevertheless, families continue to be the principal social institution enacting these functions.

The family and kinship networks are a key locus of social work intervention because of the overarching responsibilities social workers have for ensuring the well-being of children and of vulnerable adults. Historically and cross-culturally, societies have displayed a wide variety of family forms. Sociologists and anthropologists have developed a number of concepts that have helped researchers (and social workers) make sense of this diversity in relation to both family forms and kinship networks:

(1) *Conjugal/nuclear and extended families – conjugal and/or nuclear families* are those comprising a married or cohabiting couple and their children, which might include children from other/previous relationships. *Extended families* are those usually combining more than two generations living in one household. However, in contemporary research/social work practice it is acknowledged that *extended family relations* can be very important even where several generations do not live in one household but where significant

support (emotional, perhaps financial and possibly caring roles) is given and where various households involved in the extended family live in proximity to each other or other kinds of support are offered but from a distance and/or less frequently. *Nuclear families* have been thought to be especially responsive to the needs of advanced industrial societies because such families can be geographically mobile and, perhaps, are able to operate independently of extended family in terms of both kin obligations and also economically. Often, however, the picture is more complex as more active extended family relations are often re-established as elders retire and sometimes move to be closer to offspring or family breakdown may mean that remnants of a nuclear family, at least temporarily, move closer to one set of grandparents. In addition, grandparents have become key players in the care of grandchildren as parents are encouraged by successive governments to work even when their children are very young.

(2) *Step- or 'reconstituted' families* – step-families are now a very common family form given, in particular, the increased incidence of separation and divorce. Step-families also exhibit a wide variety of characteristics because of the many possible combinations of backgrounds of key players in the family where:

- one or both parties might have been married before including widowhood;
- one or both parties might have cohabited before;
- one or both parties have children that they bring to the relationship where the children are resident;
- one or both parties have non-resident children who may or may not visit regularly;
- one or both parties have an ex-partner who is still actively involved in shared care of children of that earlier relationship;
- the new relationship produces one or more children.

Step-families figure prominently in social workers' caseloads and, statistically, are more likely to 'fail' than first marriages. They also have to address significant new problems such as acknowledging that a parent–child relationship predates the new partner relationship and that each member of a step-family will bring their own ideas and expectations of family life based upon their previous experience of it. Children in particular may feel confused as they experience different expectations from their parent and step-parent and may find it especially difficult to accept attempts to exert authority by a step-parent. It is also often the case that for the new conjugal relationship to be established children of one parent may have to move to another area, community and school with perhaps associated loss of things familiar especially friends and peer group. Difficult and stressful step-family relationships figure prominently in the backgrounds of homeless teenagers.

(3) *Lone- or single-parent families* – lone parenthood also arises out of a wide variety of experiences including separation and divorce, widow(er)hood and conceptions as a result of non-cohabiting relationships. In the UK, lone-parent families account for over 20 percent of all families (and as much as 50 percent in some urban areas) and they are overwhelmingly headed by women. Lone-parent families often experience prejudice on the part of the general public fuelled by negative images of being 'a drain on the public purse' and of 'queue jumping' (especially teenaged single parents). Research has also consistently established that lone-parent families experience significant poverty and stresses associated with unremitting child care. Such families also figure prominently on social workers' case files. Men who have fathered children in lone-parent families have consistently received less attention by both social workers and governments.

(4) *Families of origin and families of procreation* – family of origin is a term that simply indicates the family in which they were born and raised or, in the case of adopted children, raised. Social workers prefer the term *'birth family'*. Family of procreation refers to a family in which a heterosexual couple conceive a child. Clearly *families of origin* and *families of procreation* may or may not be the same family.

(5) *Patriarchal, matriarchal and symmetrical families* – these terms refer to the location of power within families. *Patriarchal families* refers to any family form where men dominate (thought to be the most common family form in most cultures); *matriarchal families* refers to any family form where women dominate (unusual in most cultures but not unknown, albeit uncommon, in many cultures); and *symmetrical families* refers to any family characterized by power-sharing (the last is claimed to be on the increase in many advanced industrial societies). *Lineage*, namely patterns of *descent* and *inheritance*, is also closely associated with the locus of power within families although they are not always identical.

(6) *Locality* – refers to patterns of settlement post-marriage or of coming together namely *patrilocal, matrilocal* and *neo-local. Patrilocal* has it that couples will settle with or near the groom's parental home; with *matrilocal* settlement the couple live with or close to the bride's parental home and with *neo-local* settlement the couple would settle in a place of their own choosing.

The utility, for social workers, of noting the nature of family forms and of key aspects of their functioning both internally and in relation to kinship networks, is clear because simply asking the implied questions will mean that assessments are more comprehensive and perhaps will begin to identify stresses and pressure points within families as a prelude to helping them. (See also **divorce**, **marriage** and **separation**.)

fascism see **right, right wing**

feminism a theoretical perspective, social movement and ideology that has at its core a recognition of gender inequality, especially in relation to women's subordination to men.

Feminism, especially in the context of political struggle, has a long history. In the West, feminism as a social movement and ideology is commonly divided into two distinct periods. The first 'wave' is usually located in the late nineteenth century and early twentieth century, drawing on the earlier writings of Mary Wollstonecraft through the suffragette movement to the enfranchisement of women. The second 'wave' emerged during the second half of the 1960s alongside the creation of the New Left. Latterly feminist theory has informed wide-ranging struggles internationally to promote civil rights to votes for women, women's economic interests and women's well-being especially in relation to measures to protect them from male violence.

Contemporary thinkers identify different strands of feminism:

- *Socialist–Marxist feminism* – this perspective prioritizes social class as the prime factor in determining the place of women within capitalist societies. Consequently, this approach relies heavily on the work of Marx and Engels and argues that gender inequality is a product of capitalism and class oppression. It is critical of the essentialism inherent within radical feminism and also challenges the ahistorical approach to patriarchy. A key aspect of women's position within capitalist regimes has been as members of the 'reserve army of labour', where women's participation in the labour force has fluctuated as a response to the cyclical nature of 'booms and busts'. In this respect ideologies have been managed to encourage or discourage women from taking up work depending upon current economic circumstances; illustrated cogently in the seminal film *Rosie the Riveter*.

- *Liberal feminism* – the suffragette movement of the early 1900s was founded on the concept of basic equality and justice and rose from the abolition of slavery and equal rights through to the civil rights movements in the US. In the UK, the feminist movement gathered some momentum in the 1970s with calls for equal pay, free contraception, abortion on demand, affordable child care

online chat rooms which use the word 'friend' to indicate the status of those with access to a particular individual's communications but who may in fact have never met face to face. 'Friends', in this sense, can therefore also include members of the family.

Even before the rise of social networking, friendship was seen as an increasingly important form of social glue in contemporary society as family relationships weakened and personal communities, as opposed to geographical and work-based communities, became more central to people's lives. For individuals friendship has connotations of freedom, choice and individuality yet its very fluidity and variation has made it a difficult subject for social science.

Sociologists have previously studied friendship in terms of patterns of sociability as it is found within social class and among different age bands, in particular children. Graham Allan found that working-class friendships were formed through family links, as well as workmates and neighbours. Exchange theorists such as Peter Blau noted that people make and keep friends because they are useful and rewarding and therefore have utility – usefulness. Others who investigated the impact of consumerism have noted the fleeting nature of intimacy in the midst of some kinds of commercial transaction – for example, between customers and cabin crews on airplanes or with servers at restaurants where friendliness is commercialized.

Few studies, however, have been carried out into the changing nature and rising importance of friendship in the twenty-first century. Those that have are as interested in the changing context within which friendships are formed as in the nature of friendship itself. Ray Pahl in his part-sociological, part-philosophical investigation of friendship, conducted ethnographic studies into the nature of friendship, concluding that if it is to flourish it requires time and effort, both in short supply in contemporary society. Since friendship is the archetypal social relationship of choice, and ours is an age of choice in relation to clothes, style and identities, surely, he asks, this should be a golden age of friendship. But friends and friendship must be seen in context. Employment for both men and women is more flexible, more insecure and there is far less sense of loyalty between employers and staff. This leads to a low-trust environment in which employees have to watch their backs and be prepared to move on – an environment in which colleagues are less likely to form friendships. Pahl does see the expansion of higher and further education giving young people the time and opportunity to make friends to match their emerging identities – friendships that can survive then as families are formed. Increasingly we are culturally and socially determined by our friends yet the sources of formation of friendships remain fragile and uncertain.

Pahl, R. (2000) *On Friendship*. Cambridge: The Polity Press.

functionalism the theory that society should be understood as a system of interdependent parts dependent on each other in order to fulfil functions that contribute to social order and society's capacity to reproduce itself.

Among other conceptual problems, sociologists encounter two significant issues which functionalism addresses. First, what is it that enables any society to persist over time and to broadly retain its shape? And, second, what is it that brings about or encourages social change and thus undermines the stability of any society? In answer to the first question, functionalists in effect argue that if any institution exists and persists then it must in some sense be useful to that particular society or social system and that it must meet some social need. In answer to the second, functionalism recognizes that a particular social need does not have to be felt in the same way by all members of any social system or society; what might be functional for some might not be so for others. Such differences provide the impetus for social change, recognizing that individual actors can have an impact and that any society does not simply replicate itself.

Functionalism as a theory can be traced back to the beginnings of sociology. Early writers include Herbert Spencer and Emile Durkheim, who compared society to a living organism – the so-called 'organic analogy'. Just as organisms were construed as having quite different parts (brains, hearts, livers, kidneys etc.), so society had its separate parts, each with its own particular role to play yet also interdependent and contributing to the life of the whole.

Functionalism came to prominence in the 1950s in the US through the writings of Talcott Parsons and Robert Merton who discarded the organic analogy in favour of broader systems theory. Parsons, for example, argued that there are four interconnected systems that contribute to social action:

(1) the *human organism* – the body as the primary means for engaging in the physical environment;
(2) the *individual personality as a system* which includes conscious and unconscious motivation, responding not only to positive rewards but also to internalized feelings of guilt;
(3) the *social system* in which social **roles** are created and maintained by sanctions;
(4) the *culture system* which refers to symbols and meanings that individual actors draw upon when pursuing their personal objectives.

Parsons argued that societies as a whole could be classified in terms of their structural differences. Some societies, for example, have separated their political institutions from economic institutions more than others. On the basis of attempts at classification, Parsons flirted with the idea that some societies were of a higher order in terms of developmental complexity; implying that the US was 'leading the way'.

Merton did not regard functionalism as a general theory capable of covering all societies. In particular, he noted that integration of society may vary enormously – for example, while non-literate societies might be highly integrated it cannot be assumed that kind of integration applies as a standard for all societies. He also argued that what is functional for society is not necessarily functional for individuals or groups within that society; the reverse is also true. Alongside 'function', Merton thought it necessary to have the concept of 'dysfunction' – the negative consequences for individuals and groups. Merton made the useful distinction between 'manifest' and 'latent' functions. Using the Hopi Indians as an example he claimed that their 'rain dance' had the manifest function of trying to persuade the gods to bring rain and had the latent function of increasing social solidarity within the group. In a more contemporary setting, the existence of criminal behaviour, perhaps, has the manifest function of serving the interests of criminals but has a latent function of making clear what most people regard as right and wrong.

From its inception functionalism met criticism from a variety of social theorists, some arguing that it placed too much weight on social processes as determinants of individual action and paid insufficient attention to individual transactions as the basis of social action. Others from the perspective of conflict theories pointed to the fact that functionalism completely ignores **power** in shaping and determining the 'collective goals' of a particular society and has a predisposition to value and maintain social stability against those forces that would seek change.

Yet the case against functionalism is not open and shut – particularly for social workers who often turn to systems theory for their understanding of how society and individuals and families interact. In social work, it is useful to ask the question 'what function does any behaviour serve in any social group?' because it is an aid to assessment. For example, the behaviour of an abusive partner in a marriage would appear to serve the interests of the abuser although it may also be argued that it might maintain some kind of order, if only an 'imposed order'. This constitutes the feminist critique of family systems theory because they argue that the family is not ideologically neutral but is invariably a patriarchal institution where power is exercised disproportionately by men in their own interests. Any kind of functional analysis still has to be interpreted in historical or contemporary terms. That any behaviour or social institution serves a purpose does not imply that a more efficient or socially effective behaviour or social institution could not usefully replace it.

Functionalism covers ground relevant to social work in other ways. The debate around *social cohesion*, for instance, is a debate about social integration – how to achieve it, how to maintain it and why it is useful. Also, historically social work has been closely associated with maintaining stability in society; the theory that the main social work task is one of *maintenance*, put forward by Martin Davies, implicitly asks us to think about what constitutes 'maintenance', what it is that is being maintained and how can it be achieved. In this respect, functionalism has at the very least outlined some of the theoretical concerns that need to be explored, inviting social workers to think at a deeper level about how societies maintain themselves and what particular kinds of intervention can assist in that.

game theory a theory in which hypothetical scenarios are constructed in order to test different decision-making outcomes by participants whose interests are potentially in conflict. A 'game' is based on a constructed scenario with a set of decision-makers, called players, as participants. Each player is offered the same array of resources and the same range of possible courses of action. All participants are assumed to be rational, conscious decision-makers with well-defined goals that maximize the benefits ('utility') of the decider and able to exercise freedom of choice within prescribed limits. Game scenarios are based on two or more persons having to make a decision between two or more courses of action and the interests of each person may be partly or wholly in conflict. Often the utility arising from different courses of action is provided with a numerical value that allows the calculation of the benefits or costs of the different outcomes. Often games go through several rounds of decision-making to show how decisions are reached over a period of time by taking into account the outcomes of earlier rounds.

However hypothetical certain specific games scenarios are, they do shed light on a fundamental dilemma – how persons co-operate (or not) in a world of scarcity and finite resources? *Zero-sum games*, where one player gains only if the other loses, were the first to be explored by the early developers of game theory. They were able to show how, despite the extreme conflict of interest in such games, a relatively stable equilibrium could be reached in which each party was able to reach something approaching an optimum outcome albeit one much more successful than the other.

Other games are not zero-sum. These usually involve participants in decisions as to whether they should co-operate or not with other participants such as *prisoner's dilemma*. The collective (or public) good will only be optimized if each participant chooses the collective interest over his or her self-interest ('the public option', so to speak). Often by co-operating with one another, benefits increase for all but it is not always obvious to participants that this will be so; indeed games are often constructed so that if all participants except one are willing to co-operate, the one who intends to act solely on his or her self-interest can gain an advantage. The difficulty for the decision-makers then lies in the fact that they cannot be sure whether other participants are willing to co-operate, or trust them to do so. In simulations of such games, participants usually choose the self-interested (or selfish), distrustful option roughly two-thirds of the time with the co-operative outcome only arrived at in a small minority of instances. However, it has also been established that within much longer time frames, when the games are repeated many times (even through computer simulations), co-operative solutions do begin to emerge.

Game theory was developed by mathematically inclined economists linked to **rational choice theory** but is now applied to a wide range of settings in which decisions regarding collective action versus individual self-interest are likely to occur. Some of the basic formulations of game theory have given rise to phrases now widely used by the public such as 'the zero-sum' game or 'win–win' situations, where both parties gain benefits from an outcome. For social workers game theory reveals interesting insights into the nature of co-operation versus self-interest and how people make decisions balancing their self-interest against the need to maintain public resources available to all. It is particularly relevant for training in negotiation, a skill that social workers as brokers of services and partners in collaborative programmes require. It also sheds light on how people construct their decision-making; through the construction of complex, real-life scenarios practitioners can test out different courses of action within the game environment.

gender in everyday usage, gender refers to the anatomical differences between males and females (and also rarely 'hermaphrodites') but in sociological thinking gender is essentially a 'social construction' and a form of social differentiation based upon anatomical sexual differences.

Gender, as expressed in the adjectives 'feminine' and 'masculine', emerges from the process of both primary and secondary socialization, where individuals adapt to culturally prescribed **norms** and social roles, although as individual agents they have the possibility of accepting or rejecting aspects of the given, especially in societies where there is cultural diversity and a measure of liberality. But in broad terms gender is now construed as culturally and historically relative. For example, women's rights in the UK have changed significantly in the last two centuries so that women now have many more social, economic and political rights that were previously denied them, permitting much more socially inclusive lives and greater access to social and economic independence than was hitherto possible.

Sociology adopted it in the 1920s to describe the African American neighbourhoods on the south side of Chicago and subsequently to any area which was socially deprived, shared a cultural and ethnic identity but above all was confined to a specific limited spatial area within a city or town. Additional characteristics included poor-quality housing and welfare infrastructures as well as the features of a **culture of poverty**.

Wilson (1993) has argued that the process of 'ghettoization' is dependent on an interrelated set of phenomena primarily social and economic in origin. They demonstrate that African American ghettos – and other areas of concentrated poverty – experienced a crisis not because of a culture of welfare dependency but because joblessness and economic exclusion had reached dramatic proportions, triggering a process of 'hyperghettoization'. Their research highlighted the enormous penalties that beset African American urban neighbourhoods through deindustrialization in the 1970s and 1980s and the consequent loss of secure manufacturing jobs for the semi-skilled inner city working class. Not only did this take away the means for regular income for sustaining a family, it removed entire neighbourhoods from connections to society's main source of dignity, discipline and organization for daily life.

Social scientists have long debated whether there are ghettoes in the UK. On balance, they have concluded that American urban ghettos contain the extremes of concentrated poverty combined with physical confinement of residents that is not evident in African Caribbean and Asian neighbourhoods in British cities. However, this is a question of degree and is not to be confused with the extent of segregation, which is substantial along ethnic and faith lines or to assume that there are not intense geographic concentrations of deprivation and low-income families.

Wilson, W. (1993) *The Ghetto Underclass: Social Science Perspective.* London: Sage Publications.

gift relationship reciprocal relationships with others, both known and unknown, involving the exchange of services and goods. Several writers, notably Mauss and Levi-Strauss, have argued that patterns of taking and giving gifts express social bonds that both reflect and reveal the nature of different societies in relation to roles, expectations and obligations. More recently Titmuss in his study *The Gift Relationship* (1970) looked at the behaviour and motivation of blood donors in the UK where large numbers of people regularly donated blood without monetary reward, contrasting their behaviour with that of blood donors in other countries where donations were always rewarded. Societies where gifts are so donated can usefully be perceived as having high levels of social capital; that is, where there are high levels of activism and involvement in key community and neighbourhood activities and civic society generally.

group(s) any collection of people who are members of an association or social aggregate, where there are either formal or informal criteria used to determine membership and, by implication, who can and cannot be a member of the group. The word group is used very loosely in the social sciences to mean collections of people who *share* an experience with each other as well as more imprecise notions about people who are simply part of a larger entity such as a *reference group* or *pressure group*. Group work theory attempts to deal with the multifaceted issues associated with people sharing an experience. Some of the key ingredients, the intrinsic properties, regarding various models of group behaviour are as follows:

* *Group formation* – with any group where there are reciprocal roles and ties, there often appear to be identifiable stages that character-ize group formation. Tuckman's trajectory has it that many groups *form, storm, norm, perform* and *adjourn,* by which he meant that people coming together for the first time (*form*) begin a process of determining what the group is to be about, its ground rules and, perhaps, its aims and objectives (*storming*); once people are com-fortable with these preliminaries and have perhaps, where relevant, allocated roles it could be that the *norm*s have been broadly agreed and the group begins to more actively *perform*; later *adjourning* when the group has achieved its objectives and disbands. In practice, of course, there are many variations on these themes. For example, a group of professionals meeting to update their know-ledge and skills would already share a lot, suggesting that they could very quickly move into performing mode. Other groups may have fundamental differences about aims and objectives and disband after the storming stage and so on.

* *Leadership and self-help* – it is possible to conceive of a continuum regarding different kinds of group as being wholly reliant on a leader at one end of the continuum and functioning without a leader at the other end; and, in addition, embracing a process that starts deliberately with a leader with an agreed objective of dis-pensing with the leader at some later point. It is also possible to constitute groups deliberately without a leader such as Alcoholics or Gamblers Anonymous. Leaders may be 'teachers' or 'facilita-tors' or combine features of both roles. The considerable literature on leadership, most of it written by social psychologists, seems to cohere around the idea that the effective leader is one who is con-sultative (is interested in the opinions of group or team members),

is prepared to present new ideas (take the initiative) but in the end is prepared to be decisive and give explanations for decisions. However, the facilitator should enable the group to assume prime responsibility for these tasks.

- *Aims and objectives* – 'needs-led services' are those that reflect the needs and, hopefully, the wishes of participants. How those needs are articulated is a key process. Ideally, needs should be identified by group members and their participation in the group should be voluntary. However, although participants are supposed to consent to some group work programmes, it could be argued that there is an element of compulsion in, for example, offender groups managed by youth offending teams or the Probation Service or programmes designed to enhance the skills of parents of trouble-some teenagers where the police and/or the courts have become involved. This raises concerns about the extent to which aims and objectives are 'owned' by group members, suggesting that groups are more likely to achieve their objectives if aims are 'voluntarily' embraced and that they reflect needs and wishes and are not simply services that are offered because 'we have always done it this way'.

- *Issues of conformity and group dynamics* – a classic experiment undertaken by Asch identified the covert forces that often led to individuals conforming to group norms. In one experiment, three parallel lines were drawn on a blackboard, the one in the middle appreciably shorter than the outlying lines. 'Stool pigeons' in the experiment were asked to estimate the length of the lines and they consistently responded by asserting that all three lines were of similar length before other 'innocent' participants were asked. A small proportion of the innocents judged that one line was shorter and said so, but most people agreed that the lines were equal in length; of these most admitted that they had not wanted to 'stand out from the crowd' and a minority perceived no difference at all – under the influence of the group they simply had not noticed. In practice, group dynamics, including tendencies to conform, will actually reflect a number of complex variables including group size, agreement or disagreement about aims and objectives, the distribution of power in any group and the role, where relevant, of any leader/facilitator.

- *Inter-group relations* – groups rarely operate in isolation and it is possible that in some context groups have to deal with other groups. Where groups are required to compete for resources (or maybe territory or business, say, for street gangs), inter-group rivalry may well lead to enhanced group solidarity and identification within groups and the development of unjustified negative

views of the 'other'. However, if a group lacks coherence and consensus then it is possible that inter-group rivalry will bring about
the break-up of a social group. The German sociologist Simmel, in
his work on *formal sociology*, has explored this territory.

- *Different kinds of group* – the discussion above relates to some general properties of groups; however, it is worth noting some specific
issues in relation to particular kinds of group that would need to be
taken note of in widely varying settings:

  (1) *Peer groups and gangs* – peer groups can refer to either an age-
  related social category such as young people's peer group in
  terms of the general influence of cultural messages about (18–25
  year-olds) implicit in the media, social networking websites and
  advertising; or to a smaller peer group such as that associated
  with school or college or local community. Gangs refer to much
  tighter structured groupings that tend to persist over time and
  to offer a significant source of identity and social status.

  (2) *Therapeutic groups/treatment groups* – two perspectives are useful here. The first relates to groups that meet together under
  the guidance of a therapist with the therapist playing the key
  role, with the possibility that this constitutes an efficient use of
  the therapist's time. The second perspective consciously regards
  the group as integral to the therapy and that, if only in part, the
  group experience is an important dimension to 'healing'.

  (3) *Community groups* – a wide range of groups that might be
  wholly social or recreational in character to groups that articulate a community's wishes and needs for more resources and
  perhaps campaign to achieve improvements. Key issues relate
  to whether such groups are supported by community workers
  or perhaps local politicians and the extent to which residents
  control agendas and tactics.

  (4) *Client groups* – group work is integral to direct work with many
  different client groups and in many settings including, for
  example, support to carers which tends to be mostly social and
  emotional support with a little attention being given to accessing material resources; or the use of group work in residential
  and/or day care settings (for children and young people, adults
  with disabilities and adults with mental health problems) where
  the focus can be upon social skills, problems of communal living
  and maybe making contributions, as focus groups, to community care plans.

  (5) *Social work teams* – can be a major focus of support if the general
  environment is enabling and positive, where practitioners can

share problems in the expectation that useful ideas will emerge from colleagues. The role of team manager is critical depending upon their commitment to the team as against deferring to higher management at the cost of the team.

(6) *Multidisciplinary teams* – key issues in this context can be professional hierarchies and competing/alternative professional paradigms/priorities as they impact on practice. Much will also depend upon the organizational context to multidisciplinary teams; whether they are located in a health setting, for example, or in a more neutral agency.

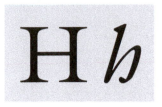

H h

human rights see **rights**

hypothesis any proposition or untested statement which is offered as a prelude to trying to establish the relationship between **variables**. Part of the process of trying to establish a particular relationship could also involve trying to falsify the hypothesis too because there is clearly a problem if a relationship can be both proved and disproved. A hypothesis has to be capable of being tested.

Normally, it would be expected that, whoever is undertaking the research, they would be required to explain why they believe that a hypothesis were likely to be true. Thus, an example of a hypothesis might be that it would be reasonable to expect that comprehensive sexual health education among teenagers, including detailed information about contraception, would be likely to lead to fewer unplanned pregnancies for this focal group. A justification for this hypothesis would be that unplanned pregnancy often arises out of ignorance about effective contraception, that young people often lack an understanding of the effect of sexually transmitted diseases upon health and, if the sexual health education should include coverage of how girls can try to be assertive, then it may be reasonable to expect fewer pregnancies from such an educational programme. (See also **data**, **research methods** and **variable**.)

hysteria see psychoanalysis, **psychopathology**.

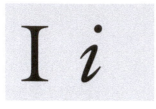

I i

identity the sense of self that develops as children and young people learn to differentiate from parents and begin to acquire social roles and attributes that they may regard as important to their understanding of themselves. Erik Erikson working in the psychoanalytic tradition argued in *Childhood and Society* (1963) that identity formation was a process that combined the individual's core sense of self and the social arrangements and values within which that self developed. He saw this process unfolding in eight different stages of the **life course** in which a person's sense of their own identity was consolidated. In particular, he proposed that **adolescence** was often a time of identity crisis in which young people construct their own sense of distinctness through different friendship or peer groups, different lifestyles and value bases and different career plans. Ideally, at the end of adolescence, the young person's sense of identity has stabilized and that person feels at ease with himself or herself.

Recent sociology has challenged the notion of identity as a single, stable concept by examining how identities – whether of individuals or seemingly homogeneous **groups** – are many sided with different elements coming into focus at different times. This is the natural consequence of migrations, the mixing of cultures, faiths and ethnicities. The contribution of sexuality and gender are also now widely explored as important aspects of identity. Michel Foucault has, in particular, inspired this line of enquiry by arguing that different **discourse**s produce different versions of ourselves, giving us multiple identities based on a range of social practices whether that of the religious adherent, local civic resident or roles based on gender. In the work of those who continue in Foucault's footsteps, class, ethnicity, 'race', gender and sexuality are all sources of differing identities that interrelate and can be located within a single person. This struggle for the 'recognition of difference' has an emancipatory objective by seeking to assert previously denied or marginalized identities. Others note, however, that the 'politics of recognition' is the primary source of social divisiveness, having displaced the older, class-based politics of wealth-based redistribution.

Understanding the different aspects of identity, particular in relation to faith, ethnicity and sexuality, has become prominent over the last two decades after a lengthy period of professional disinterest. It is critical in several fields of practice – for example in placing children for adoption or fostering where sensitivity to a child's 'race' are crucial determinants in the matching process. It is also prominent in working with adolescents as they explore different elements of their emerging identities and uncertain as to whether they should challenge or confirm aspects of their origins and backgrounds. Some of the most difficult work can arise with individual young people whose understanding of themselves may be very different, indeed marginalized by the culture in which they were raised. Sexuality, whether gay or lesbian, provides some of the clearest examples where individual young people can be marginalized and rejected by their own families. (See also **gender**.)

ideology forms of consciousness, informed by ideas, ideals, values, norms, religious beliefs, *Weltanschauungen*, moral precepts, political mantras and the like, but formed by the material conditions in which people live. In Marx's view, consciousness, located in the 'superstructure', reflects the conditions of the different social classes located in the 'economic substructure', suggesting in one formulation that the ideas of the ruling class dominate consciousness for all subordinate classes (Gramsci's *hegemony*) or, in another marginally different formulation, that each class generates its own consciousness but that the ruling-class's ideology dominates all other subordinate classes' ideologies.

In Marx's early book *The German Ideology* (1845), he argued that: 'The ideas of the ruling class are, in every age, the ruling ideas; that is, the class, which is the dominant material force in society, is at the same time its dominant intellectual force.'

For Marx, ideology in capitalist societies was evidence of *false consciousness* because people (workers and the ruling class alike) were living in an alienated world that resulted in the oppression of many. Only socialist societies, post-revolution, would manifest *true consciousness*. Many social scientists, especially sociologists and political scientists, do not accept Marx's grand theory, but they are prepared to acknowledge that ideology is dominated by a political and economic nexus that works primarily in the interests of the wealthy. Many of the media are privately owned and managed by the wealthy and those that are outwardly independent or quasi-independent, such as the BBC, are dominated by people whose social origins are also from within the same political, economic and social elite(s).

Mass media also involve, necessarily, the notion of mass society – a society atomized because of the loss of community and traditional family structures. The resultant social isolation can result in lives dominated by a kind of dependence upon mass media including

TV programmes such as *The X Factor*, *Britain's Got Talent* and *Big Brother*, enabling a kind of vicarious living born of unrealistic notions of 'instant fame'.

Another perspective has it that what Marx called the 'dull compulsion of economic relations' means that workers actually have little choice but to comply with the rules and expectations of the employer. In this discourse, workers are thought to understand fully the nature of their relationship to the means of production. In addition, if working-class culture is examined closely in folk songs, humour, trade union activities, 'alternative' political/pressure groups that are critical of the employer class, it is clear that many do not accept dominant ideologies but feel relatively powerless to substantially change them.

The social and community work tasks that arise out of challenging oppressive ideologies include offering alternative discourses about the realities of life for the poor; resisting accounts of service users' lives that blame them for their own poverty; seeking to maintain public services at no or low cost; campaigning for benefits that can maintain a reasonable standard of life; seeking to build social capital; and developing alternative social and economic institutions such as credit unions, social housing and affordable community transport.

impairment see **disability**

individualization the trend in which the disintegration of guiding social institutions, roles and communal bonds of support have compelled individuals to make critical life choices on their own, to become the 'do-it-yourself biography'. The German sociologist Ulrich Beck notes that, without the familiar signposts or collective sources of help available even in the recent past, individuals increasingly confront huge risks, including poverty and inequality, largely on their own. For him, this marks an entirely new stage in the development of society. He writes: 'The do-it-yourself biography is always a "risk biography", indeed a "tightrope biography", a state of permanent (partly overt, partly concealed) endangerment. The façade of prosperity, consumption, glitter can often mask the nearby precipice. The wrong choice of career . . . compounded by the downward spiral of private misfortune, divorce, illness, the repossessed home – all this is merely called bad luck' (Beck and Beck-Gernsheim 2002: 3). The groups with which one chooses to affiliate become smaller, less able to promote any kind of social action. Attachment to social classes become weaker, people are separated from the traditional support networks provided by family or neighbourhood, and work loses its importance as a focus of identity formation. People now choose from an array of disparate social identities, lifestyles, opinions and sub-cultures. In Beck's terms, this is capitalism without classes, but with new and still emerging forms of differentiation and inequality.

Social workers use individualization in a somewhat different sense when they link it to the 'personalization' agenda which ostensibly places services at the command of the adult who receives them. Individualization in social work's usage rests on theories of citizenship, consumer choice and autonomy, and aims to give individuals sufficient control of resources to shape the care that they determine they need. It accepts that adults are their own best experts and have the most knowledge regarding their needs.

Within the move to direct control by individuals in making their own care arrangements social work has at times struggled to find a distinctive role for itself as opposed to the other sources of support open to adults – peer groups, family relations, care support groups, and other professionals particularly in health. It has had to re-emphasize that it is a regulated graduate profession with a code of practice and constantly developing knowledge base with a key role in public protection.

While individualization means something specific to social workers it does share some of the meaning that Beck and colleagues have given it: greater levels of responsibility and risk of failure, in the sense of poorly spent money and diminished well-being, are transferred to the individual adult recipient of service. The whole edifice is based on the assumption that individuals are the best judges of their own interests and can execute their decisions competently. But for the adult, decision-making and choice is difficult arising from lack of information and lack of knowledge. While users accept choice in principle the culture and values of the care systems, the specific level and quality of services on offer often elude them. They simply do not have sufficient information and are engulfed in what Barry Schwartz has called 'the paradox of choice': facing too many options, with too many unknowns to make reasonable decisions.

Beck, U. and Beck-Gernsheim, E. (2002) *Individualization: Institutionalized Individualism and its Social and Political Consequences.* London: Sage Publications.

Schwartz, B. (2004) *The Paradox of Choice: Why More is Less.* New York: HarperCollins.

inequality large differentials in levels of reward or opportunities available to individuals and groups within a society. Inequality is found within a number of different domains – unequal rights, inequality of opportunity, educational provision, access to health care – but inequality of income and wealth attracts most of social scientists' attention simply because other forms track it so closely. The question as to whether inequality is something that is inevitable in modern societies or can be overcome runs deep, drawing on some of the most authoritative voices from among conservative, neo-liberals and other thinkers on the **right** and **Marxists**, liberals and social democrats, **functionalists** and others on the left.

Friedrich Hayek, the prominent economist and political theorist of the mid-twentieth century and his libertarian and neo-liberal followers today argued that inequality is the price to be paid for the dynamic nature of **capitalism** which develops and expands only because it can engage in 'creative destruction', as another economist Joseph Schumpeter put it – periods of expansion and contraction (with employment and unemployment) which allows capitalism to respond to the ever-changing tastes and demands of the market place. A corollary to this argument is that government policies to reduce wealth inequality – for example by setting a minimum wage, levelling up incomes through welfare payments, or creating public services to which all have access regardless of income – hobbles capitalism. This is because such efforts create an over-dominant state that siphons off money through taxes that could have been used for private capital investment. The policy of the coalition government elected in 2010 in the UK is based precisely on this assumption: it has argued that by severely cutting public expenditure and public services the private sector will be freed to expand its investment and to create many more jobs than are lost in the public sector.

In general, though, social scientists have been concerned about the impact of income inequality – both what it does to individuals and families with the least income and what inequality means for society as a whole. These efforts at analysis have described in considerable detail the extent of inequality and the process through which it is cemented in place. Much of this has focused on social class as the main source of inequality, whether in rates of mortality, educational attainment, **social mobility** or income. The assumption – or hope - behind this research is that the public and government will conclude that the large inequalities are destructive and need to be reduced. In this, very broadly, they do not argue for a utopian ideal of complete equality but what degree of inequality is acceptable.

There are different ways of measuring income inequality – for example, establishing the difference in income between the top and bottom 20 percent, or looking at the proportion of all incomes which go to the bottom half of the population. (Typically, the poorer half receive 20 to 25 percent of all income while the richer half receives the remaining 75 or 80 percent.)

Another well-known measure is the *Gini coefficient* which measures inequality across the whole of society rather than just comparing
extremes. Its scale runs from 1 – the state of complete inequality in
which a single person receives all the income with everyone else getting nothing – to 0 – the state of complete equality where everyone
receives the same income. The lower the number (always a fraction of
1) the more equal the society is, with most societies falling in between
0.3 and 0.5. For example, Britain was a relatively more equal society
in 1977 when its coefficient was 0.24 than in 1997 when it was just
under 0.35. In the course of those 20 years it had suffered as swift an
acceleration in inequality as any developed country in the world and
its degree of inequality was higher than any apart from the US. In
the following decade, under Labour, the figure remained roughly the
same, although the other main measure of inequality – the proportion
of income flowing to the bottom 10 percent – showed that Britain had
become more equal, at a time when many other developed countries,
notably the US, became more *unequal.*

Analysis of inequality goes further than compiling statistics on its
extent. In particular, it has focused on why inequalities of all kinds
are so persistent and why some social groups are subject to systematic
disadvantages in relation to other, dominant groups. Large, stable
systematic social inequalities around the world are linked to different
kinds of group identity – gender, ethnicity, religion, caste, tribe and
clan. Charles Tilly has called these 'durable inequalities'. They have
their roots in competition among groups, with each group attempting
to exclude the others from resources that they control. Two further
mechanisms – *exploitation* and *opportunity hoarding* cause the gap
between groups to widen as agents of the more powerful group patrol
organizational boundaries with their eye on available ways to secure
ever greater dominance. Tilly argues that once inequality is secured
in one domain it spreads to new domains, making the dominance
pervasive and systematic. Groups interact according to norms expressing their unequal positions in one domain acquire habits that spread
to new domains. Once durable inequality spreads people explain and
legitimate it by inventing stories about supposed inherent differences
between their groups, for example highlighting differences in intelligence, physical prowess, abilities to hold down a job. Experiences
within the dominant group *and* within subordinate groups give participants systematically different and unequal preparation for performance in any new organization.

Links have also been established between inequality and a number
of social problems. In their research, Richard Wilkinson and Kate

Pickett looked at the incidence of specific problems across a number of countries and then at the extent of inequality in those countries. After drawing on a range of international data, they found the major determinant of social problems to be the extent of inequality *within* a country rather than the overall level of wealth of a country or the average wage. Both the US and the UK are highly unequal societies by international standards and both have greater levels of social difficulties, whether in poor educational performance, obesity, mental health problems, lack of social mobility, imprisonment and interpersonal violence. Thus the paradox: material success but social failure. It arises because highly unequal societies breed greater levels of anxiety over the individual's self-worth. Individuals are more prone to anxiety arising from the intense contrast between high and low social status within such societies. Loss of face and humiliation occur more frequently. Wilkinson and Pickett write: 'If the social hierarchy is seen – as it often is – as if it were a ranking of the human race by ability, then the outward signs of success or failure (the better jobs, higher incomes, education, housing, car and clothes) all make a difference' (2010: 40). Put simply, greater inequality increases status competition and the potential shame of failure within that competition. Self-promotion becomes a necessary norm; modesty and self-deprecation become the casualties of inequality.

The studies on inequality are of profound importance for social workers for the vast majority of service users fall at the bottom end of the income scale. The social science cannot be clearer: the inequality arising from the structural conditions of society, its distribution of income, present enormous psychological difficulties such as loss of self-worth and shame. While too often the focus then falls exclusively on individuals' lack of achievement and their problems such as obesity, poor health and mental health problems, it becomes clear that there are powerful reasons embedded in society and the economy as to why this is so.

Dorling, D. (2009) *Injustice: Why Social Inequality Persists.* Bristol: The Policy Press.

Wilkinson, R. and Pickett, K. (2010) *The Spirit Level: Why Equality is Better for Everyone.* Harmondsworth: Penguin Books.

integration a process by which different ethnic groups are able to retain cultural identities while taking part equally in social, economic and political life.

Whereas **assimilation** entails either one culture absorbing another or two or more cultures combining into a new social entity, integration has different ethnic groups retaining their identities. The often used

metaphor is that assimilation is rather like a vegetable soup where the
ingredients have become an indistinguishable mush whereas integration is the bowl of salad in which the components can still be identified. Full integration is only achieved when ethnic hierarchies have
been eradicated, when equality of opportunity is equitably distributed
between ethnic groups and where all such groups are encouraged to
contribute to every aspect of society.

Elizabeth Anderson in *The Imperative of Integration* (2010) argues
that integration takes place in four states:
(1) *formal desegregation* – abolishing the laws and policies enforcing
    segregation;
(2) *spatial integration* – equal use of facilities and public spaces by
    substantial numbers of all 'races' and ethnicities;
(3) *social integration* – intergroup co-operation on terms of equality;
(4) *informal integration* – in social relationships.
In most societies with significant culturally distinct groups, integration
remains more of a political aspiration, an ideal, than a reality. The ideal
'envisions a restructuring of intergroup relations, from alienation, anxiety, awkwardness, and hostility to relaxed, competent civil association
and even intimacy; from domination and subordination to co-operation
as equals'. It aims at the abolition of racial segregation and its accompanying inequalities, not of racial identities, and consists in the full
participation on terms of equality of groups in all domains of society.
It uses ethnic-conscious policies but accepts that some degree of ethnic
solidarity and affiliation on the part of the stigmatized is needed, both
to spur integration and to cope with its stresses. Anderson distinguishes
between *formal* and *informal* integration. The first occurs when members of different 'races' co-operate in accordance with institutionally
defined social roles and all ethnic groups occupy all roles in enough
numbers that roles are not 'racially' identified. The second involves co-
operation, ease, welcome, trust, affiliation and intimacy that go beyond
the requirements of organizationally defined roles. It happens, she
writes, when members of different 'races' form friendships, date, marry,
bear children or adopt different 'race' children.

Pessimists would have it that multi-ethnic societies find it very
difficult to sustain optimal social arrangements for all groups; and that
any apparent period of stability, tolerance and inter-group harmony
will be temporary until economic difficulties, especially, develop and
groups have to compete for scarce resources. Optimists, however,
argue that equitable arrangements can be defended through strong
political institutions that enshrine power-sharing and a political ethos
that encourages co-operation between groups. It seems likely that

co-operation will only have a chance of succeeding if social arrangements also require each group to have some knowledge and understanding of 'others' and for this to happen meaningful social contact is necessary and segregated communities avoided.

Examples of how social contact might be 'engineered' include decisions about whether faith-based schools are permitted or even encouraged; whether religious/cultural clothing and jewellery is or is not to be tolerated and whether religious holidays are to be observed for all citizens and/or for separate cultural/ethnic groups. An additional issue that has preoccupied social workers includes the idea of 'trans-racial' adoption. Although there are many shades of opinion, the two most strongly expressed seem to be that all children should be placed with families sharing the same ethnic/cultural identity as against a contrasting stance that ethnicity and culture are less important than finding families for all children where they will be valued and raised in a manner that will enable them to deal with life's problems including 'racism'. (See also **assimilation, multiculturalism** and **pluralism**.)

Anderson, E. (2010) *The Imperative of Integration*. Princeton: Princeton University Press.

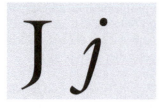

justice the idea that there should be fairness in the administration of rules, law and social transactions generally; that like cases or problems or rewards should be treated or distributed alike and in a consistent manner. Considerations of justice inevitably involve the related matters concerning equality and **punishment** as well as broader social policy issues such as income distribution.

Theories of justice have preoccupied many philosophers from Plato onwards as well as theorists and practitioners in law, the criminal and civil justice systems and politicians interested in notions of social justice. Contemporary debates embrace a very wide range of positions. For example:

- Socialists tend to stress equality of outcome and the notion of **need** at least in some formulations of the idea of justice. In fact, Marx himself was somewhat equivocal in this regard, suggesting initially that individuals should secure wages or other kinds of reward in the formula 'to each according to his labour', later changing it to 'to each according to his need' once a genuinely socialist society had been achieved and the state had withered away.
- The neo-liberal view broadly endorses the idea that the conditions for equality of opportunity should be established where possible, but that then any inequalities of outcome by virtue of hard work and/or ability are entirely legitimate.
- Variations of the conservative view have it that either hierarchies are part of the natural order and are thus to be welcomed; that elites will always emerge (without necessarily acknowledging where elites routinely originate from); that inequalities give people incentives (make them lean and hungry); or that markets will inevitably lead to differential outcomes given the entrepreneurial spirit in some and its absence in others.

These very different perspectives have a major impact on the way social work is regarded as well as having a direct bearing on the lives of service users. The following key problem areas are especially important:

- *Access to justice* – engaging a lawyer to assist with a problem is a service that is not evenly available to people. There have been recent reductions in legal aid in the UK; problems in accessing both high-quality legal representation and of being able to pay for sufficient legal advice (time) can also be a problem. Similarly, when individuals are faced with corporate interests there can be major imbalances of power in relation to accessing competent legal advice. In addition, certain problems seem less likely to be addressed legally or to secure sufficient legal support: problems faced by women in abusive relationships, cases of **discrimination** in employment and the very particular difficulties faced by asylum seekers are now well-established examples of relatively 'inaccessible' justice.

- *Equal treatment before the law* – the treatment of women and ethnic minorities by the justice system for crimes have been established as frequently harsh and disproportionate in comparison with men and white people respectively for comparable offences. The notions of systemic racism and sexism have featured in the research about sentencing; the composition of pre-sentence reports by the probation service, the behaviour of the police and punitive regimes within prisons in relation to privileges, parole and early discharge all testify to uneven access to justice.

- *Redistribution of income: criteria of need and desert* – a number of related problems are usually considered under this heading including any society's responsibility for promoting equal opportunities; its responsibility for addressing any 'unacceptable' outcomes of what is inevitably going to be an imperfect system; and the extent to which any society/government accepts broad responsibility for the maintenance of basic standards in key areas of social functioning. In recent decades the consensus on these matters has sometimes converged and at others diverged, against a backdrop of a broadly more comprehensive system of social welfare. The current debate about the cost of social care is indicative. Here some would argue that the costs of social care should be borne by general taxation just as the NHS currently is, even though it is acknowledged that some elders will need social care and others will not. Some pundits argue that costs should fall wholly on the recipient, until such times as the recipient's resources are exhausted. A sort of middle position is that some proportion of personal resources should be protected for personal use or be left to family members when the elder dies, with different arguments about what that proportion of personal resources should be.

These kinds of debate have echoes in many parts of the current welfare system in relation to paying for prescriptions, dental services, eye tests, the costs of school trips or music lessons for school children, winter fuel allowances, free bus travel and paying for community care for elders and paying for higher education, with many of these debates framed by statements that the UK has to stay competitive on the international stage. Clearly in many respects notions of justice are fundamentally affected by economic considerations and not just philosophical principles. (See also **equality of opportunity, liberty, life chances** and **social mobility**.)

Sandel, M. (2010) *Justice: What's the right thing to do?* London: Penguin.

In a sense, both sets of criticisms were responding to supposed doctrines that labelling theory had not actually put forward. It was principally concerned with investigating a social process that produced labels arising from diagnoses of delinquent acts. It was a 'middle range' theory but one that could be taken up by other theoretical, even ideological perspectives. Labelling theory does not aspire to account for all deviancy or mental health problems but seeks to explain how labels are formed and attached. It makes no claim to explain the origins of the behaviour for which labels are developed.

Streaming is a much contested idea in schools with its passionate adherents and critics among parents, teachers and policy-makers. The critics argue that streaming is *par excellence* a self-fulfilling prophecy primarily because it affects the expectations of those who made decisions about streaming as well as the children who have been streamed. Critics point to the fact that few children change streams – while advocates argue that the streamers got it right in the first place. Experiments about changing teacher expectations, however, give some credence to the idea that streaming is a kind of labelling that sticks. In one experiment, undertaken by Jacobson and Rosenthal, tests were administered to students, but were later destroyed without being assessed. The researchers then chose some students at random and told teachers that these students' scores suggested that they had been underperforming and given encouragement would blossom. Given this information it would appear that teachers responded and by 'expecting' more of these allegedly underperforming students the students' work improved significantly.

An awareness of labelling theory and the widespread operation of labelling processes is useful to social workers and indeed has become a kind of orthodoxy in the way social workers view what happens to users. They understand, first, that many users can be seen as adversely affected by the application of social labels and, second, that social workers must be aware of how they themselves operate as labellers. A concern to offset the more negative effects of labelling processes can be seen as central to the orientation of much modern social welfare, with its aim of limiting discriminatory practices both within social work and in wider society. However, it is important for social workers not to rely on a simplified, reductionist version of labelling theory. That theory arose, and continues to be anchored in, symbolic interactionism. It does not claim to be a universal theory or to suggest it can point to deep-level causation. Rather, it acknowledges that while labelling can change the intensity and direction of the experience of the user to whom a label is attached, labels can be provisional, negotiable and even rejected outright.

Adler, P. and Adler, P. (2011) *Construction of Deviance: Social Power, Context and Interaction*, 7th edition. Belmont, CA: Wadsworth.

Scheff, T. (1999) *Being Mentally Ill: A Sociological Study*, 3rd edition. Hawthome, NY: Aldine.

left, left wing the political orientation that favours government intervention in the economy, welfare benefits that provide a reasonable standard of living, public provision of services such as health and child care and, in general, aims for greater equality in society as an overarching goal of policy.

The terms 'left' and 'left wing' and 'right' and 'right wing' date back to the National Assembly set up in France in the wake of the revolution of 1789. The most radical faction, the Jacobins, simply by chance, sat as a bloc to the left of the president (chair) of the assembly, the moderate parties in the centre and the more conservative aristocratic factions to the right. Thus the designations – left, right and centre – were determined from the speaker's vantage point. In the House of Commons in Britain, where the parties sit across from each other, that original spatial reference does not literally apply as readily yet the phrases 'left wing' and 'right wing' retain their usefulness, as they do across many political systems of the developed world.

The metaphor of left and right continue in use because it is vividly clear: we all understand what is to our left and to our right; we also know that while it is difficult to decide whether what is in between – the centre – is either left or right, nevertheless there is political territory that we can see is in 'the middle'. The fact that the terminology is still in use, more than 200 years after it was first used, is thanks largely to the fundamental nature of the political distinctions it expresses. If 'left' and 'right' had not been invented then some other phrase indicating political polarity would undoubtedly have been.

Left and right are not absolute terms but relative to one another, changing over time from generation to generation as politics evolves. For example, for much of the nineteenth century, certainly in Britain, the left in the form of the Chartist movement pressed for the extension of the vote to all working men. By 1920 this objective of universal 'male' suffrage would have been considered reactionary at the time women were gaining the vote through militancy of their own.

The left has been under sustained challenge since the early 1980s – from globalization, which has compelled countries to compete in the global market place, decline of manufacturing industries and the election of right-wing governments in the US and the UK committed to privatization and restriction of trade union rights. As a result, the traditional

Figure 2 The political spectrum

labour and social democratic parties in Europe have been losing electoral appeal. This has compelled them to re-examine their policies and redefine their electoral base toward the rising middle and professional classes that are now significantly larger in the post-industrial economy. While these parties have retained some connection to the trade union movements in their various countries they made it clear to the electorate at large that when they form governments they:

- would not show special favour to the trade unions or reverse legislation on the conduct of strike ballots;
- would make commitments to reform welfare systems by linking benefits around requirements for claimants to find work;
- would underscore the point that citizens had responsibilities as well as rights;
- would not reverse privatizations or expand public ownership of production.

Despite such concessions to market forces and the influence of the right among the electorate, they remained committed to reducing poverty and inequality in society at large.

Under the general heading of the 'Third Way' – that is supporting neither unregulated market capitalism nor old socialist objectives – and describing themselves explicitly as 'centre-left', left-leaning governments came to power in the US, Britain and Germany in the 1990s based on this kind of platform. Other, smaller parties also came to fill some of the space identified as 'the left': the Green Party, Plaid Cymru, the Scottish Nationalist Party, for example, are all considered left of centre.

Distinctions between left and right remain. The left generally aims to achieve greater equality across society and use the power of government programmes to bring this about, for example through the welfare system, while the right generally favours reducing the size of government, cutting down the welfare state and allowing the **market** to operate under a minimum of regulation (see Figure 2).

Giddens, A. (1999) *The Third Way*. Cambridge: The Polity Press.

liberalism a broad range of social and political philosophies based on the belief that individual freedom and autonomy should be paramount. Beyond this, however, the words 'liberal' and 'liberalism' have a confusing array of meaning. 'Liberal' as used in the US generally refers to progressive, left-of-centre politics that favours support for government intervention in the economy, trade union rights and a strong welfare safety net for those who cannot compete in the labour market. In this sense, it overlaps with social democratic political objectives (see **left, left wing**). By way of contrast, 'liberal' as used in the UK refers to those upholding the philosophy of the Liberal Democrats and its predecessor, the Liberal Party, which, while open to state-provided welfare, nevertheless were distrustful of the trade unions and the varieties of socialism associated with the labour movement.

The term 'neo-liberalism' is different again. It refers to those who maintain that government should provide a vastly reduced welfare state (because to do more only encourages dependency), should ensure that all **market**s are deregulated with no restrictions on market activity, and should withdraw from providing public services. Neo-liberal in this sense refers to the liberal economic philosophy of the mid-nineteenth century when any government interference in the labour market was regarded as virtually violating a law of nature. On this basis, measures to limit the working day for young children, improving conditions in factories or mines or setting up a state-provided school system were rejected throughout the first half of the nineteenth century. 'Neo' in this instance means a reborn liberalism of this kind. (See also **communitarianism**.)

liberty to be without social or political constraint or confinement; a state of freedom. In another formulation, any individual's right or capacity for self-determination.

Many commentators have remarked that the concept of liberty or freedom, especially in the hands of politicians, can mean almost what the writer or speechmaker wants it to mean; although in general terms the concept implies something essentially 'good'. In relation to matters that concern social workers, there are a number of crucial debates around liberty or freedom that might affect the lives of service users:

- *Freedom and determinism* – the notion that any behaviour was *determined* has two possible interpretations: first that it can be explained as a 'causal relationship' – that is, the behaviour was caused by something; or second, that the behaviour was *unavoidable*, meaning that it could not have been otherwise. In the physical sciences, it can be said with certainty that if metal is heated in particular conditions it will expand precisely according to established rules. With human beings no such certainty appears to be possible, because although an individual's personality might predispose them to behave in a particular way, their mood or emotional state and possibly the very particular social situation they are in, might result in a variety of actual behaviours.

- *Freedom and responsibility* – the debate above also has implications for whether individuals are to be considered *responsible* for their actions. It is generally held to be true that no individual can be regarded as responsible if they were compelled to act in a particular way or were in ignorance of the consequences that might arise out of their actions or were under duress. In essence, both their freedom to act without constraint and their responsibility for their actions might well be compromised in any person by certain psychological states or social situations. These kinds of consideration include core dimensions of work in the justice systems with practitioners trying to determine the offender's capacity to act freely (and thus responsibly) and in mental health assessments of service users in relation to 'capacity'.

- *Freedom or liberty as a political ideal* – there have been many debates about the safeguards that any state should put in place to guarantee basic 'freedoms' for its citizens. In this context, *two concepts of liberty* (Isaiah Berlin's essay by the same title has been influential) have helped frame aspects of both government thinking and the behaviour and attitudes of people of different political persuasions. The first version of the concept, the positive version, has it that people should have *the freedom to do things without constraint,* so far as is possible; that leaving people to control themselves is always better. Such a view underpins ideas about, for example, low tax regimes so that individual citizens are enabled to make their own decisions about what services they wish to purchase and not have a 'nanny state' tax more heavily to pay for services for everyone. This perspective also argues that the state should be very small and that individuals should shoulder as many responsibilities for themselves and their families as possible. The alternative version of the concept, the negative formulation, is that people should be able to live *free from particular evils or adverse conditions* such as hunger, poor health, unemployment, a lack of housing and the more general concerns about any condition that might compromise or limit citizens' freedom of thought, freedom of association and assembly and freedom from unjust, oppressive laws. Contemporary thinkers who have embraced the second formulation of liberty point to the incarceration of very young offenders, the many compromises of some people's civil liberties (the indifferent treatment of asylum seekers, especially children, for example) and of lives fundamentally compromised by differential **life chances** as examples of people living in unnecessarily 'un-free' circumstances. These narratives are at the centre of current ideological debates about whether the welfare state is paternalistic and thus compromises citizens' abilities to 'stand on their own feet' or whether it is an institution guaranteeing the minimum standards by which any free citizen can begin to function at a basic level.

life chances an umbrella term that embraces a number of key social indicators of both quality of life for people and the length of their lives. Key variables include both morbidity and mortality (see **epidemiology**) (the incidence of illness and the age at death) and social achievements considered important or desirable and the avoidance of those things considered to be undesirable by any society.

The concept was devised by the German sociologist Weber in his analysis of the social consequences of class membership and varying social statuses. He acknowledged that the ownership of property had implications for purchasing power in relation to the acquisition of goods and services, that it had implications for the personal power that people might wield and thus in their abilities to maintain or enhance class position. The term is now used more generally to be an estimation of the odds faced by individuals in their attempts to achieve, say, higher education, secure a high status and well-paid job, own a decent house and have access to desirable consumer goods as well as avoiding illness and living a full and long life. It is accepted by most commentators that within advanced industrial societies marked differences in life chances have been remarkably persistent, seemingly explicable by reference to social class but with other social identifiers, such as ethnicity, gender, religious affiliation and disability sometimes also significant. Health inequalities have been similarly persistent in relation to both morbidity and mortality despite significant advances in health care, also reflecting stubborn differences in life chances experienced by the working classes. (See also **equality of opportunity** and **social mobility**.)

life course the process of personal change, from infancy through to old age and death.

Growing interest in exploring and defining the concept of life course in recent years has been from two broad perspectives: first, the biological, which emphasizes stages in physiological and psychosocial development, the common process underlying the human life course (in this usage often referred to as the *life cycle*); second, the experiential, which emphasizes the importance of unique experience and significant life events, that is, the contrasts between individuals' lives rather than their similarities. While the biological model provides a framework, each individual life course is unique; individuals have the power to make choices and each constructs his or her own biography within broad biological and social constraints. Acknowledging the importance of both age and experience when considering an individual's current concerns, an experiential psycho-social model has been proposed that describes the adult developmental process, not tied to age stages or to typical life experiences but distinguishing concerns such as the establishment of self-identity, of key relationships, the development of community interests, the maintenance of position, disengagement and the recognition of, often, increasing dependency. While this may be seen as a *life course process*, individuals may pass in and out of these areas of major concern, become stuck in one, cope well or badly, and experience crises and development as a result of the interactions within them. Sociologists, while acknowledging the very individual nature of life course experience, stress the importance of structural features of society that provide an often compelling context and sometimes constraints, of 'life chances' including, crucially, poverty, oppressive gender expectations, racism, disablism, health inequalities and differential opportunities which can seriously inhibit social mobility.

Social workers and educators particularly may find these and other models of the life course useful in interpreting reactions to crises at transition points, problems of adjustment, and failures of communication between family members, and in assisting individuals to gain insight, use their experiences developmentally and improve their social relationships.

Green, L. (2010) *Understanding the Life Course: Sociological and Psychological Perspectives.* Cambridge: The Polity Press.

loss a profound feeling of disadvantage or deprivation resulting from losing someone or something.

Loss can be associated with a wide range of human experience including bereavement, a separation from someone where there was an attachment, a stillbirth or miscarriage or a radical change in circumstances such as redundancy, retirement or loss of country because of civil war and a need to claim asylum elsewhere. Sometimes losses can be multiple and integrally related where, for example, a serious illness might lead to a loss of a job, the need to adapt to a new lifestyle because of a chronic condition and a consequent loss of status. A key issue for social workers is that of determining the significance of any loss to an individual. A death of a partner or a parent, for example, might be a profound loss or it could be liberating if the relationship that has been severed was oppressive or abusive for the person. All social and interpersonal changes, as a result of loss, are likely to bring problems of adjustment. Any really significant change, such as a move-ment from a rural area to a city, being given refugee status in another country or leaving a long-stay psychiatric hospital or prison might unsettle a person's sense of self, their feeling of personal security, their 'world view' and their social status. In relation to the problem of adjusting to loss, much will depend upon a number of factors includ-ing the person's own robustness, their support systems and the nature of their new social circumstances. It is entirely possible for the loss also to be an opportunity for positive change as new ideas may have now, post-loss, to be considered. As with all crises, some will experience the loss as quite disabling and others will deal with it comparatively equa-bly. (See also **death and dying**.)

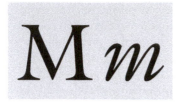

M m

market where buyers and sellers of goods or services meet to transact their business. While for centuries markets were located literally in designated places in towns and cities, markets in our own time can be detached from place, as in the electronic markets for stocks and shares or can refer to abstractions such as 'the market' for books or advertising. Economists have long taught us that the price of a commodity, product or service is determined by the point at which the quantity of supply of a good or service intersects with the demand for that product (see Figure 3).

In industrial and especially in post-industrial capitalism, markets can be formed virtually around any product or service. This total dominance of the market has led some political theorists such as Michael Sandel to argue that we have moved from a 'market economy' to a

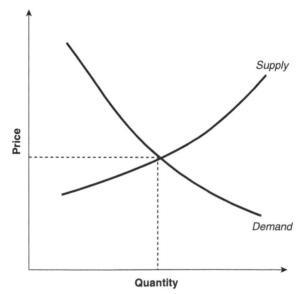

Figure 3 Supply and demand curve

'market society' in which all values, social relationships and cultural iconography are shaped by market thinking.

There are four main markets in a capitalist economy:

- the *labour market*, which determines wages for all who engage in it from care workers to senior bankers;
- the *market for production*, which sets the prices and cost of buying/leasing equipment, building and land for producing goods and services;
- the *market for consumption* of those goods and what we buy, from trainers to toothbrushes, from child care to places at university;
- the *money or capital markets* formed by the supply and demand for finance and through which its prices (interest rates) are established.

There are arguments for and against the competence of the market as the principal institution for producing and allocating goods and services across a population. Mainstream economists argue that markets generally function efficiently, that is, those who buy and sell are equipped with the knowledge and information they need to conduct the transaction. On this basis, economists maintain that markets are unique institutions that process millions of price signals and allocate goods and services in the most efficient way available. Accompanying this mainstream view is the notion that purchasers are 'rational', in other words, that they make their choice to buy x but not y on the basis of information regarding quality and price which they have sought out and understand sufficiently to make a rational decision (see **rational choice theory**).

Neo-liberal economists go even further to make the case that markets should be wholly free of government regulation precisely on this ground. Markets, they argue, are immediately responsive to people's ever-changing preferences and demands. State intervention in the workings of the market only disrupts this finely balanced interaction. In their view, no state machinery or central plan for allocating goods and services can approach the swift and continuously adjusting allocation of goods and services by the market. Rather any state-run economy (such as socialism) would have to fall back on authoritarian if not totalitarian rule in order to make such a system function at all.

In general, economists assume that markets are based on competition in that large numbers of buyers and sellers come together, so many that none of them can exert undue leverage over the price outcome. In such conditions, the market price for a product will rise or fall depending on the relative scarcity of that product and the extent to which people are willing to pay for it. Thus competition in the market place ensures efficiency – those producers that cannot provide the product at a price in line with the price that the market commands will go out of business.

But social scientists including some economists have also provided comprehensive criticism about the shortcomings of markets from the nineteenth century onwards. In general, this criticism points to the fact that markets have no in-built commitment toward achieving social justice or fairness. They refute the claim that markets are part of natural law and stress that they are human institutions with all the imperfections and faults that that implies. Both the supply side and the demand side are open to manipulation, collusion and coercion. At the extreme markets do 'fail', that is they virtually cease functioning in particular areas or in respect of particular goods and services. The housing market in 'low-demand areas' such as some neighbourhoods in the northern mill towns of England is one example where house prices have collapsed towards zero. The labour markets in towns with essentially one large employer like Corby (steel) in the early 1980s or the mining towns of Yorkshire in the later 1980s (coal) offer further examples of market failure.

Markets now shape social work and social services in ways that would have been unthinkable to an earlier generation. The 'marketization' of services began in the early 1990s following the Griffiths Report with the introduction of separate purchaser and provider functions inside what was then essentially a single service department run by the local authority. The aim was to mimic the competition that markets are said to offer – to create 'quasi-markets' – by setting up 'buyers' and 'sellers' within social services. Operation of these quasi-markets would gradually widen, inducing voluntary organizations and private providers to offer services as well.

marriage, divorce and **separation** *marriage* is a socially acknowledged relationship between two adults, often legally and religiously ratified.

Marriage in traditional or pre-industrial societies appears to serve and be regulated by *kin interests*. Within capitalist societies marriage appears to be a matter of individual choice (what sociologists call *'affective individualism'*), although choice seems to operate within a comparatively narrow range where individuals marry others of roughly comparable social status. In the UK, individual choice seems to predominate, although within some groups of Asian origin and in very rural parts of the UK more traditional forms of marriage still take place. Even in marriages that embrace affective individualism, parental approval of their offspring's choice of partner seems to be a key variable in whether the marriage persists or not. Arranged marriages play an important role within some Asian communities. Here the families of both spouses take a lead role in arranging the marriage but the choice of whether to accept the arrangement remains with the individuals. There is a distinction between an arranged marriage and a *forced marriage* in which one party does not consent to the marriage. *Forced marriages* are now a criminal offence in many advanced industrial societies, given that they are associated with coercion, assault and, possibly, kidnap. With most *forced marriages,* the victims are women but a minority of such marriages involve coerced men. For many, *cohabitation* is now a long-term alternative to marriage and it is now common for a substantial period of *cohabitation* to precede marriage. Despite relatively high rates of relationship failure in both marriages and cohabitations, remarriage continues to be popular – 'a triumph of hope over experience' as some wit has it.

For some groups, there is an expectation that individuals marry within the group (*endogamy)* or 'outside' the group (*exogamy*). Such expectations can be underpinned by convictions of religion, ethnicity, nationality and social class. Those that transgress group expectations can experience ostracism or even, occasionally, violence. *Divorce* can be defined as the legal dissolution of a marriage, often preceded by a period of separation that may or may not be legally ratified and that may or may not be recognized by religious institutions. Although there is much less stigma attached to divorce and separation, there are still major problems of adjustment for many couples and their children post-separation. The impact of separation upon adults can be traumatic and can involve considerable adjustments, although these changes will vary depending upon various factors such as the length of the relationship; whether there are children; and the emotional, economic and social investment of each partner in the relationship. There are also likely to be significantly different experiences of the adults including feelings of betrayal and abandonment or conversely considerable relief if the relationship was abusive. Although some partners may recognize that their marriage is not working at the same time, most break up because one partner is unhappy or dissatisfied 'first'; in a sense their suffering may precede the other partner's unhappiness, which is likely to be felt most keenly later. Bohannan (1970) has usefully identified different dimensions to divorce:

- The *emotional divorce* – expressing stress in the relationship and beginning to think that a marriage might be floundering, leading to a decision to separate temporarily or permanently, leading to . . .
- The *psychological divorce* – an individual begins to withdraw emotionally from an ex-partner, although emotional involvement

is rarely dissolved completely. People who have lived together for some time are unlikely to be emotionally indifferent to each other, although residual emotions are wide ranging.

- The *economic divorce* – the division of the couple's property and resources including financial arrangements concerning maintenance for an ex-spouse or dependent children.
- *The co-parental divorce* – adjustments about how parenting is to be continued and issues of custody and access.
- The *social network and community divorce* – changes in social relationships as a result of divorce involving friends, relatives including ex-in-laws and the wider community (schools and public services, for example).
- The *legal divorce* – the formal process of terminating a marriage, which may include ratifying formal arrangements.

In the UK, it was hoped that family mediation would lead to some couples staying together and others, still intent on divorce, separating on better terms, especially in relation to continued co-parenting. The outcomes for children after their parents have separated/divorced can be negative or they can result in children/young people who are content with the arrangements and more or less unaffected by the experience. The key variables affecting outcomes appear to be:

- the age of any children and their level of understanding;
- the explanations offered to children, if any;
- the quality of the conjugal relationship before separation;
- the quality of the relationships between children and their two parents before separation;
- the quality of co-parenting post-separation;
- how robust or adaptive individual children are.

After separation these factors continue to be influential but, in addition, new variables are likely to come into play especially for the resident parent such as a possible move to new accommodation, a new community, reduced income, a parent becoming a full-time carer where previously they worked, potential loss of social and family supports and new schools and peers for children. A major issue is whether children have to become parts of *step-families* where perhaps one of their parents establishes a new relationship with another person who may have children too, either resident or as visitors. Finally, a key issue in relation to outcomes is that of whether parents co-operate in relation to their offspring or whether there is distrust and conflict and the degree to which children are exposed to these problems. There is a lot of evidence that contact between a non-resident parent and children can be problematic and many men, in particular, lose contact with their children within a few years. Organizations campaigning for 'fathers' rights' argue that legal and welfare systems discriminate against men and devalue a father's contribution to the welfare of his children. By contrast, some women's groups argue that there is substantial evidence to demonstrate that fathers can be indifferent to the needs of their children and ex-partners, as evidenced by the significant lack of success of the Child Support Agency (CSA). The role of professionals in this field can be important, especially from the child's perspective. The Children and Family Court Advisory and Support Service for England and Wales (CAFCASS) has a key role to play to ensure that the 'voice of the child' is heard, when arrangements post-divorce are being determined. Family mediators are sometimes helpful in enabling disputing and separating adults/ parents to negotiate their own agreements, which subsequently can be legally ratified, although **mediation** has not been the obvious success that was at one stage hoped for. Social workers in community teams dealing with children and families routinely have to deal with parents in conflict and children experiencing stress as a result of such conflict and/or problems of adjustment to new circumstances in new communities, schools and reordered families. Interventions in these circumstances are always justifed by reference to the paramount interests of any children.

Bohannan, P. (1970) *Divorce and After.* New York: Doubleday.

Butler, I., Scanlon, L., Robinson, M., Douglas, G. and Murch, M. (2003) *Divorcing Children.* London: Jessica Kingsley.

Marxism a body of theory and political practice based on the work of Karl Marx (1811–83), his colleague Friedrich Engels (1820–95) and others who developed their main ideas in the twentieth century.

Marx began as a philosopher and came to be a radical critic of market capitalism through his connection to young philosophers' groupings in Germany during the early 1840s. He is now, however, considered one of the important pillars of the social sciences, particularly economics and sociology. He largely carried out his analysis of industrial capitalism in Britain to which he had fled when faced with probable arrest in Germany following a failed revolution there in 1848. This was a vital step in the development of his ideas for Britain was the first country to industrialize and the first to create an urban-based industrial working class.

The early years of industrialization had created vast working-class districts of poorly built housing and poor or non-existent systems of sanitation. (Marx's collaborator Friedrich Engels had already conducted a careful analysis of working-class housing in Salford in 1844, just before their collaboration began.) It was a vividly divided society – the cotton mill owners in large houses, often distinctly visible on the hills outside the major mill towns of the north, the mill hands living in cheaply built quarters around the factory. At that time, too, a nation-wide industrial working-class movement – Chartism – was agitating in mass demonstrations for a limit of 10 hours to the working day and for the vote to be made universal and no longer conferred only on property owners. It was this first such muscular show of strength on the part of the nascent industrial working class that prompted Marx to see that the future development of society lay in its hands.

Drawing on this experience and on their historical research, Marx and Engels published *The Communist Manifesto* in 1848 which, with rhetorical brilliance, praised the bourgeoisie for sweeping away the constraints on material development while confidently predicting that the industrial working class would in turn overthrow the bourgeoisie and the market economy and the society that it had created. The *Manifesto* found four major epochs in human history – 'primitive communism' (that is the tribal societies of the Bronze age and before), societies based on slavery (Greece and Rome), feudalism in the Middle Ages and capitalism. Marx's analysis led him to think that inevitably further stages would follow in the evolution of society, namely socialism (underpinned by a state owning the means of production) and eventually communism (with a vastly reduced state or no state). Each stage of history was beset with contradictions because of the constraints imposed upon the development of productive forces by the ruling ideology of those in power and each would eventually succumb to the potent productive forces of a rising social class. The bourgeoisie – the owners of capital, related professions and their retinue – would be forcefully confronted by the proletariat – the industrial working class – which would eventually prevail. This would ultimately lead to the overthrow of capitalism and usher in a new, fairer economic arrangement.

Under capitalism, Marx argued, all commodities are bought and sold on the open market. The propertyless wage labourer sells the only commodity he owns – his labour power – and can only exist by doing so. But workers create greater wealth in what they produce and the difference between the wealth they produce and the wage they receive is a 'surplus value' that accrues to the employer and the bourgeoisie as a whole. Marx referred to this as the 'labour theory of value' and, while he attempted to put this on a scientific footing, ultimately his analysis was political, one in which he took sides. In his hands, capitalism was defined relationally and in terms of power with struggle at its centre between the owners, exploiters and appropriators of capital and the workers and their families who endure long days, low wages and political exclusion to survive.

As he continued to refine his ideas Marx came to see that each epoch was dominated by a specific mode or system of production; not only was each mode of production the central motor of the economy but it created the institutions that held political power and conferred access and privileges on the social classes that staffed those institutions. Thus 'the mode of production', he wrote in 1859, 'conditions the social, political and intellectual life process in general'. The extent to which Marx was arguing that the economy actually determines everything else in society has been a source of debate since it implies that individual free will and political action is largely hopeless in the face of such determinism. Yet, after Marx's death, Engels said that neither he nor Marx argued that the economy shaped everything – but only that it exercised a 'decisive' influence on society.

Hobsbawm, E. (2011) *How to Change the World: Tales of Marx and Marxism*. London: Little, Brown.

Marx, K. and Engels, F. ([1848] 2002) *The Communist Manifesto*, with an Introduction by Gareth Stedman Jones. London: Penguin Books.

measures of central tendency (mean, median, mode) different ways of representing or calculating an average, middle or central position with regard to a data set:

(1) A *mean* is more commonly known as an average. For example, if the average income of a group of 11 people is to be calculated – and each individual earns £4000, £9000, £9000, £9000, £9000, £14,000, £17,000, £20,000, £27,000, £40,000 and £62,000, then the mean income is the aggregate income of all 11 individuals divided by 11; in this instance, £220,000 divided by 11 which equals approximately £20,000.

(2) The *median* value is the middle value where the data are presented in ascending order from the lowest value to the highest. Thus, for the same data set the median is £14,000

(3) The *mode* is the value which is the most frequent in any data set. For this data set, it is just £9000.

The usefulness of measures of central tendency for social workers can be brought into focus if the issue of poverty is considered. If the data regarding the calculation of the mean in (1) above are considered, the mean would suggest that the average income in the UK is £20,000, which might be considered by some as an adequate income. However, this figure is not really representative of UK incomes because one person is earning £62,000 and this high earner is clearly so much better off than his contemporaries that the relative poverty of the people earning £4000 and £9000 is effectively concealed. The median that figures in (2) above is helpful because it clearly indicates that the person earning £14,000 has as many people poorer then him as richer, but he is still considerably worse off than the person with the average earnings (a mean of £20,000). The mode illustrated in (3) reveals that many people live on a very low income.

In sum, it is important when presenting data about the incidence of any social problem, including measures of deprivation, that means, modes and medians are accurately depicted to reveal the intricacies of complex problems.

memory both a process for retaining and recalling information (remembering) as well as a unit of a mental process, a particular 'recollection' stored away.

An effective memory, both long term and short term, is crucial to social functioning at all levels/contexts, enabling us, for example, to find our way to work or school from where we live, operate machinery safely and to recall who it was who mugged us when presented with an identity parade. Remembering is actually a complex process that can be affected by a range of factors including brain damage and disease, emotional factors including repression, language, attempts to 'effort after meaning' (see below) context (or its lack) and other factors. Some key issues are as follow:

(1) Individuals' tendencies to try to make sense of their memories can often mean that their personal *schemata* (frameworks for interpreting events based upon earlier experiences of the same phenomenon) are brought into play to shape memories to make them consistent with schemata. This is the notion of 'efforting after meaning'. For example, earlier experiences of PE lessons may predispose a schoolboy to remember all games sessions in the same way regardless of variations in actual experiences.

(2) Experiments with visual presentations of events, say a film about an accident involving two cars, have been undertaken to demonstrate that when groups of respondents are later questioned about what they had seen, their answers will depend upon how the questions have been framed. Questions involving the word 'crash' will evoke more dramatic accounts of the accident then questions that include the word 'collision'. Law court judges' advice to lawyers to avoid 'leading questions' is a practical example of where testimony (recall) can be influenced. Cues to aid recall have, in general, been shown to be an aid to remembering including, for example, students having examinations involving multiple-choice questions. To see a list that

must include the 'right answer' can often assist with recall if the student had already undertaken some work about the topic.

(3) Failure to remember well can be attributed to a variety of additional causes including brain damage and disease (especially stroke, dementia, Alzheimer's disease and various other neurological conditions) as well as poor nutrition.

(4) Repression of painful and/or traumatic events has been shown to affect memory. Women's aid and rape crisis centres both testify to the importance of sympathetic and painstaking questioning to be able to 'reconstruct' very painful events to determine what has happened, especially given the now well-established predisposition of women to blame themselves.

(5) Interference occurs where different narratives or procedures affect understandings of closely related fields. For example, the learning of one language might inhibit the learning of another because different rules of grammar apply.

(6) The influence of drugs and/or alcohol can both distort and weaken both memorizing and recall. People who drink a lot for long periods often have their immediate judgements affected as well as running the risk of not being able to memorize things well. A particular kind of amnesia, Korsakoff's syndrome, affects alcoholics who both drink a lot and eat very little.

(7) Mental health problems can also affect memory in very profound ways twisting memories because of, for example, the effects of neuroses and especially psychoses where powerful auditory and visual hallucinations distort reality.

The social work tasks with service users who are experiencing significant problems of memory and recall mostly concern working on the issues that are affecting social functioning; for example, working on problems of addiction or helping a woman or a child recover from traumatic or abusive experiences – both of which can help 'resurrect' memory. However, direct work on the problems of memorizing and recall, especially the latter, can be a core focus of intervention. One locus of this kind of work is with *reminiscence* therapy often conducted in residential establishments for elders. Such therapists argue that reminiscence can have a positive effect upon social functioning in general because it is an active process that involves mental stimulation that might also involve physical activities such as dancing to music that might have featured in the early lives of elders. In addition, it is suggested that reminiscence can arouse and animate memories so that they are reclaimed by the individual. Although life-story books have mostly been used with children who have entered the care system and/or have been adopted, life-story work has also been found to be very enlivening in direct work with elders. Assessments of mental capacity, concerning adults of any age, involve issues around competence and decision-making abilities and memory is clearly a key component to both issues. If a person is deemed to lack capacity, then it is possible that a person or persons (often a relative) will be appointed with lasting power of attorney (LPA) to manage key decisions concerning care, medication and health provision as well as financial matters.

Another major context for direct work with memory is counselling and psychotherapy. Here the recall of memories, sometimes painful, together with work that is essentially concerned with restructuring or contextualizing such memories can be very important in promoting mental health. Although many service users might reasonably be regarded as 'experts' in relation to their own problems and needs, sometimes the task of the social worker, counsellor or therapist is to help them reinterpret experience to locate blame or responsibilities for abuse, for example, elsewhere. If a woman has had a childhood where she has witnessed the abuse of a mother and maybe been abused herself and has then gone on to contract unfortunate relationships with men in adulthood, it will be a major task to help her to understand that the abuse of women is not a necessary feature of life. However, this will require unpacking memories accurately and re-ordering them to provide a non-oppressive environment to aid recovery.

migration the movement of people across political and/or symbolic boundaries, voluntarily or under duress, to resettle in another location. The term *diaspora* has been used when there has been an element of compulsion underpinning the migration. Migration has been a feature of life since prehistory with, for example, hunter–gatherers leading a nomadic existence, and movement as a result of climate change and natural disasters, both of which might have resulted in famine, aggressive and acquisitive acts, genocide and imperialism/colonialism. Some forms of migration have been motivated by ethnic tensions, religious, and racist discourses.

Since 1945, researchers have identified different forms of migration globally: first, the displacement of peoples as a result of post-colonial or post-war state formations or adjustments (the creation of India and Pakistan, the dissolution of Yugoslavia and the recent division of Sudan are examples); second, the migration of unskilled labour to Europe from north Africa and Turkey and to the US from Mexico; third, the growth of international migration of skilled labour especially doctors, people working in finance, nurses, plumbers and electricians from Eastern to Western Europe; fourth, asylum seekers and refugees migrating to Western Europe from Asia and Africa; fifth, migration of people from rural to urban areas within many industrial and developing societies; and finally, the trafficking of women and children.

Some aspects of migration identified above are clearly associated with the needs of capitalism. Migrant labour has become part of the *reserve army of labour* to be taken up or put down as the economy requires. The management of this process has sometimes led to tensions as migrants begin to feel part of the host society and wish to assume citizenship. These tensions can be exacerbated when the host society was earlier the colonial power. Some Western societies have sought to manage this situation in the provision of visas specifying how long an immigrant can stay in the country, as in the UK.

Social workers often have very specific roles to play in, for example, assisting those given refugee status to integrate; sometimes supporting unaccompanied asylum seekers (minors under the age of 18); and helping women and children who have been trafficked and have managed to get away from the traffickers. Kohli has conceptualized three domains for social work practice. While he has developed these in relation to unaccompanied children seeking asylum in Britain they are useful in mapping the practice terrain for all refugees and asylum seekers.

The first is the domain of *cohesion*, in which the primary focus is on the 'here and now', the practicalities of settlement such as providing shelter, care, food, money, schooling, medical support, welfare advice, a support network and ensuring good legal representation in relation to any claim for asylum. Social workers in this domain follow humanitarian efforts of non-governmental organizations (NGOs) abroad, offering material and practical help. Kohli describes them as 'realists, pragmatists' who want 'to deal with the present first, the future next and the past last' (Kohli 2007: 156).

The second is the domain of *connection*, which focuses on resettlement of the 'inner world' of the refugee. Here, social workers respond to the emotional distress of leaving the country of origin and helping the person connect events, people and feelings that will assist in making sense of them. Kohli observes that while few needed psychiatric or therapeutic services many were 'psychologically disheveled as a consequence of dislocation'. The social worker then is mindful of making connections between past and present and between inner and outer worlds, to free up emotions to cope with resettlement.

The third is the domain of *coherence*, where social workers frame the experiences of asylum seekers within a broader view of how children especially cope with extraordinarily adverse circumstances by making the best use of their own capabilities. These workers – Kohli dubs them 'the Confederates' – looked for and found resilience, expressed fondness and attachment towards them, making 'the line between friendship and professional help less distinct' and in so doing tried to make the young person feel more at home.

Kohli, R. (2007) *Social Work with Unaccompanied Asylum Seeking Children*. Basingstoke: Palgrave.

model an attempt to identify the key components including, perhaps, a diagrammatic or formal representation of any social phenomenon as a prelude to theorizing about the relationship between those components.

In practice, social scientists have used the term *model* very loosely so that for some a model approximates to a theory and for others a hypothetical causal relationship between two or more variables. In social work, the word *model* is frequently applied to the study of disability where the *medical model* is invariably contrasted with the *social model*. Here the first perspective relies on notions of 'deficits' associated with impairments managed by medical practitioners; whereas the second perspective locates the problems in a generalized negative response of most people and institutions to those with impairments. This use of the term *model* seems to be closer to what others have termed a *paradigm* because different sets of assumptions and perspectives are more or less active.

In sociology, Weber's model (his *ideal type*) of **bureaucracy** attempts to capture the key elements of organizations. His *ideal type* offers a heuristic device by which to compare both historical and contemporary forms of any social phenomenon. In practice, researchers actually compare Weber's separate features of bureaucracy with what they have found in their empirical investigations as a way of further understanding how organizations might respond to particular historical or cultural contexts.

In research, the concept of *maternal deprivation* has been influential and in its simplest formulation it argues that any significant deprivation of a mother experienced by a child can lead to problems of maladjustment. As the model has developed, various researchers have insisted that additional variables need to be taken into account including, crucially, the age and understanding of the child when the deprivation occurred (could the child understand what was going on?); the quality of the relationship between mother and child prior to the deprivation and whether there were other carers in the family, such as a father or older sibling to which the child may have had continued access; the length of deprivation; the quality of the care provided during separation; whether deprivation was experienced alone or with siblings; and finally, how the child was handled on being reunited with a mother, if indeed it happened at all. What began as an apparently simple hypothesis has become a much more complex model where further important ingredients have been acknowledged. However, a comprehensive theory enabling both researchers and social work practitioners alike to locate and understand a particular child's experience has yet to be fully articulated and thus 'applied' in practice with confidence.

modernity the term used to denote the broad cultural, social and political epoch in Europe and the US that began at the end of the eighteenth century with the onset of the Industrial Revolution in the economy and the French Revolution in politics. Supporting these twin revolutions stood the philosophical and intellectual achievement of the Enlightenment that developed doctrines on universal morality and law, the importance of objective natural sciences and the independence of art and literature from state patronage. There was also the conviction that knowledge accumulates by many individuals working freely and creatively in pursuit of human emancipation and the enrichment of daily life. The scientific domination of nature promised freedom from scarcity and poverty and could overcome the arbitrary, destructive power of natural calamities. The development of rational forms of social organization and rational modes of thought would free humankind from the irrationalities of religion and superstition. Together these advances would show the universal, eternal and unchanging qualities of humanity.

Modernity recognizes that order in human society is neither natural nor god-given but arises through the development and application of science under human control. The world is not preordained or eternally fixed. Instead, rational men and women can understand both the natural and social world and as a result change it: human actions therefore have meaning and purpose. No longer were human actions rendered pointless by an unchanging natural world but could achieve specifically designed goals on the basis of rational investigation of objects, events and even politics. Human reason in the modernist view was capable of discovering and establishing foundational truths that underpinned all natural and social phenomena. Discovery of such truths would harness the natural world to human needs and point to the creation of a harmonious social order.

The certainty of science, of complete conviction of being able to determine the 'laws' of both the natural and social world, reached its high point in the late nineteenth and early twentieth centuries. Both Marx and Freud regarded their theories as science, which they verified

storms – and moral hazards such as playing with matches, which the industry attributed to 'carelessness and roguery'.

Today the term is widely applied in economics and in analysis of welfare policy. It refers to the indiscriminate risks that people are apt to take if they do not have to bear the consequences of their actions. The term has been widely used, largely from the political **right wing** as an element within **rational choice theory** in describing the behaviour of those on welfare. For example, because welfare payments are made to those eligible the argument is that recipients will spend it on any purchase they choose, sensible or not. In other words, if the money is free, why not spend it on a designer purse? Neither will they have learned the lesson as to why they had to apply for welfare in the first place. In short, the concept of moral hazard alleges that if the consequences of bad behaviour are cushioned in any way it only encourages that behaviour in the future.

Since the bailout of the banks on both sides of the Atlantic the term has been applied to whole institutions. Since no punishment, in the form of financial failure, was experienced why should these institutions change their behaviour in the future? If a bank knows that it will be bailed out, why not again speculate on some risky investments? Accusations of moral hazard, in the hands of the right, quickly devolve into the question 'why subsidise losers?'.

Historically the sentiment, if not the term itself, has dominated discussion of welfare from the nineteenth century on when the thought that even a small portion of money would be misspent and encourage lack of thrift was enough to reduce welfare payments to the minimum and to introduce stringent tests to see who is a truly legitimate applicant. Moral hazard also raises the question of whether an individual has done enough to prevent themselves falling into poverty with this reverse twist – the greater the financial difficulty you are in the more irresponsible you are and therefore the less deserving of public assistance.

One can see the political bias within the concept of moral hazard – it in fact implies that any public responsibility for those in poverty or social exclusion is misguided, that the system will be manipulated by those eager to evade their responsibilities. In relation to welfare it is essentially saying that 'less is more' – that criteria for welfare should be stringent and benefits kept to a minimum, sufficient for subsistence but little else. (See also **need**.)

morbidity and **mortality** see **epidemiology**

motivation the driving force behind human activity that sustains 'goal-directed' behaviour. In very general terms, motivation is the 'energizer' for what people do. Motivation is regarded as having a biological basis in sexual drives and the need for food and water, as well as social components such as the need to feel a part of a social group or a need, perhaps, for 'self-actualization'. Psychologists have found a number of different approaches fruitful:

(1) *Instinct* theories – instincts are thought to have a biological basis (not learned), to be found in all human beings and to be similar in the way that they are expressed. Although considered to be useful, theories based upon instincts have met with criticism mostly because it has proved difficult to agree a definitive list of instincts. In addition, any suggestion that an instinct must be expressed has also been acknowledged as false. It is entirely possible, for example, *not* to express one's sexual drives (celibate monks and nuns are thought to do it) or even to satisfy the need for food and water (people have starved themselves to death when making a political statement or if they suffer from anorexia nervosa).

(2) *Drive* theories – the notion of psychological drives has proved persuasive as a development of instinct theory. Drive theories rely upon the idea of 'homeostasis', which can broadly be understood as a tendency to want to maintain the status quo in the body/ mind. Thus, shivering is a physiological response to the cooling of the body, just as sweating is a physiological response to a rise in body temperature. This kind of motivation is thought to rest upon 'primary drives'. At an entirely different level the need to 'self-actualize' might be heightened if an impediment to achieve one's personal goals should unexpectedly appear. This is what has been labelled as a 'secondary drive'. A useful example might be where a much valued music teacher decides to move away from an area with the result that an able pupil's plans become uncertain and s/he is motivated to identify another able teacher very quickly.

The many ways in which individuals maintain and express motivation has preoccupied many writers; for example, ego defence mechanisms, in the form of *repression*, might lead someone with homosexual tendencies to refute such feelings by vigorously asserting anti-gay sentiments to the world at large. Another perspective arises out of the use of **personal construct theory** where individuals put together their own unique set of ideas, theories and concepts to make sense of the world including others' behaviour; thus a bold, outspoken extrovert might be interpreted as positive and decisive by one observer and opinionated and unsympathetic by another. Yet another perspective on motivation has been identified as *approach avoidance*, where a strong inclination to, say, explore something entirely new (a 'gap year', perhaps) is counterbalanced by an expectation that the young person will miss his or her friends very much. Other writers have speculated on what they have deemed to be an individual's *locus of control* – essentially an issue about whether people locate the origins of problems within themselves or whether they have a predilection to blame external forces. The *internal* locus of control is considered to be psychologically a more robust position than the *external* locus of control. A useful connection here has been made with the concept of *learned helplessness*. Depressed people often feel that their efforts are entirely pointless because nothing they can do will address or ameliorate their problems. This perspective may well be closely related to another perspective: the notion of *self-efficacy*. Here individuals' confidence in relation to their abilities or natural aptitudes seems to be key, because the evidence suggests that people make more effort if they have self-belief than if they do not have it. Both *locus of control* and *self-efficacy* are related to what yet other writers have dubbed **attribution theory**, where ideas individuals have about the characteristics and/or behaviour of others determines how they interpret and respond to others' behaviour. Parents who are having a lot of problems with their son, who has been involved in, say, minor criminality, may well be predisposed to interpret other innocent behaviour as deviant because their relationship with their son is currently very tense. Other dimensions of motivation that have been debated include those based clearly upon social influences including the ideas of wishing to be positively regarded by others, especially others we value, or groups that we aspire to join. Empathy and the desire to live or work constructively with others in a spirit of co-operation seems as likely a motivator as competitive or even aggressive behaviour but has probably received less attention in research.

Overall social workers need to understand the origins of motivations influencing any service users and of the social context that might be influencing their behaviour including, especially, their apparent inability to engage with problem-solving that is in their interests. Effective *task-centred* working and the appropriate use of *motivational interviewing techniques,* the *strengths perspective* and *solution-focused therapies* are all useful methods of intervening that try to take account of the current circumstances and morale of individuals and harness what remnants of motivation they can in problem-solving based on a realistic assessment of individuals' current capacities.

motor skills see **child development**

multiculturalism societies or social entities in which different ethnic and cultural groups coexist in a reasonably harmonious manner. It is closely associated with the idea of pluralism.

In relation to the state, multiculturalism suggests two political tasks for any government. First, that it should be interested in maintaining harmonious relationships between culturally diverse groups. Second, that any government should seek to directly establish a responsible and responsive relationship with any cultural or ethnic group acting, in effect, as honest broker in relation to the distribution of state-managed resources and in sponsoring equality of opportunity.

Supporters of multiculturalism argue that there are many acceptable ways of managing social, political and economic affairs and that it is inappropriate for any monocultural system to impose conformist policies across all ethnic groups. But multiculturalism cannot succeed, its advocates have argued, if different groups are not treated reasonably equitably. However, the feminist and anti-racist critiques of multiculturalism argue that the appeal to cultural and ethnic tolerance in practice often masks racist and sexist oppression both within ethnic and cultural groups and by the state, which invariably represents the interests of the most powerful ethnic/cultural group. They argue that it cannot replace efforts to address the continuing reality of racial inequality, for example over-representation of black youth within the criminal justice system or disparities in health or educational outcomes.

In relation to social policy, governments have to make decisions about whether multiculturalism is to be supported in any way. Multiculturalism may be thought of as compatible with integration, but it is clearly at odds with any notion of assimilation. Examples of policy dilemmas include ideas about supporting faith-based schools or care homes or family placement agencies, same 'race' or trans-racial adoption or whether there should be government support for public information to be provided in many languages. (See also **assimilation**, **integration** and **pluralism**.)

N n

need the necessary requirements for maintaining life at a certain
standard. This standard may be little more than subsistence living,
such as that provided by the nineteenth-century workhouse for its
inmates. Or the standard may relate to specific necessities that are
widely regarded as essential for a reasonable life in a specific society
(see **poverty**) or it may be of a higher order and relate to what a
person needs for their well-being or fulfilment in life. The issue for
some social scientists is whether this complexity of needs, in part or in
whole, indicates some universal functional prerequisites for meeting
need. Debates over the concept of need always centre on the
question of what these prerequisites should be and who should define
them. Often the standards for determining need are set by a mixture
of influences, such as social consensus, acts of Parliament, activist
groups and professionals in the field. As a result, what constitutes
need changes over time. A good example is provided by campaigns
against **domestic violence** and the need for women's refuge where
physical safety is guaranteed. Such a need was scarcely recognized a
generation ago, although is now widely accepted both by the public
and government.

Abraham Maslow argued that human needs are inborn and exist
in an ascending hierarchy: physiological needs such as sleep, and
food, come first, structure and order providing security second, the
need to belong and be loved is third. Fourth in the hierarchy is the
need for self-esteem in the form of self-respect and the esteem of
others. Fifth is the need for self-actualization, the desire to become
everything one can become. Maslow himself later added extra
dimensions – 'self-transcendence' as a motivational step beyond
self-actualization. This took his thought more in the direction of the
psychology of religion and the foundations of altruism rather than
the empirical definition of 'needs' per se with which his work was
previously associated.

Maslow's hierarchy of needs is found in virtually every psychology
textbook and remains, after some 60 years or more since its first
formulation and despite limited empirical validation, the major

departure point for a discussion on needs. Yet there are criticisms. He largely thought that needs were inborn and downplayed questions of social interaction, culture and social structure as the framers of need. His later work was also more concerned with exploring transcendent or 'peak' experiences, which took his work in the direction of **spirituality**.

Needs – what a person requires to live – are often distinguished in theory from 'wants' or what a person prefers or desires. In practice, however, defining what a person needs as opposed to what he or she wants is fraught with difficulty. For example, a homeless person can be said to need shelter, but shelter can mean many things: a temporary bed in a hostel, a room in bed and breakfast accommodation, a permanently rented room, a rented flat or an owner-occupied house. What are the real needs of a homeless person and who decides?

In the attempt to resolve some of the conflicts over the definition of needs, Jonathon Bradshaw developed a taxonomy of needs:

- *normative* needs, that is, needs as defined by a norm or standard set by professionals;
- *felt* needs, which individuals themselves declare as their needs (the same as 'wants');
- *expressed* needs, that is, felt needs turned into a demand through some action;
- *comparative* needs, which are defined by the fact that others, living in the same conditions, have been recognized as having a similar need and receive a service.

Social theorists, sociologists and economists continue to explore need in an ever-increasing stream of publications. Among the more important are Doyal and Gough's theory on human need that begins with what they consider to be the all-pervading goal of humans – the wish to participate in human affairs in some form without serious or arbitrary limitation. Thus their central reference point for need is not the individual's inborn needs or psychological development but the capacity for social engagement. From this they work out their own hierarchy of needs based on the universal preconditions for participation.

Amartya Sen's concept of *capability* has certain parallels with Doyal and Gough's analysis of needs. By capability, Sen means the capacity of an individual to undertake certain functionings. Some of these functionings are basic such as being adequately nourished and enjoy good health while others are more complex but still widely valued such as achieving self-respect or being socially integrated. Individuals may differ a good deal from each other in the weights they attach to these different functionings – although all are valuable – and assessment of individual and social advantages must be sensitive to these variations. Much like Doyal and Gough's central goal of participation, Sen links capability to freedom: the individual's freedom to choose to live in a particular way is the overarching goal of capability.

In general, the discussion of need in these different explorations extends beyond those needs necessary for survival and in each case involves steps toward higher goals, whether transcendence (Maslow), participation (Doyal and Gough) or freedom (Sen). A thoroughgoing understanding of need and of the various ways it has been theorized is essential for social workers because human need is primarily what they deal with. The creation of the welfare state in the middle decades of the twentieth century focused the discussion of needs around the kinds of services that were available, such as housing needs, income assistance, and care for long-term incapacitating illness or disability. Social workers in general came tacitly to understand need as defined in light of these specific services. That older way of looking at need has now shifted to more individually defined models of need, although debates around need are still heavily influenced by statutory definitions and the eligibility for services criteria that go along with them. When social workers define need they usually do so on the basis of the definitions used by their agency and from formal guidance issued by government, such as the Department of Children, Schools and Families or the Department of Health.

In assessing need, social workers often have to consider a broad range of needs, such as physical care, the provision of shelter and food, cultural and religious sustenance, emotional and psychological needs arising from isolation or violent personal relationships and social contacts. Very often people in the same household have different needs that have to be met in different ways. Because needs are a matter of interpretation and judgement, it is common practice that service users participate in the process of deciding what their needs are and that their wishes and preferences are taken into account.

Needs can be met only if there are the means to do so. Because resources are limited, social services professionals have recourse to systems of prioritizing needs and of developing criteria for eligibility. This invariably places greatest importance on the need to protect the health and physical safety of the client and less importance on those needs that would improve the person's well-being but are not essential to physical survival. At the same time, there are pressures to widen definitions of need and to at least log *unmet* need. Groups of users and their advocates are urging this across a number of services, including those for children and families, disabled people and people with mental health problems. Such groups can be involved in setting local policies on need, since community care reforms in particular envisage a growth of new services from the independent sector.

Doyal, L. and Gough, I. (1991) *A Theory of Human Need*. Basingstoke: Palgrave.

Sen, A. (2007) *Development as Freedom*. Oxford: Oxford University Press.

neighbourhood a geographic zone or area which is continuous and is definable by certain characteristics such as recognizable boundaries, local institutions or common ethnic culture. Neighbourhoods are smaller in size than other recognized spatial entities, such as a city sector or a city district. They do not have precise borders but are practical, informal judgements about who and what to include in an everyday sense.

For most people, 'the neighbourhood' means the small area immediately around where they live, while 'neighbours' are those who live in households nearby with whom social relations, by no means always close, are generally based on face-to-face contact. In government policy, 'neighbourhood' is generally used to denote far larger geographical areas than is commonly understood by most of us. There are several rules of thumb used to define neighbourhoods in this larger sense. Some of these are: an area mapped out by how far a person can walk in any direction in 15 minutes; an area defined by landmarks as recognized by most residents who live near them; common boundaries established by roads or housing tenure; political ward boundaries or areas with an historical identity such as parishes. These in turn often reflect population clusters and natural boundary points; street patterns, housing tenures, social networks – all are important constituents of neighbourhood definition. The neighbourhoods referred to in this volume are often defined by a mixture of these and may embrace 3000 or so households with perhaps as many as 6000 residents.

The fact that **social exclusion** is spatially concentrated has prompted research on the dynamics of excluded neighbourhoods – how high levels of unemployment, poor health and high crime reinforce one another in ways that affect the behaviour and choices of all residents living there. A formidable amount of research on such 'neighbourhood effects' now exists. William Wilson's classic study *The Truly Disadvantaged* (1987) demonstrated how the lives of residents in excluded neighbourhoods are shaped by where they live: through poor services (especially schools), lack of jobs, poor health, social isolation and lack of transport. They act in combination to restrict individual choice and undermine residents' lives at every turn regardless of individual character and behaviour.

Subsequent research has clarified neighbourhood effects further. All of the following have been shown to be heavily influenced by where people live:

- Child and adolescent outcomes such as infant mortality, low birth weight, teenage child-bearing, school exclusion and drop-out rates, child abuse and neglect, anti-social behaviour by young people.
- Employment prospects for people from ethnic minorities living in relatively deprived urban areas, for example higher rates of unemployment and lower rates of self-employment than in ethnically balanced areas.
- A strongly negative effect on the behaviour of pre-school children exposed to neighbourhood violence.
- A neighbourhood impact on a range of health outcomes, such as low-weight births, health protective behaviours, levels of adult mortality, cardiovascular risk factors and many others.

Lupton and Power (2002) have well described the cycle by which entire housing estates are excluded in a process that once underway is difficult to break. Their research established how evidence of anti-social behaviour and loss of social control leads to less social contact and less informal supervision of pro-social norms, which in turn changes public attitudes toward the estate as its reputation declines and those who can leave do so. A tipping point can then be quickly reached as the neighbourhood becomes more unpopular: properties are empty, there is less rent income and more disrepair and neglect, families with little housing choice available to them are moved in, more problems emerge with fewer resources to fix them (see Figure 4).

Social work has periodically addressed directly the needs of a whole neighbourhood. While community work used to be taught as a social work method and developments such as 'patch'-based social work teams were prominent in the 1980s, today practitioners have been reluctant to address 'whole neighbourhood' issues, to recognize the interdependence between people and the local environment and the willingness to act as a change agent in those environments. This is in part simply due to the lack of time and other resource constraints: intervention with individuals and families are the first priority for practitioners and managers alike. But the reluctance to engage in neighbourhood development of any kind is also due to the limits of social work methods that focus exclusively on the individual. As the relationship between individual behaviour and neighbourhood stresses becomes theoretically much clearer, local 'capacity-building' – helping residents to acquire the skills and knowledge that allows them to create or influence responses to

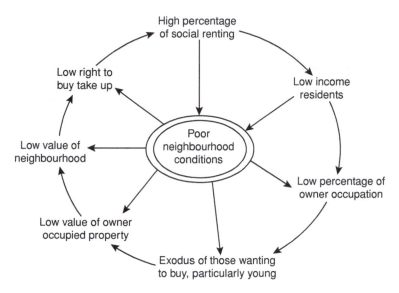

Figure 4 Cycle of decline (adapted from Lupton and Power 2002)

problems they face – becomes more urgent. (See also **community development**.)

Lupton, R. and Power, A. (2002) Social exclusion and neighbourhoods, in J. Hills, J. Legrand and D. Piachaud (eds) *Understanding Social Exclusion*. Oxford: Oxford University Press.

Pierson, J. (2007) *Going Local: Working in Communities and Neighbourhoods*. London: Routledge.

Wilson, W. (1987) *The Truly Disadvantaged: The Inner City, the Underclass and Public Policy*. Chicago, IL: University of Chicago Press.

neurosis a mental or personality disturbance that is distressing and unsettling in its consequences for the individual experiencing it. Neuroses are thought not to be associated with either an organic or neurological source and are considered to be less serious than psychoses in that an individual's contact with reality is essentially intact and social norms are mostly enacted and observed. Freudian theory has been influential in locating neuroses in unconscious conflicts, perhaps as a result of childhood experiences, resulting in the excessive use of *ego-defence mechanisms* (especially *denial, introjection, isolation, projection, reaction formation, regression, repression, reversal, splitting* and *sublimation*).

Typologies of neuroses are thought to be useful ways of capturing particular behavioural and cognitive difficulties but it is also recognized that these labels are approximations of symptom clusters that mental health professionals should use with caution:

- *Depression* – a mood state characterized by a sense of despondency, sadness, low self-esteem and low energy levels with often additional associations of fatigue, insomnia (but also sleeping for significantly longer time and a reluctance to leave one's bed), poor concentration and possibly suicidal thoughts. Some practitioners have found it useful to distinguish between endogenous depression (for which there is no known psychological or social cause) and other forms of depression where a likely cause has been identified; others do not recognize such a distinction, arguing that failure to identify cause does not mean that there is no cause. Brown and Harris's *The Social Origins of Depression: A Study of Psychiatric Disorder in Women* (1978) has been influential in identifying stressful life events as likely, tangible causes of depression.

- *Anxiety states* – an emotional state characterized by uneasiness, apprehension and distress, sometimes with associated physical symptoms such as nausea, a raised pulse rate, perspiration and blushing. It is usual to distinguish between an anxiety state that may be *appropriate*, say as a preparation for an interview, an examination or public performance or as a response to the threatening behaviour of another person, and an anxiety state that is thought to be disproportionate and disabling.

- *Obsessional compulsive disorders* – emotionally disabling conditions, closely related to an anxiety state, in which the individual experiences persistent thoughts and urges to behave in irrational ways. In essence, the individual is compelled to act out ritualized and repetitive thoughts and behaviour such as repeated hand-washing, and experiences considerable distress if he or she attempts to resist such preoccupations and rarely any satisfaction or pleasure, beyond the release of tension, should the compulsion be satisfied.

- *Post-traumatic stress syndrome* – another condition, thought to be similar in its presentation to anxiety states, originating very specifically in an emotionally scarring event(s). The symptoms associated with this condition include vivid re-experiencing of the trauma in both dreams and recurrent 'conscious' images, disturbed sleep patterns, a lack of involvement in everyday events and sometimes guilt if the individual has survived and others have not.

- *Phobias* – an emotional or psychological state associated with a feeling of fear and dread; where the reaction to the feared object or situation is persistent, intense and the individual has a strong desire to avoid or leave the situation. The phobia must be unreasonable or irrational and not reflect a sound estimation of risk. Phobias may have their origins in traumatic events/experiences.

- *Psychosomatic disorders* – emotional and disabling conditions that involve elements of both psychological and physiological responses to events; such disorders can either be 'precipitated' by the psychological (people who are anxious can often have breathing problems such as asthma or raised respiratory states) or the physical (blood pressure or hypertension or gastric problems can lead to anxiety states).

- *Eating disorders* – several conditions involving serious disturbances in eating habits or unusual desires about food. Three conditions are recognized by therapists including, first, *pica* – a condition where individuals have cravings for unusual foods; second, *anorexia nervosa* – a condition where individuals experience intense fear of becoming fat and where their body image does not reflect reality (individuals perceive themselves as fat when they are emaciated); and third, *bulimia* – a condition involving binge eating followed by induced vomiting; the binge eating often involves rapid gorging with little chewing. Bulimia and anorexia nervosa can be experienced by the same person simultaneously. The majority of people experiencing eating disorders are women, leading to analyses located in the social science of the body and body image. Orbach's *Fat is a Feminist Issue* (2006) locates these problems in oppressive expectations of women and preoccupations with particular unnatural discourses on beauty.

Orbach, S. (2006) *Fat is a Feminist Issue*. London: Arrow.

norm a standard, expectation or prescription governing or influencing social behaviour but often falling short of either a rule or law, although a norm might become enshrined in either.

Sociologists, in their attempts to understand how societies persist over time, have sought to identify processes and structures that underpin ordered and continuous social behaviour. Norms are considered to be a key aspect of social life because they provide the adhesion of shared obligations and expectations characterizing any society or social group, and in this respect they offer an indication of likely 'future behaviour'. Thus, Durkheim conceives of societies as enduring entities characterized by a shared moral order or at least where there is a significant degree of consensus about acceptable behaviour. Similarly, Parsons also refers to the concept of a 'normative order' that is to be found in all stable social systems. Parsons identified

socialization and the taking on of social *roles* as the principal mechanisms by which norms are transmitted between generations – norms
that might deal with everyday matters such as behaviour at work,
in schools, parenting or the compiling of tax returns. However,
people may adopt norms because they want to conform or perhaps
to have a particular social identity acknowledged. The latter perspective accepts that norms are not simply imprinted in the socialization
process; in effect, the acquisition of norms is a more interactive and
dynamic process.

Clearly many societies, communities and social groups might not
have all their members or citizens agreeing about norms. This will be
true in times of flux where forces of conservatism and modernization
might be at odds with varying pressures for change. It will also be
true of societies in which conformity is imposed through the exercise
of power and coercion, as with totalitarian regimes or in closed or
traditional societies that have not experienced any alternative narratives about how life is to be lived. Pluralistic societies will also evidence
wide-ranging beliefs and adherence to different and perhaps competing norms.

Social workers have an interest in norms in different contexts.
Identifying the norms underpinning the behaviour of service users
as individuals, family members, groups and communities can be
crucial in understanding social behaviour and being able to intervene most effectively. For example, membership of peer groups,
especially gangs, can be a significant source of personal identity
through close adherence to the group's norms. If such norms are
deviant or criminal in nature it may be that the most useful forms
of intervention to address offending behaviour will include attention to individual factors as well as work with the whole group to
try to reconfigure norms and thus, perhaps, group loyalties. In
other contexts, the formation of group norms in self-help groups or
in therapeutic groups can be key to working effectively with service
users sharing the same problems, such as addictions, or in preparing for the same roles such as foster parenting. Norms established
by constructive consensus can provide the optimal conditions for
effective problem-solving.

normal distribution the commonly found distribution of data drawn
from **variables** under investigation, in which the means, mode and
median are the same. Plotting these data on a graph produces a symmetrical pattern and suggests the shape of a bell, hence the phrase 'bell
curve'. In general, normal distribution shows the most commonly
occurring or largest number of instances of a variable with the lower

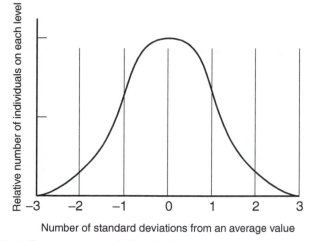

Figure 5 Bell curve – normal distribution

ends of the bell (see Figure 5) indicating fewer instances as relative
outliers. The concept of normal distribution is often used as a hypothetical measure against which data from a specific research sample
may be compared to see how far they coincide with or depart from it.

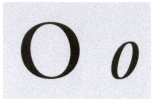

O o

observation see research methods

opportunity costs a measure of the value of the other opportunities or alternative projects, services or strategies that have had to be given up or not considered, because funds and resources have been spent on a particular project.

Debates in political circles, trade unions, think tanks and institutions of higher education inevitably involve different perspectives about both social and economic goals and the means to achieve them. The concept of an opportunity cost can be a helpful way of focusing attention on how scarce resources can be used most effectively. However, analyses and calculations may have to construct sometimes complex models to attempt to make rational choices.

Here issues about opportunity costs stray into the related territory of **cost–benefit analyses** that could have either a short-term or a long-term evaluative framework. For example, it is now well established that young people who have had any substantial period in the care system are likely to figure disproportionately much later among the homeless, in prisons and psychiatric hospitals, and among users of addiction counselling services. A significant investment in services to improve the 'care experience' might reduce the incidence of these 'downstream problems' and thus overall costs. However, the same funds might also be usefully used to support vulnerable families, leading to fewer children entering the care system in the first place – a measure that might also save costs. The comparative value of projects or services has to be studied very closely on the basis of evidence-based practice and rigorous evaluations.

P p

paradigm any broad conceptual structure – for example, Newtonian mechanics, Darwinian theory, psychoanalytical theory – for understanding physical or social phenomena. For a time, particular paradigms enjoy wide agreement within the field to which they apply. Because of these qualities, however, they can get locked in place, as it were, and inhibit acceptance of new data and new understandings of the social or natural world that arise.

The exploration of paradigms is traceable to the work of Thomas Kuhn, in particular his *Structure of Scientific Revolutions*, first published in 1961. While lecturing on the history of science at Harvard University, Kuhn came to see that the linear, cumulative process of scientific knowledge was only partially correct. Yes, science did gradually accumulate knowledge and facts about the universe and the natural world but Kuhn, with a longer view in mind, noticed that the development of science was more dramatic and interrupted than gradual accumulation or steady progress would suggest. He developed the concept of the paradigm to represent the consensus that arises within particular scientific communities about the theoretical and methodological rules and procedures to be used, the problems to be investigated and the standards by which research is to be judged. Scientific training involves familiarization with and socializing within a paradigm.

He developed the now widely used phrase 'paradigm shift' to capture the revolutionary nature of scientific progress. To qualify as a new paradigm the scientific work must provide convincing answers to previously recognized problems, sufficient to attract enough – often younger – scientists to form the core of the new paradigm. For Kuhn, the important thing to notice is that the paradigm brings together the scientific facts of the time. It is also an active working construct that describes things as they are but is also used to flesh out other areas where previous research was thin or non-existent. A paradigm is useful because it suggests ways to understand and manipulate the world – until a point is reached when it does not account for new knowledge and data and is supplanted by a new paradigm. However, the older paradigms can linger since scientists do not lightly discard ideas in which they have a long-standing personal intellectual investment. Thus science is never a straightforward matter of simple empirical test but rather involves competitive groupings of scientists and social scientists.

The classic example of a paradigm shift is found in the move from the astronomy of the classical Greek and Roman era to that of Copernicus in the late fifteenth century. According to the first, the cosmos was made up of bodies moving in a series of concentric circles with the earth stationary in the middle. The planets moved around the earth in perfect circles and there was nothing beyond them except God. Copernicus overturned that view when he established that the sun was the centre of the solar system and the planets, including the earth, travelled around it. The point is that the earlier paradigm was honestly held in its time when no other data suggesting otherwise were available. Indeed, its most brilliant scientist, Ptolemy, working in Egypt around 140 CE, generated extremely accurate data on the position of the stars and planets, sufficient for shipping navigation for example.

Kuhn, T. (1996) *The Structure of Scientific Revolutions*, 3rd edn. London: University of Chicago Press.

participant observation see **research methods**

patriarchy see **family** and **kinship**

perception an act or process by which individuals translate or give coherence to sensory experience. Perception is to be understood as a complex combination of emotional, cognitive, physical and neurological processes all interacting with each other. Although physical stimulation is often prominent in a process of perceiving anything, a number of other factors can be significant depending upon the person, the location and the situation:

(1) *Attention* – in order to perceive another person, scene, situation or event, an individual has to both notice it and concentrate upon it, thus giving less attention to other phenomena or perhaps not noticing other things/people at all. Attention is in essence a very selective and more or less active process.

(2) *Consistency* – through a process of learning, an individual is able to understand that a mountain seen from a distance as small is the same phenomenon as the mountain seen from just a few miles. Experience allows us to make adjustments for light, distance and angles to accept that an object or person can appear to be different but is in fact the same. The rules of perspective underpin the issue of consistent identity of any phenomenon despite apparent changes to anything observed.

(3) *Organization* – perception is both selective and a combining process in that we tend to choose from a bewildering 'landscape' of stimuli to focus upon particular elements to construct a coherent 'whole'. This process is evident when we respond to particular human faces, perceiving them as attractive or not; or to the construction of a painting where we choose to focus upon some elements to the exclusion of others. **Gestalt theory** provides a convincing account of how in music, for example, a well-known melody can be played in different styles, with different instruments and at different speeds but will still be recognizable to most people because they have understood the 'whole' that is that melody. Elements of different kinds of design (style) can be understood in the same way.

(4) *Motivation* – individuals who feel particular senses keenly, such as thirst, or fear because of a pub brawl, might well experience sharp perceptual responses to, say, the sight of water or the sound of an approaching police car. In this context, some writers have found it useful to use the phrase *perceptual vigilance* – accepting that the process can be both conscious and unconscious.

(5) *Set* – an individual's emotional state and the way they think will fundamentally affect what is 'selected' from a sensory landscape. Panicking parents, who have temporarily lost sight of their 3-year-old son in a supermarket, will be predisposed to focus upon red clothing because their son was wearing a red jumper.

(6) *Learning* – it is now understood that perception is part innate and partly learned. For example, experiments about very young babies responding more actively to cartoons of a face with eyes, nose and mouth in the usual positions and less actively to cartoons of the same elements randomly arranged, suggest an innate predisposition to interpret some elements of their world in a particular way. In another context, art students are taught to look more closely at, say, a riverscape to be able to understand that reflected light might be depicted with white and/or silver paint on a canvas. In other words, the tutor is asking the students to look more closely than they have hitherto.

(7) *Distortion, illusion and hallucination* – it is now widely understood that some drugs (both illegal and prescribed), physical illness (involving perhaps a high temperature), mental health problems, sleeplessness or sleep deprivation, heightened emotional states and sustained stress can all lead to 'false' perceptions, altered states or 'misperceptions'; none of which could be said to be a 'reasonable' response to apparent stimuli.

(8) *Social dimensions of perception* – it is now known that immediate social groupings can influence how people see or perceive the
world. The classic experiments of two psychologists, Asch and
Sherif, have been persuasive in demonstrating how groups can
influence social behaviour, by establishing group **norms** in relation
to perceptions. In these experiments, individuals were often not
aware of the extent to which their perceptions were distorted by
group influences and where they were, sometimes admitted to
feeling that they did not want to stand out from the crowd.

Perception is a key concept for social workers in several contexts. In
direct work with children, the issue of a child's ability to concentrate
in an age-appropriate way is important in relation to assessments of
normal or abnormal development. Thus an ability to recognize some
colours, pictures of animals or of family members and cartoon characters from favourite DVDs is construed as a 'normal' milestone for,
say, a 3-year-old child. 'Reception year' primary school teachers will
be especially vigilant about the perceptual framework children bring to
school and their ability to concentrate on tasks as diagnostic tools for
beginning to help children from family backgrounds that have lacked
stimulation. Similarly, attention deficit hyperactivity disorder (ADHD)
is a source of considerable difficulties for some children, offering many
challenges to social workers working closely with parents/carers,
psychologists and teachers.

In relation to adults, misperceptions can be symptomatic of significant mental health problems, especially psychoses in conditions such
as schizophrenia and bipolar disorder and with physical health-related
problems such as dementia, stroke and brain damage/disorder as a
result of accident or trauma. The social worker's tasks, in these contexts, are to determine the extent of any delusions and hallucinations,
whether they imply any risks to the individual or to others, and how
best to support any recovery programme. One key issue is whether to
'confront' any delusional behaviour ('you cannot possibly have been
visited by the devil') or whether such delusions are simply put to one
side until a recovery programme is implemented and has shown some
signs of being therapeutic. Some support groups, supporting individuals experiencing auditory stimuli, now take the view that 'hearing
voices' does not have to be an entirely negative experience and that it
may be helpful to work 'with the voices' by exploring them and ren-
dering them less threatening. It is now accepted that people without
any kind of mental health problems sometimes hear voices.

Social workers' own abilities to assess problems effectively are
also vulnerable to many of the potential influences upon perception

outlined above. A predisposition to believe that some kind of religious faith is an important ingredient (or not, as the case may be) for potential foster carers could possibly affect or even distort a social worker's assessment of parenting capacity. Issues of perception might also affect notions of how social workers should present themselves to the world – say, in relation to a dress code or the badges they might or might not consider wearing. For example, should social workers be able to wear a badge that bears the slogan 'a woman's place is in the union' or 'Jesus loves you'? (See also **attitude, stereotype** and **values**.)

personal construct theory the ways in which individuals attempt to understand or make sense of their world; a process that involves individuals' perceptual framework but also their attempts to control their world and perhaps predict it, the latter sometimes as a 'self-fulfilling prophecy'.

Personal constructs can become so embedded in the individual's persona that they can become an integral part of an individual's personality. However, it is also possible that personal constructs will change and adapt in the light of experience. An 'open-minded' individual dealing with conflicting information by sustaining *cognitive dissonance* (young men are all predisposed to be noisy and self-seeking, but my neighbour's son is a nice young man who is often very kind and considerate) might eventually resolve dissonance by altering his or her personal construct. According to Kelly (1955), individuals tend to develop small-scale theories about how the world might be understood and these theories often have bipolar dimensions to them or can be experienced as continuums. For example, one important construct might focus upon whether people are friendly and emotionally warm compared with others that are experienced as distant and lacking warmth. This construct could be really important to particular individuals but they could also have less important constructs as part of their personality about whether individuals are good cooks or not. Kelly's view of personality could usefully be located in a phenomenological paradigm in its insistence upon subjective meanings for individuals that need to be painstakingly described before any kind of understanding is possible.

The potential use of personal construct theory for social work practice is significant. Kelly developed a useful technique called a *repertory grid*. Here the social worker would invite individuals to describe a number of other people that were important to them. These descriptions, in Kelly's view, would almost certainly reveal the key personal constructs that individuals use to make sense of their world. Such a grid also has the potential to reveal whether people are reasonably happy with their lot, feel low or depressed and how they view their relationships with others that are important to them.

Kelly, G. (1955) *The Psychology of Personal Constructs*. New York: Norton.

personality general orientations and dispositions, thought to be reasonably stable, that characterize the behaviour of any individual. Personality is construed as the 'cause' of individual behaviour and, in addition, that it can reasonably be implied or inferred from any person's behaviour. Thus, a football fan with an extrovert and aggressive personality might reasonably be expected to be someone who will shout a lot at football matches, insult the referee and be hostile towards opposition fans. Conversely, a person who would find it difficult to ask someone out on a date would be likely to have a personality that is shy and perhaps introverted. However, the manifestation of personality will be closely affected by concrete situations that will be more or less influential. For example, an approaching mob during urban disturbances might lead to the same evasive behaviour by both extrovert and introvert alike, whereas vacation time is more likely to reveal personality differences where choices are not so constrained.

Some theorists have tried to explain how personality develops, especially during childhood and adolescence. Other theorists have sought to devise ways of classifying various dimensions of personalities that will enable useful conclusions to be drawn about, for example, someone's suitability to do a particular job competently.

Among the theories about how personality develops are the following:

- *Psychodynamic theories* – these refer to the work of Freud and others who later developed his ideas. Freud's psychoanalytic theory has it that the mind has both unconscious (the id) and conscious components (the ego and super ego). Driven by a life force (libido) the id pursues the 'pleasure principle', but it has to adjust to the surrounding social world. In confronting the 'reality principle', it develops a more socially acceptable self in the form of the ego, as well as a conscience, the super-ego – construed as the internalized authority of the father or parental figure. Individual personalities develop as a function of the very particular dynamic between id, ego and super-ego that transpires as a child adjusts to its family and immediate social environment. Problems of adjustment occur, which may lead to neuroses or even psychoses, because of stress or oppressive experiences in childhood. Although psychoanalysis has many admirers, it probably has many more critics who regard it as essentially unproven.

- *Learning theories* – take the view that personality is formed from behaviour changing as a response to experience. Three kinds of associative learning account for how behaviour is learned and then perhaps reinforced – behaviour that includes emotional, cognitive (including language) and motor responses. The three kinds of learning that have been identified are – first, classical or respondent conditioning; second, operant or instrumental conditioning; and, finally, vicarious learning or modelling. Classical conditioning has it that people learn by associating a particular stimulus with a particular outcome (a father's return from work is identified, with the statement 'I'm home', followed by the father trying to find the child, who will be hiding). Operant conditioning requires a more active role from the person such as stroking the cat, which will in turn lead to the cat purring, which will result in the person feeling pleasure. Vicarious learning or modelling simply relies upon the person observing the behaviour of others and copying it. Crucially, many children do imitate and adopt the behaviour of parents and/ or siblings. Complexity can be built into this system of learning where a person falsely associates an outcome with a particular stimulus or an individual stimulus, such as being mugged by someone from a particular ethnic minority, leading to a generalized fear of all people from that ethnic background. Problematic behaviour is construed as a failure to learn 'appropriately'.

- *Humanistic theory* – an entirely different approach to the study of personality has been undertaken by Carl Rogers. In Rogers's view, psychoanalytic thinking offered very limited opportunities to understand what might lead to a happy, well-adjusted personality except in terms of reducing the psychological tensions between the three components of id, ego and super-ego. Rogers's humanistic theory argued that there is a need in all people to 'self-actualize' – in effect, to aspire to one's potential. Consistent with this view was Rogers's idea that everyone has a 'self-concept' and that psychological distress occurs when people feel that there is a substantial discrepancy between their 'self-concept' and any behaviour on their part which did not seem to be consistent with the 'self-concept'. Rogers also claimed that relationships with others were crucial to good mental health and that the 'positive regard' of others was fundamental. However, it is entirely possible that the influence of others' positive regard might be at odds with the impulse to 'self-actualize' (for example, 'my husband would like me to work to generate enough income to sustain a particular kind of lifestyle, whereas I am content to live more simply and stay at home with the kids until they reach a certain age').

- *Sociological theory* – that integrates personality with history/social structure. Sociologists have also sought to understand, in terms of broad structures, the relationship between what some have dubbed 'biography and history' and others 'character and social structure'. These perspectives have it that much of what appears as individual is in fact shaped by very broad social forces and there are often many similarities in the personalities of substantial proportions of, say, national groups at any one point in history. Similarly, gender is often subject to prescriptions underpinned by particular norms and clearly defined roles. In essence, there can be major **paradigm** shifts in the social assumptions underpinning, say, medieval societies in comparison to nineteenth-century capitalist societies or twenty-first-century capitalist cultures – paradigm shifts that might have meant a strong sense of fatalism and of fixed social roles in medieval societies changing in recent centuries to a sense of individual free-dom and the possibility of achievement in a more open and fluid society. Using this notion of personality, it is of more importance to recognize the social constructs of gender, social class and ethnic-ity as likely to bring about major continuities in identities and thus personalities.

Personality trait theories are more concerned with identifying psycho-logical traits that can hypothetically be used to 'measure' aspects of personalities for pragmatic purposes. Thus the behaviourist Eysenck, using *factor analysis*, hypothesized that personality could be under-stood in terms of two essential dimensions, namely extroversion/intro-version and neuroticism/stability. Plotting each dimension against the other in the form of a cross, he claimed to be able to plot individual 'subordinate' characteristics against this superstructure (see Figure 6).

Another prominent 'trait' theory is that of Cattell who claimed to have identified 16 different dichotomous 'factors', namely: reserved–outgoing; less intelligent–more intelligent; affected by feelings–emotionally stable; submissive–dominant; serious–happy-go-lucky; expedient–conscientious; timid–venturesome; tough minded–sensitive; trusting–suspicious; practical–imaginative; forthright–shrewd; self-assured–apprehensive; conservative–experimenting; group dependent–self-sufficient; uncontrolled–controlled; and finally, relaxed–tense. Critics of trait theories argue that they do not take sufficient account of two issues: first, that personalities can develop and change and, sec-ond, that any individual's behaviour may well be different in different circumstances or with different people.

The use of personality theory in social work practice is uneven and in some regards both eclectic and poorly developed. In general social work practice, learning theory has been used to good effect in helping parents to deal with parenting issues and in offering consistent parenting

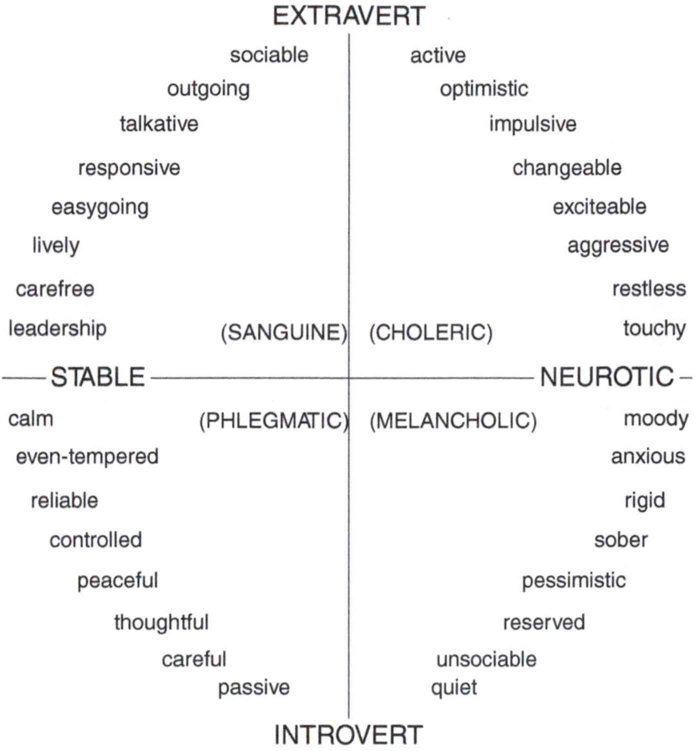

EXTRAVERT

sociable	active
outgoing	optimistic
talkative	impulsive
responsive	changeable
easygoing	exciteable
lively	aggressive
carefree	restless
leadership (SANGUINE)	(CHOLERIC) touchy

——— STABLE ———————————————————— NEUROTIC –

calm (PHLEGMATIC)	(MELANCHOLIC) moody
even-tempered	anxious
reliable	rigid
controlled	sober
peaceful	pessimistic
thoughtful	reserved
careful	unsociable
passive	quiet

INTROVERT

Figure 6 Eysenck's model of personality

in relation to some agreed behavioural targets. There are also substantial sections of set pieces such as the common assessment framework and the Prospective Adopters' Report (the former form F1) that require social workers to assess parents and 'would-be parents', but both forms are essentially descriptive, based around prompts concerning emotional warmth, ability to be consistent, ability to offer boundaries and other interpersonal skills. However, more rigorous assessments of personality are often carried out by psychologists associated with children and adolescent mental health service teams or other specialist units.

personality disorder psychological conditions that involve enduring, persistent and deeply ingrained maladaptive patterns of behaviour that impair normal social and behavioural functioning. The term has been regarded as contentious by many commentators who argue that it lacks precision because it is often presented as a 'residual' category of disorders that cannot be classified as either neuroses or psychoses.

In addition, some argue that personality disorders are not amenable to treatment or social support/intervention because the condition is not a mental illness, a view not shared by others. Some have associated *dangerousness* with such disorders. The principal disorders included under this general umbrella term, which should be regarded as clusters of characteristics or symptoms rather than absolute diagnoses, include the following:

- *Paranoid personality disorder* – a condition where individuals express extreme suspicion, sensitivity or even hostility because of a perceived threat to self, or from another person's character that is unjustified by the evidence or circumstances.
- *Schizoid personality* – a psychological condition, not thought to be related to schizophrenia, characterized by an inability to form emotionally close attachments as well as remoteness, and a predisposition to solitude and secrecy.
- *Anti-social personality disorder* – the preferred generic term that includes conditions earlier dubbed as psychopathic and/or sociopathic, where individuals appear not to experience any disquiet, anxiety or guilt in compromising or even violating others' rights. In adolescence, this general syndrome is sometimes labelled as a *conduct disorder,* defined by a predisposition to criminal activity, an inability to attend school or work regularly, addictions and possibly vagrancy.
- *Histrionic personality disorder* – also known as hysterical behaviour, this condition is thought to include extreme egoism, attention-seeking and a preparedness to manipulate situations in favour of self. Other associations include a willingness to play the 'prima donna' or the victim in dramatic fashion. The condition is closely allied to *narcissistic personality disorder*, which can entail 'fantastic' claims to achievements or perhaps wealth or social connections that are either false or much exaggerated.

Research has, however, found that critical life events that appear to lead to personality disorders may be amenable to treatment (National Institute for Mental Health in England (2003) *Personality Disorder: No Longer a Diagnosis of Exclusion.* London: NIMHE).

pilot study see **research methods**

pluralism the organization of social arrangements in which culturally distinct groups share some aspects of social and political behaviour in order to maintain a reasonably stable and co-operative social whole. In this arrangement, distinct cultural and/or ethnic groups would continue to maintain differences through religious institutions, social institutions, media and possibly exclusive education and particular economic activities. In addition, primary group relations are likely to be sustained by intra-group marriages as well as family, friendship and community support systems.

Sociologists usefully distinguish between cultural and structural pluralism. Cultural pluralism is where individual groups have their own beliefs, values, attitudes and lifestyles but where they have some of these attributes in common with other distinct cultural or ethnic groups. An example of cultural pluralism is to be found in the United States where Hispanic, African American and different white communities have their own very distinct cultural differences but may also share a vision of the 'American Dream', support the same sports teams and vote for the same political figures. Structural pluralism entails groups having some separate social and political institutions while sharing others. Belgium's two principal groups of Flemish-speaking and French-speaking peoples and Canada's English-speaking and French-speaking groups are perhaps among the best-known examples, having both regional and local governments that predominantly serve the separate communities while having a national government that serves all. It is worth noting, however, that each of these countries have both separatist and integrationist movements as well as minorities, in Canada at least, of indigenous peoples who have little access to political processes. (See also **assimilation, integration** and **multiculturalism.**)

political correctness a term used largely by the **right** to indicate excessive attention to using particular terminology when discussing gender, 'race', disability and sexual preference. Although there were antecedents to political correctness from within the **left**, particularly within Western communism of the 1970s, when some members noted the necessity of using accepted jargon to fit with party doctrine, by the 1990s the charge of political correctness was levelled by conservative politicians and media personnel to ridicule the language and objectives of gays and lesbians, feminists, disability activists, anti-racist campaigners and, particularly, social workers.

The more thoughtful users of the term on the political right would point out that some of these new social movements and their allies were prone to adopting implicit linguistic conventions to describe themselves and their objectives and that these conventions were then used to assess whether the beliefs of individual members conformed to these norms. This, they argued, opened up the possibility of self-censure and limited debate. Largely, however, the charge was used simply to denigrate the attempts to promote equal rights for oppressed groups and to encourage the public to laugh at these aspirations.

Social work was in advance of all other professions in making the combatting of racial discrimination a professional duty and for this reason it became a kind of lightning rod for those who opposed this project as well as a target for right-wing commentators who knew nothing about social work but welcomed the opportunity to ridicule its practices. The publication of Paper 30 in 1991 by the Central Council for Education and Training in Social Work (CCETSW) crystallized the hostility. In it, CCETSW stipulated that social work education should include a strategy for tackling racism as an institutional phenomenon as a matter for professional training. The right attacked this with calls for CCETSW 'to be stopped in its tracks'. Although the anti-racist strategy was also criticized within social work for what seemed to be its excessive emphasis on language as a vehicle for social change, 20 years later it is clear that the profession was in the vanguard in developing anti-racist – and later anti-oppressive – strategies. It is deeply ironic that the political right, which laid the charge of political correctness with such regularity throughout the 1990s, has now embraced the very agenda that social work was outlining then: combatting racism at an institutional level, promoting gay and lesbian rights and adopting the objectives of the disability movement.

population see demography

positive action measures permitted by the Race Relations Act 1976 and the Sex Discrimination Act 1975 to help members of ethnic minorities and women achieve more equality (in comparison with white people and men respectively) in relation to seeking employment or promotion.

British law does not permit discrimination at the point of selection for employment or promotion. Positive action measures mostly concern training opportunities targeted at women and members of ethnic minorities. Such training might include special attempts to equip and encourage women to apply for jobs in areas of employment hitherto dominated by men, such as in engineering. Similarly, it might be demonstrated that black people are a substantial proportion of the population within a particular area but are practically invisible as local authority employees. Training in these circumstances might be to familiarize black people with an area of work or occupation relatively unknown to them and to help them acquire the specific skills necessary to secure a job. Other measures might include networking, that is, telling particular community groups that an organization really does want to recruit more people from ethnic minorities. The use of particular newspapers and advertisements in various languages would send strong signals to particular communities about the seriousness of an organization's equal opportunities policies. It is also possible to appoint a black person or a woman to a post (in competition with a white person or a man respectively) if he or she is considered to be equally competent to do a job and women or black people are under-represented at that level within the organization.

A limited number of posts can also be 'reserved' for black people and for women where the job could be said to offer a personal service that only somebody of that ethnicity or gender could reasonably be expected to provide. Thus a woman and only a woman should be considered for a job in a rape crisis centre, and only a black person for a job as an African Caribbean advice worker. Some employers have also made attempts to recruit older workers, although such initiatives are not required by law despite recent legislation giving people the right to claim discrimination on grounds of age.

Affirmative action is regarded as a more vigorous attempt designed to reverse past discrimination in any society in relation to both ethnic minority groups and women. US President Lyndon Johnson said in 1965 that 'You do not take a person who, for years, has been hobbled by chains and liberate him, bring him up to the starting line of a race and then say, "you are free to compete with the others", and still justly believe that you have been completely fair.' In essence, Johnson's statement implied that those used to discrimination will take a considerable time to adjust to the idea that they can compete on equal terms and that their efforts will be justly recognized. In addition, those accustomed to discriminate will have to be challenged to change their behaviour. Although many if not most commentators can agree with Johnson's statement, opinion has been divided about how discrimination can be avoided in the future and a more genuinely meritocratic system established for all.

The first key element of programmes based on affirmative action principles has been about setting quotas, as distinct from setting targets. The second important strand of affirmative action programmes has been the willingness of some governments to use wide-ranging sanctions to achieve their goals. The use of fines has been one strand of direct government interventions. A second and potentially very persuasive strand is the willingness of governments to use their considerable power as purchasers of goods and services from the private sector. In essence, governments can insist that companies employ a specified proportion of ethnic minority and/or female workers by a particular date and that failure to do so will lead to a loss of a government contract.

post-modernism the term for a cultural and intellectual trend that
broadly declares there is no single overarching social reality but only
multiple points of view each with their own validity. Post-modernism
literally means 'after modernism' and as a term appeared at various
points in the twentieth century within different contexts including in
the 1960s when it was used to celebrate or mourn the passing of modernist art and literature (see **modernity**). The term came definitively
into use in social theory in the 1980s under the influence of French
philosophers Michel Foucault, Jean Baudrillard and Jacques Derrida,
and spread rapidly across Europe and the US. This tells us that it is not
so much an actual historical epoch as a social philosophy suited to a
social world of continuous change, moral relativism and social uncertainty. The social sciences were initially resistant to post-modernist ideas
in part because they saw themselves as the product of modernity – with
claims to objectivity, measurement of various social behaviours and
theoretical insights into the structure of society itself that are the
antithesis of post-modernism.

But post-modernism proved a powerful wave – within higher education at least – and by the late 1980s social scientists began to bring
post-modernism into mainstream sociological theory even if they had
to confront the uncomfortable fact that it not only appeared to trans-
form social theory but even to indicate its demise altogether. Some
sociologists took this to be its logical conclusion, arguing that 'the
truth claims' of social science no longer warranted any privileged status
and that sociologists were free to develop any narrative or story they
liked regarding society and an individual's place within it.

Post-modernism broadly has been defined as a crisis of representation
of society and loss of coherence in institutions (especially political institutions). It particularly denies the existence of categories that had conventionally been relied on to instil social ideals – community, the state,
class, ethics. It asserts that the reality of the social world is too complex,
too 'contingent' (i.e. left to chance) and too disputed by conflicting
points of view to permit such universal concepts. Rather, 'reality' itself
is **socially constructed** and therefore is constantly being remade. How
it is constructed varies depending on who is doing the constructing –
whether a group, social movement or intellectual orientation. These
are localized, context dependent, complex and often in conflict with
one another. As the principal post-modernist sociologist in Britain,
Zygmunt Bauman (1992), has argued, there is no longer any certainty
grounded in an established, universally recognized set of values.

Post-modernism also relishes cultural and moral 'relativism': each
culture is legitimate, regardless of specific practices and values. In a

world of many different cultural groups, each will have its own system of meaning and its own criteria of what is right and wrong. Such practices can only be judged within the context of the group's own culture or discourse, some post-modernists would argue.

Many critics have noted the central paradox of post-modernism – that although it claims that there is no such thing as universal truth, this one statement is nevertheless universally true. Other critics have noted that the emphasis on language as the main source of power overlooks the fact that power is also embedded in institutions, wealth, social classes and political regimes. If language is the principal source of power, these critics argue, then power as a social phenomenon becomes difficult to pin down – power is everywhere and nowhere, so to speak. Other more philosophically oriented critics agree that while there is no such thing as universally accepted truths, nonetheless people reasoning and deliberating together on the basis of experience can progressively arrive at clearer understandings of complex social problems. While there is no 'Truth' with a capital T there is still the struggle to define what is real and true through formulating principles and knowledge that apply widely to human behaviour.

Whatever the criticisms within social sciences, post-modernists have generally sought to obtain a clearer view of what is actually going on within capitalist societies in a time of rapid globalization. In such efforts, there are distinct parallels with classical sociologists such as Marx, Weber and Durkheim, who also struggled to find new ways to understand the dramatic changes in social structure and everyday life. Post-modernists have particularly explored the increasing superficiality in social relationships and the destructive consequences of this for the development of strong, stable identities. This line of analysis points to the disintegrating effects of relentless **commodification**, accelerated by the pervasive presence of all forms of media. Many post-modernists also deal with the effect of commodification on society as a whole, noting in particular the loss of normative consensus and widely accepted social norms.

The first excursions into post-modernism by social work academics used it to confirm elements of social work practice that were already in existence. Howe, for example (1994), noted post-modernism's emphasis on diversity. Post-modernity, he wrote, 'feels comfortable with *difference* and multiplicity, variety and conflict', so that difference should be celebrated as part of a 'polymorphous, non-unitary and non-consensual' social world. He also noted the growing emphasis on service users' participation in matters that affect their lives; this reflects the fact that there are no privileged perspectives, no centres of truth or absolute authority on individual behaviour. Users' participation in decision-making is essential to putting together a workable plan as knowledge is no longer confined to the all-seeing professional. Finally he observed that social workers are now aware that in statute and practice they find themselves in positions of power, able to shape how situations are to be understood and the specific knowledge that is to count as relevant. Much of the critique of power draws on how social workers may be completely unaware of the ways in which social work discourse can disadvantage users.

Perhaps the most disturbing element for social work in post-modernism is the radical loss of self that it projects – the 'decentring' of the transcendental self – upon which social work has based its approach through its entire history. The most unflinching post-modernists, such as Ulrich Beck and Zygmunt Bauman, have dissected the position of the self in contemporary society and found that the personal self is essentially wholly on its own, bereft of the roles and motivating ideas which provided a sense of self-worth in the past. (See also **modernity**, **risk society** and **social constructionism**.)

Bauman, Z. (1992) *Intimations of Postmodernity*. London: Routledge.

Howe, D. (1994) Modernity, postmodernity and social work, *British Journal of Social Work*, 24(5): 513–32.

Pardek, J., Murphy, J. and Meinert, R. (1998) *Postmodernism, Religion and the Future of Social Work*. London: Routledge.

poverty the lack of sufficient material resources to sustain health and well-being.

Sociologists have defined poverty in one of two ways – as either absolute or relative. *Absolute poverty* has conventionally been defined as a fixed standard below which individuals and families experience complete destitution and so cannot meet even minimum needs for food and shelter in order to sustain life. The Poor Law in nineteenth-century Britain based its services on just such a standard: only a person or family facing the threat of starvation would turn to the local workhouse where the regime offered only the barest necessities for continued existence. Many aid agencies as well as the World Bank and the United Nations Development Programme (UNDP) today use an absolute standard for measuring poverty in the developing world which they have fixed at two US dollars of income per person per day. The absolute standard of poverty is broadly fixed at the level of income necessary for basic subsistence. Above that level families can survive, if only barely. Below that level they face severe malnutrition or starvation. Absolute standards of poverty, defined in this way, have the virtue of allowing us to calculate poverty across different countries – the UNDP was able to estimate in the mid-1990s that 30 percent of all children under 5 in the developing world were malnourished on that basis.

Relative poverty, by the same token, refers to the lack of resources needed to obtain the minimum standards of a particular society – for example in relation to diet, activities, social connections and living conditions that are widely approved and generally obtained by the great majority of people in that society. A person in relative poverty has resources so seriously inferior to those commanded by the average individual or household that they are excluded from ordinary social activity.

It is important to note that increasingly the definitions of absolute and relative poverty are used in a different way. For example, the Child Poverty Act of 2010 defines an individual in relative poverty if his or her household's income is below 60 percent of the median in the given year that it is measured, and that he or she is in absolute poverty if the household's income is below 60 percent of the 2010–11 median income, adjusted for inflation. In this formulation, the definition of absolute poverty is very different from the historical meaning of absolute poverty, which always centred on the minimum income necessary for survival. It is deemed absolute here because it fixes on a single baseline (the median income of 2010–11) on which to calculate poverty for each succeeding year in the future.

Generally social scientists have accepted that if a household's income falls below 60 percent or less of the average household income in any given year that household is in relative poverty. On that basis in 2005/06 nearly 13 million people or one-fifth of the UK population were living below this income threshold; four years later the headline total was 13.4 million.

A different measurement for determining relative poverty has developed around what the public considers to be the *necessities* for achieving a minimum standard of living in Britain. One of the most influential studies, *Breadline Britain*, through a series of surveys, showed a striking consensus around those items that all adults should be able to afford and not have to do without. In the most recent of these surveys, 95 percent thought beds and bedding were necessary (leaving 4 percent, of course, who thought they were not), while 94 percent thought heating for the living areas of the home was necessary. Other items deemed necessary by the vast majority of the public were:

- two meals a day – 91 percent;
- a refrigerator – 89 percent;
- fresh fruit and vegetables daily – 86 percent;

- money to keep the home in a decent state of decoration – 82 percent;
- a washing machine – 76 percent.

In their research in 2003, Bradshaw and Finch combined three different measures of poverty to determine the number of poor households in Britain. They looked at the percentage of households that first, cannot afford basic necessities, second, subjectively consider themselves poor and, third, live on income below the poverty threshold (two-thirds of the median wage in Britain). They found that 5.6 percent of British households were poor by all three standards and 16.3 percent poor by two of the standards while households found to be poor by one standard approached 30 percent. By using the three different criteria, they discovered that some households have an income above the poverty line but would not be able to afford things seen as essential by most people. Families that fall into two of these categories are considered excluded from the norms of society, a differentiated social class that cannot escape taking on debt that they are unable to repay.

Why and how people are poor has been hotly contested since the beginnings of social science. The issue is whether poverty arises as a consequence of individual, family and group behaviour (such as individual laziness, dependency on benefits, attitudes toward work discipline and education), or as a consequence of the economy, social constraints or social structure (such as unemployment during economic downturns, restructuring which closes local industries or discrimination on the basis of age, ethnicity or gender). In general, the research that social scientists have produced tends to point to the second cluster of reasons, that poverty is largely a product of social and economic forces *beyond* the control of the individual. But over the last 30 years there has been a strong counter-attack from social theorists who have argued that the first cluster is more important.

Conservative-minded social theorists, in particular Americans such as James Q. Wilson and Charles Murray, point to the first cluster of causes of poverty – the changes in cultural outlook, moral attitudes and above all family breakdown. In general, the research conducted from this perspective does not focus on defining poverty or trying to establish the number of poor people but on investigating the effects on children of lone parenthood and rising levels of divorce, of absent fathers as role models, particularly for boys, dependency on welfare benefits and how moral relativism has led to acceptance of what was in earlier times unacceptable, especially children born out of wedlock. (See also **child poverty**, **culture of poverty** and **underclass**.)

That social workers largely engage with people on very low incomes is beyond dispute. Knowing what social science has to say about poverty – how it is defined, the conflicting reasons for it, the ways out of it, the link between welfare benefits and the labour market – is part of the essential social worker understanding of social processes. Thinking through how and why some families are poor and others not is both a general issue *and* an individual issue. Why is *this* particular family in poverty? How, if at all, does poverty feed into parental stresses and parental attitudes? What is the relationship between neighbourhood environments and individual behaviour? These are the kinds of question that poverty research and social science theorizing about poverty raise for the reflective practitioner. (See also **social exclusion**.)

Bradshaw, J. and Finch, N. (2003) Overlaps in dimensions of poverty, *Journal of Social Policy,* 32(4): 513–25.

Parekh, A., MacInnes, T. and Kenway, P. (2010) *Monitoring Poverty and Social Exclusion.* York: New Policy Institute/Joseph Rowntree Foundation.

Townsend, P. (1979) *Poverty in the United Kingdom.* Harmondsworth: Penguin Books.

power the capacity to change, alter or influence another person or social structure or institution, perhaps despite resistance. Power may also involve some element of discipline or punishment and often is ultimately rooted in the use of physical violence or its threat.

Although power is often seen in negative terms – the capacity of one person to compel another to do her or his bidding – it can also be seen in more positive terms, as enabling people to achieve certain goals or objectives. This dichotomy between 'power over' others and 'power with' others is what makes the subject such a compelling one for political theorists and social scientists.

Within Western democracies debate has focused upon whether political power essentially rests with 'power' elites in a small number of decision-making forums which control political and cultural affairs or whether it is dispersed across many decision-making centres, which affords access to all sectors of the population (**pluralism**). Other social scientists have noted that the study of power cannot be confined simply to observable instances where power is exercised but that it is necessary to study the hidden forces that shape decision-making. One of the most celebrated of such analyses is by Stephen Lukes. According to Lukes, power has an ideological dimension, the operation of which is not always observable. While some post-modernist thinkers have found power to be dispersed so widely and in so many different forms that it has led some to call for it to be abandoned as a concept, Lukes finds it a useful analytical tool relevant to understanding domination and the role that ideology plays in maintaining it.

In *Power: A Radical View* (2005), Lukes writes: 'Is it not the supreme and most insidious exercise of power to prevent people, to whatever degree, from having grievances by shaping their perceptions, cognitions and preferences in such a way that they accept their role in the existing order of things, either because they can see or imagine no alternative to it, or because they see it as natural and unchangeable, or because they value it as divinely ordained and beneficial?'

Michel Foucault adopted a different position that blended elements of power-elite theory and pluralism. He started his analysis at what can only be described as the micro-level, looking into the smallest mechanisms for exercising power each with their own techniques and tactics, often embodied in the specific language that each employed. He concluded that there is a very close relationship between systems of knowledge or **discourses** that codify techniques and practices for the exercise of social control and domination. The prison, the asylum, the hospital, the university, the school, the psychiatrist's office are all examples of sites where a dispersed and piecemeal organization of power is built up independently of any systematic strategy of class domination. The only way to mount resistance is to develop open qualities in human discourse and thereby intervene in knowledge. Foucault himself undertook what he called 'localized resistances' in his work with gays and prisoners.

Within agencies and organizations, power and control are evident in the hierarchies in which superiors exert power over subordinates. But there are reciprocities in this relationship. Control is never total and no subordinate is ever totally powerless since their active compliance is needed if a power relationship is not to become burdensome and inefficient.

Social workers are involved in many activities that have power at their core. The social work role involves the use of professional power and it can be combined with the use of statutory powers if the intervention is underpinned by law. In either context relationships with service users or clients can be governed by commitments to consult them or even to devolve power to them. Arnstein's ladder describes a continuum ranging from a position where service users have control to one where they are virtually powerless. From the highest rung on Arnstein's ladder, in descending order, are citizen control, delegated power, partnership, placation, consultation, informing, therapy and manipulation. The commitment to anti-oppressive practice in current social work education and practice requires that the service users' voice be heeded unless there are good reasons not to do so or where their interests conflict with the interests of others.

Influencing or altering the power dimensions of relationships also features in social work interventions as, for example, social workers support women trying to persuade their partners not to be violent or parents to avoid using physical chastisement to discipline their children, or to help a carer resist a domineering elder who does not acknowledge the carer's right to a life independent of caring.

Power is at the heart of agencies delivering social work services in relation to organizational arrangements for supervision, accountability and the allocation of scarce resources. Supervisory arrangements can be hierarchical with each social worker having to account for him or herself to a person on the next rung of a ladder. Some agencies, however, are prepared to use other forms of supervision including peer supervision, especially where there are experienced social workers. In this context, professional authority can be valued as much as bureaucratic or hier-archical authority. Accountability can also have several dimensions as social workers have to answer to professional bodies, but also to politi-cal masters in the form of councillors on local authority committees. Last, competition for scarce resources is an inevitable part of local and national politics as social work services vie for funds with other statutory services such as education or health. (See also **discourse** and **ideology**.)

Lukes, S. (2005) *Power: A Radical View*. Basingstoke: Palgrave Macmillan.

prejudice pre-judgements, biased opinion and attitudes that are not justified by reality. Although it is possible for prejudice to be in favour of a person or other social entity, prejudice is usually a reflection of a negative stance.

Prejudice can be rooted in communities and passed down from one generation to another and thus can be construed as evidence of social learning. In this sense, prejudices may be acquired by an indi-vidual without having had any personal experience of the social entity attracting the negative attitude. Although the study of prejudice has historically focused upon individual propensities to express unjustified negative views, sociologists have also been interested in wider connec-tions that relate to social structure and to issues associated with human rights. Structurally prejudice is useful in underpinning exploitative rela-tionships especially in the economy where a view that a particular ethnic group, for example, is only capable of certain kinds of unskilled work, thus justifying poor conditions and low pay. In this sense, prejudice leads to unjust policies and practices. Prejudice, in its failure to assess every individual and every situation on its merits, is irrational because it justifies an unreasoned response. Finally, prejudice also compromises human dignity and begins to undermine any claims to treat people equally and humanely. (See also **discrimination** and **ethnocentrism**.)

pressure group association of people including, for example, community groups, companies, quangos, professional bodies, research bodies/think tanks and trade unions that seek to influence both local and central government, or, even further afield, institutions such as the European Union or the United Nations. Pressure groups can also be *interest groups.*

Some pressure groups may be formed to campaign around a single issue and are therefore likely to dissolve when the issue is either settled or interest in it is waning, for example a campaign group with the sole objective of preventing a new airport being located in a particular locality. Other pressure groups such as the CBI (Confederation of British Industry) or the TUC (Trades Union Conference) are more or less permanent features of the political landscape. Some pressure groups associate themselves with particular political forces or parties, such as the close connections between the TUC and the Labour Party or the CBI's association with the Conservative Party; indeed it is frequently the case that such bodies sponsor particular MPs in the expectation that they will try to enhance the aims or objectives of the sponsoring body in parliament.

The existence of pressure groups is seen by some political scientists as evidence of an open civil society characterized by **pluralism** – the notion that advanced industrial *democratic* societies permit the formation of pressure groups and that governments are required to act as *honest brokers,* adjudicating between the demands of competing interests. Other more sceptical commentators would point to the close association between some long-established pressure groups and governments of a particular political persuasion, that the political class and particular pressure groups are often drawn from the same *elites* and that, in essence, despite the appearance of influence where governments make the odd strategic concession to relatively less powerful pressure groups, the overwhelming evidence has it that power is entrenched in certain groups with their close associations with all three arms of government: the executive, the civil service and the judiciary.

Some have found it useful to distinguish between pressure groups that are deemed to be *protective* and those that are *promotional.* The former would encompass any trade union or professional association that was seeking to preserve or enhance the group's interests and the latter, groups that were seeking to achieve an objective, say in relation

to tackling poverty (Child Poverty Action Group) or homelessness
(Shelter) that might, perhaps, have a 'public interest' focus. Two issues
in relation to social work present themselves including the participation of social workers in political parties, trade unions, professional
bodies or other pressure groups to enhance their own interests and
their participation in other groups that may have broader, say, social
policy interests. Current evidence indicates that social workers are
divided on whether they wish to associate themselves with trade unions
or professional bodies, or perhaps both. And in relation to pressure
group activity to enhance the interests of service users, social workers
seem currently to be relatively uninvolved, suggesting that the current
paradigm influencing how social work duties are discharged is personal
and not structural/political.

profession an occupational group that has consolidated its status and
reputation with the public at large by demonstrating that:
(1) it commands a high level of unique expertise based on years of
     training in what the public regards as a difficult body of knowledge;
(2) it maintains dedication to public service;
(3) it is autonomous in regulating its own affairs.

The widely accepted professions are doctors, lawyers, clergy,
architects and the military. Other occupations such as teaching and
social work have attempted at different points in their history to attain
professional status but have not succeeded to the extent of those listed
above.

The professional ideal has been closely examined and is regarded now
as more motivated by self-interest, with professional associations seen as
anti-competitive cartels unwilling for others to perform the same duties
for a lower fee. Breaking into barristers' monopoly on higher court
representation and solicitors' monopoly on conveyancing are cases in
point, while consultants in the health service are wary of trust commis-
sioners influencing clinical decisions. Other social changes – the rise
of celebrity culture, the huge salaries paid in the financial and sports
industries, the rise of determined consumer advocacy groups – have
also undermined some of the professions' prestige.

Social work has made repeated efforts throughout the last 100
years to attain professional status on a par with medicine and the law.
It seemed on the verge of achieving this aspiration in the early 1970s
when the formation of the British Association of Social Workers
and the establishment of large, unified social services departments
brought social work a higher national profile. However, the succeeding decades were marked by setbacks in seeking professional
status. There was division among social workers themselves with a

significant proportion regarding themselves as trade unionists and salaried employees rather than members of a profession. Efforts to distinguish specifically social work tasks from more general (and, it was implied, less skilled) social care also faltered because defining social work was difficult without becoming overly abstract. This undermined attempts to draw clear lines around what precisely it is that professionally qualified social workers do that allied staff do not and cannot do. The creation of a College of Social Work in 2010 was another attempt in a long line of efforts at cementing social work's professional status – an effort undermined by the conflict between the new college and BASW as to who should be the lead voice of the profession.

Sociologists generally place social work (and teachers) among the *semi-professions* – occupations that claim professional status but differ significantly from the established professions:

- their training is shorter;
- status and authority is less accepted by the public at large;
- their body of knowledge and expertise is less specialized;
- the autonomy of individual practitioners is less because they remain under supervision and are controlled by senior managers.

These characteristics are relative – social work is only a 'semi-profession' as a result of not enjoying the pre-eminence of the traditional professions. In terms of dedication to users and undertaking their work to the highest standard, social workers can be described as 'professional'.

psychopathology the study of conscious, abnormal psychic events involving the classification, diagnosis and treatment of mental disorders as well as investigation into causes of disorders. In general, particularly since Karl Jaspers's *Clinical Psychopathology* was published in English in 1959, it has focused on reaching as precise a definition as possible of each particular disorder and establishing specific criteria for each. In so doing, it places great emphasis on selecting, differentiating and describing the particular abnormal mental experience. While the term overlaps substantially with 'abnormal psychology', psychopathology as a discipline is largely the province of psychiatry, the medically trained profession that deals with severe mental health problems.

The descriptive psychopathology of Jaspers – and those who followed his lead – concentrates on the identification of particular mental experiences. The process of identification involves giving a name to a condition along with criteria that define the condition and makes it capable of being defined again and again. In this way, phenomena such as delusions, hallucinations, compulsive behaviour, grandiose ideas and inability to pick up social cues have been named and described. A diagnosis of this kind depends on the person's own experiences, his or her *subjective* accounts as understood by the psychiatrist/diagnostician. Broadly, psychiatrists are empathic in this role, able to put themselves into the patient's position; they seek the missing connection, making sense of incoherent and fragmented communications.

By contrast is the direct observance of *objective* physiological phenomena – such as sweating during episodes of fear, facial expressions indicating euphoria or depression, or measurable performance such as memory tests or work output. Behavioural psychologists who emphasize objective phenomena attempt to measure intelligence, cognitive abilities, task performances, sense of perception and levels of fatigue, all of which lend themselves more to generating data such as scaling that is replicable and allows for comparison with average standards. In this role, the psychiatrist acts more as the uninvolved observer.

Psychcopathology therefore is not only descriptive but interpretative as well – understanding the meaning, making connections, recognizing the subjective experience of the individual person's inner world. In reaction to behavioural description, a strand of psychiatry particularly in the 1960s and 1970s placed heavy emphasis on interpreting the inner world of individual patients, and understanding what they, through their symptoms and behaviour, were trying to say. R.D. Laing, within the **anti-psychiatry** movement, perhaps took this approach to its furthest extreme but others such as Ludwig Binswanger explored the thoughts and inner experiences of patients through their mental constructs. The work of Aaron Beck in **cognitive behaviour** and **personal construct theory** can also be traced to this broad effort to understand the experiences from the individual's point of view and the meanings that person attaches to them.

Overall, psychopathology remains firmly based in symptom diagnosis and classification of what psychiatry still calls mental illness. Symptoms fall into different categories:

- disorders of sensory perception such as distortion of smells or colour, illusion (based on an object present) or hallucination (no object present);
- disorders of thought and speech through which speech has haphazard sequences, occurs extremely rapidly or slows with little content, or is subject to thought blocking – abruptly stopping one line of thought and beginning another completely different one;

- possession of thought – people experience a loss of control over their own thinking, that it has been overtaken by other forces;
- disorders of thought content such as delusions about self and holding false beliefs.

The standard reference in psychopathology is the *Diagnostic and Statistical Manual of Mental Disorders*, familiarly referred to as 'DSM'. Such is its influence in defining diagnoses of mental illness that it also shapes treatment, drug development pipelines and, in the US at least, decisions on health insurance. The process of updating is in the hands of some 160 specialists, some of whom are under sustained criticism for their links to the pharmaceutical industry.

The manual is currently undergoing revision for its fifth edition – the last was in 1994 – amid some contentious debate. (In early editions, homosexuality was considered a mental disorder.) There are accusations that criteria are widening for specific diagnoses to enlarge the numbers defined as requiring psychiatric attention. For example, the definition of depression is now to include bereavement, which had been excluded from previous editions on the basis that it is a normal reaction to loss that millions experience every year. 'Bipolar disorder' – formerly simply 'manic depression' – now has different levels of intensity, all of which are regarded as symptomatic. The new edition will also introduce a new diagnosis, 'attenuated psychosis syndrome', that will apply to children and young people with some symptoms of delusions, hallucinations and saying things that do not make sense. The aim is in effect to diagnose a 'pre-schizophrenic condition' in children in order to treat it early. Critics argue that such studies show that 70 to 80 percent of young people who show these symptoms do not progress to full-blown schizophrenia and that any such diagnosis would then be treated with anti-psychosis drugs, where there is already overuse of drugs among children and young people.

The new DSM is also reconsidering its definition of autism and the related but less severe conditions of Asperger's syndrome and 'pervasive developmental disorder, not otherwise specified'. Criticized for years for its ever-widening definitions of autism and related conditions – resulting in more and more children diagnosed – the DSM is now tightening those definitions. The consequence of this is that families who now receive state assistance for their child diagnosed under the previous criteria will lose that support when the child is reassessed under the new criteria.

Social workers have long been part of the collaborative treatment and support provided for those with mental disorders, often working closely with psychiatric nurses, floating support workers and psychiatrists. Broadly, their role is to work on the border between mental disorder and the social context within which it occurs. This has, rightly, tilted social work toward questioning the limits of psycho-pathology and the diagnostic regimes that define disorders. Without necessarily adopting the position of the anti-psychiatry movement it is important to understand that the elements of any given diagnosis of a specific disorder are to a degree culture specific. The approach of descriptive psychopathology, at its extreme, suggests a detached diag-nostician who accumulates data and treats the sufferer as an object, reducing her or his experiences to a set of discrete symptoms and initi-ating a process over which that person then has little control.

Getting the balance right, however, between certifying the accuracy of a diagnosis, protecting the community at large from risk of dan-gerous behaviour, maintaining the connections that the person with mental disorder has with society and serving as advocate is extremely difficult. The number of psychiatric beds in England has fallen from a peak of 150,000 in 1955 to 28,000 by 2007, giving a rough indica-tor of how far the care of those with mental disorder has fallen on the community and community-based services. High-profile instances of violence committed by those under supervision in the community and the incidence of self-harm and suicides, together with high rates of homelessness of those discharged from hospitals, have formed a kind of undertow to the general policy. For social workers, this has increased focus on *risk management* – amid perceptions that different groups are more, or less, suitable to community care. There is, for example, a pronounced gendered dimension to this: women are regarded as more suitable for community care than men, who are more likely to be regarded as 'mad' and 'dangerous'.

Scull, A. (2011) *Madness: A Very Short Introduction*. Oxford: Oxford University Press.

Jaspers, K. ([1969] 1997) *General Psychopathology*. Baltimore: Johns Hopkins University Press.

psychoses severe and incapacitating mental illnesses or disorders that are thought to have emotional and/or organic origins and that can fundamentally disrupt cognition, perception, behaviour, the ability to manage and/or sustain relationships and social functioning generally. Distortions of reality and delusions together with auditory or visual hallucinations are also sometimes features of some psychotic condi-tions.

As with other mental health problems, psychoses are best thought of as clusters of symptoms that can be more or less prominent with indi-viduals experiencing distress. The following typologies are indicative:

the public sphere and at the same time making it less obviously 'public' as public meetings and especially political gatherings went into sharp decline. By the first decade of the twenty-first century the physical aspect of the public sphere had once again been turned on its head with the spread of the internet and the web. Whether the internet has facilitated dialogue and the coming together of people to deliberate and inform or whether it only further constructs walls between individuals as each retreat to the online 'communities' with which they feel most at home and which echo their own views most completely is a question that social scientists are still wrestling with.

Social scientists investigating the functioning of the public sphere have generally found that it is dominated by bias and power. Nancy Fraser, for example, in her exploration of the changing nature of the public sphere, criticizes the conventional assumption that 'confinement of public life to a single, overarching public sphere is a positive and desirable state of affairs'. Fraser contends that, in unequal, stratified societies it is more realistic to talk about contests between competing publics that allow for a greater range of participation. She points to subordinate groups such as women, workers, people of colour and gays and lesbians as forming alternative publics that she calls 'subaltern counterpublics' in which members of subordinated social groups 'invent and circulate counterdiscourses'.

Understanding the distinction between public and private spheres and the sphere open to state action is critical for social workers, particularly now that the boundaries between the three spheres are blurring. Sexuality and religion, for example, are generally still regarded as matters private to the individual or family yet debates over gay marriage and gay rights generally indicate how easily the boundary between what is private and public can be overrun. Parenting styles were once firmly within the private sphere but some parenting behaviours are now openly questioned in the public domain – in relation, say, to diet and obesity, physical chastisement, school attendance or whether child rearing is best done by one or two parents.

Social workers have historically worked at the boundary between the private and public spheres with responsibility often to probe what is generally deemed private by the wider public. With the increasing complexity and uncertainty over what is public and what is private, sensitivity in this role and an understanding of where the boundary actually lies is an important element of the work.

Fraser, N. (1990) Rethinking the public sphere: a contribution to the critique of actually existing democracy, *Social Text*, 25/26: 56–89.

punishment a social process, usually 'officially' sanctioned, by which
individuals are required to experience, either voluntarily or more usually compulsorily, a penalty or sanction or treatment because they have
committed some crime or misdemeanour.

Various theorists have identified some key prerequisites or criteria
that must be met for punishment to be, in any sense, legitimate. These
include:

(1) the punishment must be the response to a violation, 'evil' or some
     unpleasantness committed on a victim;
(2) the punishment must relate to an offence;
(3) the punishment must be of an offender who committed the offence;
(4) the punishment must involve *personal agency* (there must be
     intent) and not be an accident or some unintended consequence
     of an action;
(5) the punishment must be imposed by a legitimate authority, where
     the authority arises out of a system of rules that are widely known
     and understood.

Most writers concerned with social philosophy distinguish between
four major themes in relation to the justification of punishment as a
necessary feature for all civilized societies; the first relates to retribution and the others to various utilitarian notions. The key strands are:

- *Retribution* – this view is not interested in the consequences of
  punishment, but only that an individual has committed a crime
  and that she or he must experience some discomfort or hurt. The
  biblical notion of retribution as 'it is fitting' simply reasserts this
  basic rationale for punishment. In one very particular formulation
  by the philosopher and social work ethicist Bernard Bosanquet, the
  criminal is considered to have 'a right to punishment'; the penalty
  is owed and punishment needs no other justification.
- *Prevention* – this view relates to contriving arrangements that will
  make it impossible for the criminal to offend again. The idea of
  'preventive detention' encapsulates this view, but it only applies
  in full if a criminal is put to death, imprisoned for life, deported
  where possible or perhaps, under earlier regimes, transported. It
  cannot apply to circumstances where the criminal at some stage is
  returned to the community, unless it is assumed that repetition of
  the crime is unlikely.
- *Deterrence* – here the key idea is that punishment deters potential
  offenders by punishing actual offenders. This form of punishment
  is, in effect, a threat to others; a threat that fails, should anyone
  subsequently commit an offence. There is sometimes an implied
  notion that the punishment of the individual offender was harsher

than it might have been had it not been that the judge 'wanted to send a message' to others who were 'considering' criminal actions.

- *Rehabilitation* – here the key objective is to help offenders to become 'reformed' characters; that is perhaps to show remorse, have some kind of insight into the consequences of their criminal activity for the victims and perhaps their own family, but, crucially, to accept that their acts were wrong and to resolve not to offend again.

In the contemporary criminal justice system in the UK, these four justifications for punishment appear in varying guises in the general framework underpinning sentencing options. For example, the Probation Service practice is currently informed by a four-tier response to offenders: the first tier is wholly focused on punishment; the second on punishment and help; the third upon punishment, help and change; and the fourth on punishment, help, change and control. The punishment element involves some measure of retribution; the help element refers to acknowledging that offenders might need assistance with accommodation, work or preparation for work opportunities, advice on benefits and other practical assistance; change refers to specific interventions to help to, say, address the violent behaviour of a man with a track record of abusing his partner or to confront and deconstruct the behaviour of sex offenders; and finally, control refers to putting in place measures to confine, monitor closely and constrain offenders.

Some take the view that rehabilitation should include an element of *reparation* as an essential component of *restorative* justice. Reparation could include restoring matters to the pre-offence situation so that stolen goods might be given back to the owners, that anything 'criminally damaged' would be repaired or restored to their original condition by the offender or financial penalties would compensate the victim for damages. Reparation might also include meeting with victims, hearing their account of the repercussions for them as a result of the offence(s) and apologising in person for the injuries caused; in a sense trying to establish a 'moral discussion' with offenders. Another form of reparation includes an element of 'community payback' such as clearing litter, decorating communal buildings or working with vulnerable people needing various forms of assistance. Some take the view that community payback should include an element of 'shaming' by requiring offenders to wear, say, bright clothing that would indicate that these are offenders working in the community.

Other key contemporary debates in relation to punishment include the seriousness of crimes and proportionality in relation to sentencing and human rights; issues that are clearly closely related. The social construction of crime is evident in a changing landscape where domestic violence, for example, can now be considered a crime, whereas not many decades ago, it was not; homosexuality was previously considered a crime and now is not. Seriousness is also a matter of debate with, for example, white-collar crime routinely being treated more leniently than, say, burglary where the value of goods or money stolen is similar. Similarly, feminists argue that crimes against women in general, but sexual crimes in particular, are not regarded as seriously as they ought to be and that given that conviction rates are also very low, this amounts to compelling testimony that the criminal justice system's notion of punishment is systemically discriminatory and that women's human rights are being compromised.

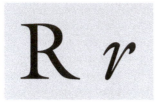

rational choice theory (RCT) is derived from economic theories of capitalism and argues that many elements of human behaviour can be understood by the wish to maximize benefits at the least cost. RCT theories are convinced this rationality applies to many different kinds of decision, even those that we would regard as falling outside any kind of economic calculation such as choosing a marriage partner or friends. RCT theorists have even studied and analysed religious adherence on these grounds.

In most areas of life, then, RCT assumes that humans make rational choices within the limits of their information and understanding, and view the range of options open to them on that basis. They weigh anticipated rewards against costs, including the **opportunity cost** of *not* taking some other course of action. Rewards are relatively scarce and limited in supply and can be anything which human beings desire and are willing to incur some cost to obtain. They may be subjective, diffuse and specific to the individual, such as peace and happiness, but that does not undermine the principle that people decide essentially on a benefits versus costs calculation. As rational choosers humans implicitly construct explanations of how rewards can be obtained and costs minimized. These are evaluated on the basis of the results they yield: the most beneficial are retained and the others discarded.

reference group a social group, institution or other social category which individuals identify and use to compare and evaluate themselves and their social circumstances.

It is possible for individuals already to be members of the reference groups (sociologists call them *membership group*s) that are important to them; or the reference group is one with which they identify and aspire to join or associate with more closely in some way.

Some commentators argue that the concept of a reference group lacks precision but it nevertheless seems to offer some interesting insights that are relevant to social work. Pertinent examples are:
- The role of team leader is critical in providing a positive and enabling environment for social workers. Team leaders should have the needs of the individual team members, the frontline workers,

as their primary focus, ensuring crucially that they are offered the necessary support to deliver an effective service. Allocating a reasonable workload is one very important dimension of a team manager's responsibilities. Yet ambitious team managers can choose to associate themselves with more senior management (a group that they perhaps wish to join at some stage) and thus be more inclined to do their bidding, say, by distributing work to workers who are already under pressure because all cases must be allocated and have a named 'responsible' worker. Alternatively, a team manager who identifies more closely with frontline workers may not be prepared to allocate work and might either request additional resources (more workers) or have the cases sit on her or his desk until such times as a worker becomes available – maybe offering to deal only with emergencies themselves that arise on unallocated cases.

- The concept of *relative deprivation* is useful in trying to understand how people react to feelings of being disadvantaged within a general framework of what might be dubbed *reasonable expectations.* Here the core notion is that an individual's objective position, say, as a member of the lower middle class, might be at odds with their aspirations and that they still feel that they are at some distance from the reference groups they identify with, leading them to feel that they are relatively deprived. This kind of reasoning has been associated with both morbidity and mortality in studies of health inequalities. Researchers have been surprised to find that health outcomes for the highest ranks of the civil service were better than those of middle-ranking civil servants, the surprise arising out of the notion that the middle-ranking individuals still enjoyed a good salary and employment conditions that were sufficient to support a good standard of living. The key explanation here might well be to identify the extent to which people are exposed to difference and the extent to which they *feel* difference. Life in mass society with daily exposure to the 'good life' in consumer terms through, for example, TV advertisements may lead to disaffection whereas people living in rural Wales are rarely exposed to such marked social differences leading, perhaps, to a level of greater satisfaction with their place in the general scheme of things.

- In relation to the idea of *class consciousness*, Marx was entirely aware of the lack of class awareness in the minds of many working-class people and of the mechanisms by which the ruling class (bourgeoisie) managed to inhibit the growth of such consciousness, sowing division within the working class, encouraging status differences and the purchasing of goods associated with status

differences. Being interested in status differences, and consciousness of status groups (reference groups) of which individuals were
either members or sought to join, are key mechanisms by which the
working class is persuaded to be distracted from recognizing class
realities.

religion from the Latin *relegere*, to bring together, to harvest or
to gather in, and *religare*, to tie or bind together. Religion can be
defined broadly as a system of beliefs, symbols and practices that are
shared and considered sacred for a group of adherents. The attempt
to understand religion and its relationship to society was one of the
driving forces that brought sociology into being in the first place and
major figures among social theorists and sociologists have explored its
meaning and significance including Émile Durkheim and Max Weber.
Sigmund Freud also investigated religion from a psychoanalytic point
of view. This preoccupation has continued right through the twentieth
and into the twenty-first century – as the competing trends of **secularization** and the revival of religion and its place in public life have
stimulated a fresh sense of urgency to understand what is going on.

There are immediate difficulties in defining religion from a social science standpoint since it refers to a reality that is unable to be explored
in any empirical or scientific way. Sociologists have resolved these
issues by investigating religion as a collective and symbolic search for
meaning, particularly focusing on ritual and symbolism, and on the
devotional practices of the religious communities themselves. In his *The
Elementary Forms of Religious Life*, first published towards the end of
the nineteenth century, Durkheim noted the distinction between 'the
sacred' and 'the profane'. The sacred, from the Latin *sacer* meaning
forbidden, is that which 'the profane must not and cannot touch with
impunity'; it is an area that is forbidden or restricted from common use.
Religion he defined as 'a unified system of beliefs and practices relative
to sacred things, that is . . . things set apart and forbidden – beliefs and
practices which unite in one single moral community'. To gain access to
the sacred, Durkheim argued, requires 'abstention – the gate of access
to achieving sanctity through such things as costly renunciations of
the world of attachments'. 'Man' he wrote 'cannot approach his god
intimately while still bearing the marks of his profane life.'

While Durkheim was interested in the social functions of religion and particularly in their impact on social cohesion, Max Weber
examined the modes of religious belief – which he divided broadly
between asceticism and mysticism – and undertook comparative and
historical studies on the impact of belief on economics and society.
In *The Protestant Ethic and the Spirit of Capitalism* ([1904] 2001) he

examined how religious practices were taken out of the monastery and into the ordinary household. From there Protestant piety spread into the daily routine of commercial life with meticulous habits of accounting and willingness to postpone reward and gratification.

Social theorists in the late twentieth century have been heavily influenced by Durkheim's and Weber's analysis of religion while making some adjustments to their thought. Social scientists still draw on the concept of the sacred which continues to describe the signature formations of new and traditional religious groups. But with a bow to **post-modernism** some argue further that a religious group is a kind of linguistic construct that then appears to convert specific events or physical items into the foundation of belief. These then take on the appearance of 'objectivity', so deeply sacred that they become fixed and unalterable, such as female circumcision, 'Remember Kosovo' campaigns for Serbian nationalists, the Western Wall for Jews, and headscarves for Muslim women.

Social work's relationship to religion is ambivalent. Social work itself emerged from a Christian context in the later nineteenth century, blending Protestant social thinking with philosophical idealism. One of its earliest theorist-practitioners in the nineteenth century, Octavia Hill, was influenced by Christian socialist thinking (socialism did not yet have its twentieth-century meaning), as were many of the founders of the Charity Organization Society. The pioneers of children's homes, such as George Stephenson, were also inspired by Church of England or Methodist theology.

But as social work strove to achieve professional status in the first third of the twentieth century it distanced itself from its Christian and charitable roots and sought to develop distinctive methods of working with users for which training was required – chiefly casework. In the course of this, it learned to examine human motivation purely in terms of behaviour and personality. Thus while social workers held to a variety of beliefs (or none) throughout much of the twentieth century, their work and their organizations were secular. In addition, there was little research or professional interest in religion, either as an aspect of users' lives or as part of practice for much of the time. As late as the 1980s the discussion among social work academics centred on the distance between what was regarded as a thoroughly secular, scientific profession and the world of faith. There was ambivalence on both sides of the religion–social work divide: some social workers were personally religious but believed social workers should stay away from religious discussions with users, while believers outside social work often supported social work ideals even though it was secular in its orientation.

This began to change as social work responded to what has been called the 'third great awakening' in the 1990s – the upsurge of religious commitment which has taken various forms across the globe, from a more vigorous and politicized Islam to the rapid spread of evangelical Protestantism and Catholicism in the developing world, from the rise of Hindu nationalism in India to renewed calls in both Britain and the US to regard both as Christian nations.

Social work's lack of knowledge of religion and its secular orientation was seen to impede understanding of the beliefs and faiths of service users and to obscure how social workers could explicitly introduce matters of faith and **spirituality** into their work with users. Beginning roughly in the mid-1990s with small research projects and some general discussion, social work's reawakened interest in religion had by 2010 resulted in a flow of books, articles and research findings that seek to shed further light on how practitioners should conduct themselves in matters of faith.

Durkheim, E. (2008) *Elementary Forms of Religious Life*, edited by Mark Cladis. Oxford: Oxford University Press.

Weber, M. (2001) *The Protestant Ethic and the Spirit of Capitalism* (Routledge Classics). London: Routledge.

research design the overall plan for any research presenting key information about the research 'problem', the aims and objectives of the research, the methods to be used, a rationale for the use of such methods, relevant detail on the size and composition of any sample, the possible benefits of the research for social work policies and practice and a consideration of research ethics. In addition, it is possible that additional issues will be presented for consideration including the use of, for example, *triangulation* – that is, combining several methods of social research in the hope that any findings will be confirmed by the use of, say, both quantitative and qualitative techniques.

research methods systematic methods of social investigation to try to understand the nature of social behaviour and of social problems. For social work, social research can be used to inform ways of intervening with evidence-based practice and effective social policies.

The range of methods for social research in the social sciences is wide ranging. Established methods include quantitative methods such as surveys, interviews (both using predominantly structured questionnaires), cross-sectional studies and panel studies. Qualitative techniques include case studies/histories and life studies; documentary research; observation and participant observation. Qualitative data can also be gathered by the use of questionnaires where many or most of the questions are 'open'. Additional useful techniques include sequence analysis, content analysis, secondary analysis and triangulation.

Surveys can involve observations of people's behaviour but are most often conducted through the use of prepared questionnaires for interviews conducted face to face, on the telephone, by post or possibly over the net. Potential problems include poor survey design; the use of inappropriate, obscure or technical language; inadequate interviewing skills on the part of interviewer; and the kind of sample and sample size that are not 'fit for purpose'. Structured questionnaires, especially in their use of closed questions, will only be effective if the formulation of questions is the result of careful preparation including pilot studies. Another problem is the possibility of there being social distance between interviewer and the interviewee or a felt power imbalance. Questionnaires administered by an interviewer do at least offer the opportunity for clarification to be offered if a respondent appears not to understand a question. For questionnaires sent through the post, no such opportunities are available. In constructing questionnaires it is useful to note the following:

- Locate any sensitive questions to the latter part of a questionnaire in the hope that some kind of rapport has been established between respondent and interviewer in relation to non-contentious questions asked earlier.
- The use of closed questions (asking about a person's age, occupation, how long they have been at their current address) or open questions (how do you feel about asylum seekers coming in to the country?) depends upon the nature of the research topic or problem. If the problem/topic is relatively unrehearsed then it is likely that the use of open questions will be more productive.
- Some researchers have found it useful to adopt the 'split half' technique where some questions are in effect asked twice in a slightly different way but where there is a reasonable expectation, if respondents are being honest, that they will provide similar answers. Comparing the 'split halves' will help to determine whether respondents were focused and not giving ad hoc and inconsistent answers.

Postal questionnaires are thought to be most effective if they are primarily designed to capture hard data with many or a majority of closed questions. They are also cheaper than questionnaires administered by interviewers. But postal questionnaires are notorious for achieving low response rates, often as low as 10 percent or less.

Panel studies are a form of longitudinal study where the focus is upon changes in the attitudes of a defined cohort or sample of people. Such studies, usually using surveys, are suitable where the focus is upon changes over time, say, in attitudes to education if the focal group have shared an experience but where some are from a particular

background and others another background; for example, where all
children have experienced the Sure Start programme but one group
has gone on to schools that differ markedly in performance. A further
example might be comparing the outcomes for 'looked-after children'
who all experienced the care system – but one group kept in touch
with the after-care teams for longer than the other group. In general
terms, panel studies offer the opportunity to identify the influence
of critical life events for a cohort of people sharing the same experience or being of the same age or sharing some other common social
characteristic.

Cross-sectional studies are where the focus of any survey tries to capture the same experience for a cross-section of any society or focal social
group. For example, the annual *Household Expenditure Survey* provides
information on household expenditure for all social classes, revealing that
for poorer sections of the population very high proportions of income
are devoted to housing costs, fuel and food and that, as a consequence,
funds available for holidays are either scant or non-existent.

Secondary analysis involves the analysis of data sets (often official
data sets arising out of government-sponsored research such as the census or the *Family Expenditure Survey*) in relation to hypotheses or questions that the original compiler of the data set was not concerned about.

Case studies/histories and *life studies* relate to attempts to compile
detailed histories or biographies about individuals but, perhaps, with a
focus upon particular events or experiences. For example, a researcher
might be investigating the backgrounds of women who have been
in abusive relationships as adults and might be particularly interested
in these women's childhood experiences of abuse in their families of
origin. Should these case studies reveal some patterns a researcher may
then want to use other methods, a survey perhaps to find out whether
material revealed in a small number of case studies/histories were
in fact commonplace and a key feature in the backgrounds of many
abused women.

Documentary research involves investigations that use paper sources
as the raw material; such paper sources could include personal diaries, correspondence, newspapers and magazines, posters, leaflets and
written programmes, official government reports, Hansard, minutes
of meetings, electronic sources, local records of all kinds (records of
births, deaths, marriages and divorces) including parish records, land
registry and recordings of TV and radio broadcasts. Although some
documents are the result of systematic research (for example analyses
of census data), most will be devised for other purposes. For these
documents the key issues are:

- authenticity – documents have sometimes been found to be entirely false and fabricated; for example, a book purporting to be Hitler's diaries;
- credibility – is the document in any sense a reasonable account of an event or is it so skewed because of political or religious convictions that it has to be discounted?
- representativeness – is the document representative of the range of all available documents exploring the same issues or problems? The criteria of credibility and representativeness both acknowledge that no document is entirely objective and that all or most documents will be to some extent partial;
- meaning – here the key questions are about whether a document is of the era we are interested in and whether it can be fully understood. The latter refers to whether the document can be 'interpreted' accurately to determine the social and cultural significance of it. Here, the skills of the researcher will be to focus on the cultural and social context to unravel insights into contemporary narratives and discourses and for this content analyses will be necessary.

Observation and *participant observation* has been found to be a useful form of research although it is not without its difficulties and may, in some circumstances, be flawed and perhaps even compromised. The study of gangs in the US (*Street Corner Society*, 1943) by Whyte is now regarded as a classic. Whyte lived in an Italian community for over three years and was able to study at close quarters the behaviour of an immigrant Italian community and gangs within their midst. Social anthropologists also use what they have dubbed ethnography, a form of participant observation; in essence a detailed written account of the societies/communities they have lived in together with their attempts at 'interpreting' what these descriptions 'mean' together with their cultural significance. Researchers who use participant observation claim that the observed cease to be influenced by the observer after some time if the researcher plays a low-profile role and offers some empathy for the behaviour of the people being observed. Others have argued that the observer inevitably affects the behaviour of the observed. (For example, the *Hawthorne effect* – a study of behaviour in a factory that was ostensibly about the effects of improved lighting on performance, but changes in performance were found to be the result of the workers being observed by a researcher.) In other circumstances, it is possible that observations may involve criminal behaviour and put researchers in a difficult position ethically.

A particular form of participatory social enquiry has been labelled *emancipatory research*, sometimes associated with action research. Here the involvement of service users in identifying the research problem, its aims and objectives and in the delivery of the research programme, and the fact that the researcher keeps in touch with the service users throughout the research project, is seen as key. The work of Paolo Freire and his concept of 'conscientization' has been influential in the emergence of this kind of research paradigm where the researcher is in some senses 'accountable' to the service users who have an interest in the research problem and, in a sense, are in a unique position to decide on the efficacy of any findings.

Sequence analysis is research that is focused upon the sequence of events and whether that sequence is a necessary feature of that person's or group's experience and/or whether an alternative sequence is possible or even desirable. For example, it is known that high-achieving women who take time out to have children and to raise them, on their return to work, often find they have to accept lower status posts than those they occupied before they took maternity leave. Such a sequence is justified by some employers on the grounds that the women have to 'catch up' with key features of the industry they have been out of for some years before they can become fully operational. Others argue that the comparatively low-status women have to endure on their return to work is simply a reflection of patriarchy and the willingness of employers to exploit able women. Sequencing analyses should be able to unravel what happens in practice in the 'return to work' scenario and whether such possibly discriminatory behaviour by employers is justified.

Content analysis involves the close examination of written or recorded data to count the number of references to a particular idea or theme to determine its frequency. The data might concern the answers given by respondents to open-ended questions in exploratory interviews, analyses of themes that recur in the press or on a particular TV channel, or the propaganda disseminated by political parties. Content analysis has to contend with a number of methodological problems. For example, it is possible that the omission of themes or ideas in any narrative may be more interesting and revealing than the presence of other themes. Further, there can be problems with regard to the classification of data. Is a remark about the undeserving poor similar to another remark about poverty being the result of individual weakness? Despite these problems, content analysis can be an extremely effective empirical tool helping researchers to uncover how people really feel about their worlds.

Triangulation concerns the use of different methods of social research as a means of increasing the levels of confidence in any findings. For example, if an idea emerges from a few exploratory qualitative interviews using a wide-ranging set of open questions (say, about people's belief in capital punishment) and these issues are then explored with a number of surveys of particular segments of the population which confirm these findings and later in a content analysis of letters and emails sent to the prime minister, then it is probably quite safe to conclude that a majority of citizens in the UK are in favour of capital punishment. Replication of research findings, where researchers repeat other researchers' studies using the same research design, can also be a key part of triangulation.

right, right wing the range of political, social and economic orientations on the right of the political spectrum (see **left, left wing**) associated with conservatism, fascism and **neo-liberalism**. As with the left, this span of orientations is broad and often further broken down into far right, right wing and centre right.

A breakdown of the spectrum of the right is as follows:

- *Fascism* – the most extreme variant promoting hatred and violence toward specified minorities or ethnic or racialized groups; calls for national renewal on the basis of some superior cultural and nationalist traits that its members embody; an element of street-based violence and intimidation; trade unions are viewed as disloyal to the nation; people with disability are considered genetically inferior and a danger to national strength. Fascism most notably came to power in Italy and Germany in the 1920s and 1930s based on violent oppression of trade unionists, the Jews, Roma and people with disability. There are more recent, racist movements that have developed small but violent fascist parties across Europe and the US displaying hatred for foreigners and a willingness to engage in street violence in the name of a superior 'race' which they embody.

- *Conservative parties* – often a blend of politics that combines Christian, old aristocratic lineages, small and large business entrepreneurs, monarchists and assorted traditionalists as well as the *far right*. The perspective is itself wide, embracing a range of 'social conservatives' – opposed to abortion, marriage for gays, lone-parent families – and 'economic conservatives' (or **neo-liberals**) who believe fervently in the free market being allowed to take its course, within a regime of low taxes and vastly reduced government expenditure. The politics of this segment of the right was relatively moderate for 30 years after the Second World War – in France, Germany, Italy, Britain and the US – often headed by genial, avuncular leaders such as Harold Macmillan, prime minister in Britain and Dwight Eisenhower, president of the US in the 1950s. Both governments were conservative yet maintained highly progressive tax structures which redistributed income and supported the welfare state. Their policies produced the greatest levels of income equality – far greater than today.

This broad consensus around moderate conservatism has entirely broken down in the last 30 years with the moderates in retreat as 'far right' positions have come to dominate conservatism following the electoral victories of Margaret Thatcher in 1979 in the UK and Ronald Reagan in 1980 in the US. This is most evident in the US where the Republican Party by 2010 had been completely captured by elements totally and irredeemably opposed to public spending and to any role for government in fostering national prosperity and well-being. The Conservative-dominated coalition government elected in 2010 in Britain does not have the same degree of hostility to taxes but its policies to tackle national debt entail draconian cuts in public sector spending that reflect some of this far-right thinking.

- *Centre-right* – embodies some of the moderate social and eco-nomic positions of the older conservatism. It broadly supports the notion of the 'social market' economy, namely that markets need to be regulated with the aim of offering reasonable levels of welfare benefits and improving social mobility. Trade unions should be regarded as partners and incorporated within decision-making structures of companies while firms have responsibilities toward their workers to maintain and improve conditions, hours and wages. Often it is centre-right thinking that is associated with continental European conservative parties, accounting for the dif-ference between the 'Anglo-American' model of capitalism and the European 'social model' of capitalism.

There are some points, however, on which all elements of the right agree:
- a limit on trade union rights to organize and call strikes;
- a belief in unequal endowments in intelligence, motivation and physical strength;
- the belief that inequality is a spur to economic activity; it promotes wealth creation by rewarding entrepreneurs, and underpins eco-nomic elites;
- support for tax structures that favour the wealthy as 'wealth creators';
- limits on the immigration of groups they consider to be antagonis-tic toward the national culture;
- reduction of the size of government and in particular a paring back of welfare spending and tighter criteria for claiming benefits;
- they regard the public sector as constricting the free market and aim to deregulate and cut red tape.

rights claims to treatment, benefit or protection that an individual can make on the basis of a law, code of practice or declaration.

There are several kinds of right. *Political and civil rights* both protect citizens of a particular country from the arbitrary use of power by state authorities and entitle them to undertake certain **positive actions** that enable them to exert some influence, however nominal, in the political process and in influencing public opinion. *Social and economic rights* lay claims to publicly provided goods and services; these rights are not dependent on whether an individual is eligible for them or in some way is deserving. *Human rights* claim a universal status and are usually framed in global terms pertaining to all peoples. *Procedural rights* lay claim to giving people a fair hearing before any decision is made regarding a social benefit or service, such as setting a level of an individual's income support, meeting the special educational needs of a child with a learning disability or taking a child into local authority care.

Those political and civil rights that protect a citizen against abuse of state power include the right of free speech, the right to vote, the right to trial by jury, the right to personal security and the right not to be discriminated against on the basis of race. Such rights were established in law, often as the consequence of considerable struggle, from the seventeenth century onwards in Britain. They are not universal, neither can they be assumed to be permanently irreversible, as recent discussions about the right to silence of the accused in criminal trials indicate.

Social and economic rights include the right to medical care, the right to social security, the right to vocational training and the right to housing. The concept of social and economic rights does not enlist the same consensus as political and civil rights. There is fierce argument as to whether they should exist as rights at all. In general, conservative commentators think that, because such claims involve a call on resources such as money and the time of those who would deliver the services or benefits, they cannot be considered as rights because the resources needed to provide them may not always be available and the concept of a right as an unconditional, automatic entitlement would be undermined. Others at the political centre and on the left argue that the difference between civil rights and social rights is not as great as it seems because they both depend on a sufficient level of resources being available. The right to personal security, for example, requires an effective police force and the right to a fair trial requires court time and the provision of legal aid.

The best instances of global human rights provision are found in United Nations human rights declarations regarding, for example, the right to work, education, social security and health care. Nations may have such rights enshrined in their laws, but most do not. In practice, they are often ignored even by countries that have assented to particular UN conventions. They continue to exert influence, however, by their claim to universality and through the work of many organizations, both governmental and non-governmental, such as the UN Commission on Human Rights and the World Court.

Procedural rights have a broad political consensus behind them. Increasingly, they are seen by the public as the most effective way for individuals to guard against arbitrary decisions by government bureaucracies, including those of the local authority. This trend has important implications for social work and social care. The right of a person to participate in the process of defining his or her own needs, the right to be told about the worker's role and powers in a specific situation, the right to give explicit consent or to refuse intervention (except where the worker has statutory protective duties), the right of people to receive information in their first language, the right to written agreements as the basis of any service provided are all powerful examples of procedural rights affecting how welfare professionals undertake their work with users.

The incorporation of the European Convention of Human Rights into British law came through the Human Rights Act 1998. Historically, the European Convention on Human Rights has its roots in the philosophical tradition of universal rights that stretches back to the Enlightenment of the eighteenth century and the French Revolution, although formal adoption of the Universal Declaration of Human Rights actually came through the United Nations in December 1948.

There is continuous and evolving discussion on the place of rights in social policy and social work. Commentators on both left and right sometimes argue that an overemphasis on rights or 'rights talk' leads to 'entitlement thinking', that is that a person or group of people will assume they have a 'right' to a source of income, service or other privilege while ignoring the responsibilities that go with it. The notion of parental rights offers an instructive example in which there are those who argue that simply being the parent of a child entitles the adult to a certain level of mastery over that child without acknowledging any explicit responsibilities in providing for the child.

Ife, J. (2001) *Human Rights and Social Work: Toward a Rights-Based Practice*. Cambridge: Cambridge University Press.

risk the chance that the health or development of a person may be damaged by certain conditions, natural disasters or actions of others.

Care professionals use the phrase 'at risk' to indicate that a service user is exposed to some source of harm and that possibly some protective measures should be taken. These sources of harm to a service user may be external, such as assault by someone else, or arise from the client's own habits, such as not feeding himself or herself. For example, a 'child at risk' is regarded as vulnerable to physical or sexual abuse by one or more people or to other sources of harm through parental neglect. What is rarely stated is the probability that the child will suffer some harm. This is the drawback of the phrase; it is used widely but with little agreement over the actual chance that a service user deemed at risk will come to some harm. Care professionals also use the word in the sense of 'risk-taking', which means making a conscious decision to put something at stake in order to make possible a worthwhile gain or benefit for the client.

(See also **risk assessment**.)

risk assessment   assessing the chances of some harm occurring to a service user or other person.

Risk assessment means carefully weighing the chances that particular forms of harm might or will happen to a service user or be caused by a service user in a given situation. Analysing the degree of risk is necessary, for example, when discharging from psychiatric hospital a person who has previously been violent, when returning a child home from care who has been physically abused by his or her parents, or when leaving in his or her home an elderly confused person who refuses to turn on the heat in the winter. In each instance, the practitioner has to try to gauge the chance of harm occurring against the benefits. It is often necessary to accept a certain level of risk, because to try to minimize risk has its own costs and can be detrimental to the interests of a service user. Although the risk could be reduced or eliminated in each of the cases above, to do that would require taking action that would be highly restrictive for the person concerned and might itself present different risks to the service user's health or development. The person in difficulty, if not released, could become institutionalized, the child placed long term with foster parents would suffer from loss of family contacts, the older person if removed to a home could become severely disoriented.

With risk assessment, the care professional must be clear as to the specific benefits and harms that may result from proposed action. Increasingly, this is a joint task, discussed with the service user and the service user's family and carers. After both the benefits and harms are itemized, some attempt must be made to judge the probability or likelihood of each occurring. One of the most difficult examples of risk assessment concerns the level of danger to a physically or sexually abused child if left at home. To undertake risk assessment it is important to know precisely what the nature of the abuse was, whether or not it was committed by a member of the family and what the likelihood is of its happening again. Both the severity of the abuse and the probability of its happening again are important considerations. Often the assessment will be difficult, since it must try to balance the possibility of immediate harm against the long-term harm the child could suffer if removed from home for a lengthy period of time.

Risk assessment is also a key part of the health and safety policies, especially 'lone working policies' – when a practitioner is working alone in potentially threatening situations – of health and social work agencies. Should a service user have a history of aggressive or even violent behaviour social workers will need to devise strategies to minimize harm to themselves and others. Working in pairs, involving the police where necessary and making decisions about where service users are to be met are all examples of risk assessments in everyday practice.

As resources available to social work agencies become more constrained it has been argued that services become wholly focused upon the 'management of risk' and decreasingly on therapeutic interventions and 'healing'. The pressures on social work agencies to manage risk effectively is clear evidence of social work being asked to devise technical solutions to what are essentially political problems.

risk society the shorthand term indicating the degree to which all aspects of risk permeate and drive society at large. The origin of the phrase stems from the work of the German sociologist Ulrich Beck who published his path-breaking book *Risk Society: Towards a New Modernity* in 1986. Its translation into English in 1992 initiated a wide-ranging discussion on the impact of risk in contemporary society, a discussion that continues to this day, marking Beck's book as one of the most influential works of social analysis of the late twentieth century.

Risk, Beck argues, is no longer confined to the sense of personal threat that historically defined the word – the risks in childbirth or sea travel, coming down with the plague, being a victim of crime. This kind of risk was understood by individuals and directly perceptible by them, albeit often perceived as beyond human control and subject to fate. The risks today typically escape individual perception and are beyond the powers of individual calculation based on their everyday knowledge – global warming, corruption of the food chain, financial collapse, pollution of the oceans or the air we breathe. These arise from physical and chemical formulas obscure to the public, such as toxins in food or radiation, that are essentially uninsurable. They are global rather than national and their impact rolls through all social divisions such as class and gender. What limited understanding the public have of such risks actually comes from within the very organizations and institutions tasked with managing and controlling those risks. The magnitude of these risks therefore is a direct function of social systems and is dependent on the social relations with those systems. The actual *primary* risk arises from dependency upon these organizations and their staff who are remote and inaccessible to those most affected by the specific risks in question – the public.

Beck's concept of *reflexive modernization* suggests that professional agencies and political authorities have to confront the widespread impact of risk across many dimensions, a task fraught with complexity and often producing unintended social and environmental consequences that only compound the problem. In this process, he recognizes that the knowledge of experts and scientists of regulatory institutions is not the only knowledge on which to base decisions but that there are social and situational issues to address that require negotiations between different forms of knowledge held by people other than scientists and based on different social or moral identities. In this and later writings, Beck suggests that the risk dynamic undercuts the public's respect for technical competence so that scientific reasoning itself comes under challenge. In the wake of this, a broader political morality emerges, one less beholden to rationality and scientific expertise. To accommodate the tensions inherent in all decision-making regarding risk requires examining the discourses of the non-intellectual lay public groups.

(See also **individualization, risk** and **risk assessment.**)

rite of passage the rituals, ceremonies and social processes involved in significant changes of social status over the **life course**.

Rites of passage are socially constructed and within societies liable to change over time. In many advanced industrial societies, there are some socially 'confusing' messages in relation to rites of passage. In the UK, it is legal to have sex at the age of 16, but in broad terms adulthood was achieved until relatively recently at the age of 21 and is now celebrated when young people become 18 years of age. In many respects, such a transition is partly symbolic because few young people aged 18 are in a position to sustain an independent life. Other widely recognized rites of passage include marriage (which may also mean leaving the *family of origin* for the first time), retirement and maybe acknowledging that one has a terminal illness or adjusting to the results of a really awful traffic accident that has resulted in serious impairments. Although coming of age and retirement are regarded as important changes, the significance for the individual may well vary substantially. For example, if someone's employment carried social status and their

work was an important, perhaps the most important, activity in their
lives, then the rite of passage that is retirement may well be hard to
adjust to and manage. However, for the person who disliked her or
his work, retirement could be experienced as liberation. And for both
individuals, the income now available to them is likely to have a bearing on how welcome the transition to retirement is regarded.

role theory   a role amounts to a set of expectations and obligations to
behave in a particular way, arising from a recognized social position,
function or status. Roles often carry with them specified rights
as well as obligations.

The theory has its origins in the language of the theatre: that is,
people play parts in everyday life in ways that resemble actors' performances. The difference is that social roles are learned so effectively
that a person *becomes* the role, such as daughter, son, soldier or doctor.
People identify themselves as the role, having learned and internalized
the script (expectations) through socialization processes. Thus roles
are a key part of a person's social identity. The theory has been sum-
marized in terms of people's self-concepts being based on how they
think others see them and these perceptions in turn being partially
based on the roles people occupy.

People can play many roles – for example, the role of parent,
worker and neighbour. People belong to *role sets*, that is, all the people
associated with the playing of a particular role. Some people have
many role sets; others have fewer, perhaps even as few as one (or none
in the case of hermits or recluses). Role sets can be quite separate or
they can overlap. For example, the people that a person relates to at
work might be called the 'work set' and the people a person relates
to in the community might be called the 'community set'. Sometimes there will be other people who are part of both sets such as a
neighbour or friend who also works in the same company. People can
occupy a number of sets and have varying status in each. So the vicar
might occupy a powerful position in the church but a lowly position
in the village cricket team. It is more likely that in urban contexts
people will occupy many different role sets than in rural locations.
And it is also more likely that in rural locations the same people will be
members of various role sets but with different statuses in each. The
analyses of roles and role sets in relation to particular individuals can
be helpful in understanding issues of social stress and social solidarity
or their lack.

Roles can conflict in two ways. First, there can be 'conflict within
a role' – for example, a team leader might be expected, by members
of the team, to protect them from further pressure if they are already

working to capacity, but the same team leader could be expected by senior management to get workers to work harder if there are many unallocated cases. Such role conflict is referred to as 'intra-role conflict'. The second kind of role conflict refers to conflicts between roles, that is, 'inter-role conflict' – an example might be a person having to work long hours (role of worker) who is very worried about his or her children (role of parent) but feels unable to alter the situation to meet the obligations of both roles. Roles can also usefully be seen as 'ascribed or achieved'. Here sociologists look at the issues of whether roles are given and are unchanged (as in some traditional societies) or might be developed in later life. Some interesting problems, for example, arise about how first-generation Asian children adapt to both traditional expectations of them from their families and those of their peers. Similarly, some roles might be considered to be tightly defined (specific) and others to be of a more general nature (diffuse). This typology of roles can be helpful in looking at the range of responsibilities that may be built into a role. A shift from a tightly defined role to something more diffuse, or the same process in reverse, can have interesting repercussions for the parties involved with the role-player. Some social workers, for example, feel constrained by the expectations of statutory social work where roles are closely defined and in some cases such individuals find that there is more room to experiment in social work roles in the voluntary sector.

Role theory has useful applications for social work in its attempts to make general sense of particular problems or situations (say, women's roles in modern Britain) and in its potential for helping to understand individual and family problems. Family therapy is an area of work that has developed and applied role theory. Family stress can arise when there are changes to roles that members have occupied for some time. A woman who returns to work after a period of being a full-time parent takes on a new role with the potential for experiencing inter-role conflict. A man who is made redundant may feel a loss of a key role and may find adjusting to the unemployed role very difficult. These kinds of changes can have a major impact on individual morale and family functioning.

Role theory places a strong emphasis on understanding the individual within the context of social networks and organizations. Thus the concept of role is useful in explaining why a person's behaviour changes when he or she changes social position. Hence if a person's social position is known, it may be possible broadly to predict his or her behaviour. The theory maintains that attitudes and beliefs are shaped by the role a person occupies and that a person tends to bring his or her attitudes into line with the expectations of the role. It follows that a change in role will lead to a change in attitudes. Role theory argues that people spend much of their lives participating in organizations and groups where they occupy distinct positions, formally or informally assigned. Role theory suggests that, in general, people conform to the expectations of others, and an individual is evaluated by others on his or her level of conformity to norms. However, some commentators have criticized role theory for seeming to imply that people are endlessly compliant to the expectations of those around them, and for suggesting that people receive information about role performance during socialization and interaction processes and then willingly set out to meet those expectations. Thus role theory, it is claimed, ignores the impact of individual determinants of behaviour, motivation and personality. The extent to which people are allowed to innovate with a role may be related to the pressures for conformity and tradition in a society or social institution. Clearly some people do exercise **agency** but that may only be permissible in a society that tolerates change.

rural–urban continuum the idea that rural and urban communities can be plotted on a continuum that charts differences in terms of community relations and social organization including role sets, more or less social isolation, the size and densities of populations, division of labour and differential rates of social change. Some writers have preferred the notion of a *folk–urban continuum* or of *traditional versus modern* societies.

A number of sociologists, including Tonnies, Sorokin, Maine and Parsons, have tried to identify significant differences in relation to a rural–urban continuum. For example, rural communities are more likely to have people working in multifaceted jobs, whereas people in urban centres are more likely to have specialized occupations. This is thought to be a reflection of the need for people in rural locations to be self-sufficient, especially agricultural workers in remote locations. Community solidarity is also thought to be greater in rural areas with a much greater degree of social support and reciprocity provided by extended family, neighbours and other community members. In urban locations, social networks are more likely to be fragmented or divided, with people working with a designated group of people, pursuing leisure activities with others, participating in political and community activities with yet others and living in particular areas with yet another group of people. Social status can also vary in each of these settings, so that a person may have, say, a low-status job, but occupy an important position in a trade union, political party or community organization.

It is possible for people to achieve much more in differing social groups because of greater fluidity in urban settings and fewer social constraints. Rural relationships are narrower where there is a much greater chance of enacting all roles within the same social group; what sociologists have called *role set*. Social status is also likely to be consistent or ascribed because of the social pressure implied by the force of tradition and more or less fixed social relationships. This is most evident in the now diminishing phenomenon of tied accommodation, where the landlord is also the employer, a position of considerable influence over an employee.

Some commentators have pointed out that the concepts of the rural and the urban are now more fluid. First, many people can live in the country and commute. Second, given the advances in technology, in particular IT, some people can work for urban companies and live in rural areas. Third, there is the influence of urban values on rural areas promoted by the media, especially television. Finally, there is much evidence of the spread of technology and of the capitalization of much rural economic activity. Small farms are disappearing to be absorbed by large companies applying highly mechanized and highly capitalized methods. There is also the possibility of rural values, of social and community supports and reciprocity, emerging in urban areas, especially where there are very settled communities and including ethnic minority communities.

The extent to which extended families are living in proximity and offering support to each other may be a critical factor in both rural and urban locations. Even if the rural and the urban are becoming less distinct, there are often still residual differences that have repercussions for how social and personal needs are manifested and how services are delivered. There is evidence to suggest that it is more likely that needs will be hidden or repressed in rural areas. It may well be easier to keep secrets in very remote areas with regard, for example, to child and adult abuse and domestic violence. Similarly, and paradoxically, given the alleged greater knowledge of neighbours in small communities, it is apparently more likely that community secrets will be kept rather than divulged to public social bodies.

If people in rural areas are poor or have limited resources, access to services can be a major problem. Rural public transport is scant in many areas. This can mean that the siting of health and social welfare services is critical if there can be no alternative to the service user having to travel to the service. It may be that services have to think in terms of an integrated package of providing services as well as the means to access them. Alternatively, or in addition, there must be some rationalization of location in order that health services can be had in the same location as social services, advice services, day or respite care and so on. Other services, such as advice services, have been offered by the development of outreach facilities, such as offering a service one day per week in a parish or village hall or the provision of a free telephone in a travelling library that can access advice from any number of public services. For very specialized needs, such as children with Asperger's syndrome or autism, it will be very hard to make the economic case to provide services locally. An interesting alternative model is to require one professional to take on a wider assessment role in order to provide information to service users about appropriate services or make referrals to such services. The delivery of health and social welfare services to rural areas demonstrates the overarching need to conduct periodic community audits and to require health and social welfare services to commit themselves to organizing services in the most cost-efficient way to meet identified needs.

S s

sample, sampling is a research device for selecting either individuals or households from a larger group, community or society. It is intended that the sample will be representative of the group, community or society so that any social characteristics revealed (in relation to, for example, attitudes, values or any variable such as income, household composition or expenditure) can reasonably be expected to represent the 'parent population'.

Sampling is widely used in social research because it is cheaper than studying whole populations, enabling closer and more detailed scrutiny of any social group so long as the sample is genuinely representative and can be said to have 'validity'. Validity rests upon two key factors. First, samples should be random; that is, every individual or household or social entity within a 'parent population' should have an equal chance of being selected. Second, the size of the sample should be appropriate to the size of the 'parent population'. Clearly samples of, say, just one person in a million are going to be less representative of a population than one person in a hundred. Most large government statistical reports (for example, the *Family Expenditure Survey*) rely upon samples of approximately 2000 to 3000 households as representative of the broader population in the UK, with apparently minimal 'sampling error' (because the sample is both random and sufficiently large).

Other kinds of sample include the following:

- *Stratified sampling* – dividing any parent population into strata such as ethnic or age groups, occupational groups/social classes, male/female or rural/urban to ensure that samples more accurately reflect the focus of any study and the size of the sample from each stratum is a more accurate reflection of the proportionate size of each stratum or sub-group relative to the whole 'parent population'.
- *Cluster sampling* – selecting from identifiable groups within any 'parent population'. For example, if the focus of the research was upon an investigation into possible associations between social class and racist attitudes, the researcher may decide that it will be fruitful to compare working-class attitudes in communities where there are

few members of ethnic minorities with communities where there
are high proportions of ethnic minorities. A key issue about representativeness could arise if these communities were not a reasonable reflection of the wider 'parent population', leading to some
misleading findings.

- *Quota sampling* – selecting a predetermined number of people or
  households from strata (social classes, communities, ethnic groups
  or whatever) from the 'parent population' but without attempting
  randomness. Quota samples are often adopted by market researchers or pollsters trying to research support for political parties
  during elections. Often they will stop people in town centres who
  appear, by virtue of their clothing, the quality of the car they are
  driving or the shops they emerge from, to be from a particular
  social class. Such measures can lead to sample error.

- *Snowball sampling* – a method for selecting respondents by starting
  with a few people sharing some particular social characteristics and
  then asking them if they know of more people who also have said
  characteristics. This method of sampling people from a 'parent
  population' is likely to be utilized where the topic being researched
  is especially sensitive or where a problem is quite rare and people
  with the problem are hard to trace. People with HIV/Aids were
  sometimes tracked down in this way as were women who had experienced abuse at the hands of the partners or ex-partners. Other
  groups that might fit this 'hard to trace' criterion might include
  illegal immigrants. Snowball sampling is almost always a form of
  investigation where qualitative rather than quantitative data are
  being collected.

scales, scaling methods for measuring attitudes, personality traits,
social status and similar social and cultural phenomenon, usually represented as a continuum ranging from one extreme of, say, an attitude
to the other extreme. For example, the Bogardus social distance scale
attempts to capture the range of feelings a person might have towards
'outsiders' ranging from being prepared, in principle, for the outsider to marry into the family (relative social intimacy) to an attitude
of wanting to exclude all outsiders from the country (relative social
distance).

Most scales rely upon responses given by people to questions or
statements. There are several methodological problems in relation to
the construction of scales. First, the issue being investigated should
involve just one dimension, theme or subject. To ask one question
which includes sub-clauses might confuse respondents if they were
inclined to, say, strongly agree to one clause and strongly disagree to

another. Second, it is important to try to check whether people are responding consistently. This can be done by using positive and negative versions of the same issue/statement so that opposite responses could reasonably be expected and the split half technique where the two halves of a questionnaire contain very similar items to see if people are answering in like fashion to each half.

Different kinds of scale have been found to be useful to researchers, viz:

*   *Likert scales* – typically use a five-point response scale comprising strongly agree, agree, don't know, disagree and strongly disagree. Questions used in an interview schedule or in a questionnaire often try to include a positive and negative question or statement regarding the same issue. For example, one positive question might be 'that all young people over the age of 16 should be given the vote' to be compared with a negative version of the same issue, namely 'that the vote should not be given to anyone under the age of 18 because they lack the necessary life experience to be able to make a mature assessment about politics'. Given these two statements it would be reasonable to expect a person answering strongly agree to the first question to answer strongly disagree to the second. Likert scales are useful in determining the strength of feeling(s) in respondents.
*   *Guttman scales* – a method for ordering statements that imply particular attitudes; suggesting that to agree with a particular statement will mean that respondents will also agree with all remaining or other statements of less intensity/emphasis. For example, using the Bogardus social distance scale it is assumed that if individuals would not like ethnic minority families to settle in their community, they can also be assumed not to like the idea of an ethnic minority family living next door or marrying into their family.

secularization the process through which industrial and post-industrial societies lose religious faith in the beliefs, practices and institutions that defined religious commitment.

Social theorists in the nineteenth and early twentieth century, especially Marx, Weber and Durkheim, all pointed to the decline in the overt demonstrations of religiosity and religious values in personal and public life. It was assumed that progressive secularization would take place when affluence and education eliminated the need for religion. The immense changes in family structures and social mores from the 1960s on only confirmed sociologists' thinking that the waning of religion was an inevitable social process. As evidence they pointed to the decline in church attendance, especially in the numbers who attend church weekly and the numbers of those who declare adherence to the principal religions.

Those espousing this secularization thesis argued that the advance of a rationalist, scientific view of nature, the earth and the cosmos explained how they actually function, not as the work of a deity but as a consequence of laws of nature. Other trends are also identified that contribute to secularization:

- cross-cultural influences that have broken the monopolies that specific faiths enjoyed in particular countries;
- consumerism and urbanization, which have gone hand in hand with a heightened sense of individualism and individual autonomy;
- technological developments that provide greater levels of mastery over the natural world.

The re-emergence of acute conflicts at the interface between religion and politics in the later twentieth and early twenty-first centuries has posed questions for the secularization thesis. Social scientists now generally think that secularization is not a single, inevitable process that applies to all countries but that it is partial and is accompanied by sacralization (increasing religiosity) in other spheres. Other sociologists who reject the secularization thesis altogether define religion very broadly as any system of beliefs and practices concerned with ultimate meaning. This includes forms of **spirituality** outside formal religious institutions that fluctuate in strength over time. On that basis, they find no evidence of secularization in Europe and urge the term be dropped.

Others argue that secularization confuses personal behaviour with institutional decline. Grace Davie's examination of religious belief in England, where arguably secularization began the earliest and has run the deepest, concluded that while formal membership of religious institutions has fallen away, religious belief itself has not (Davie 2004). Still other critics point to the fact that the secularization thesis does not account for different countries' experiences, such as the US where new churches, broadly Christian but not linked to long-established faith institutions, have been founded; neither does it account for the upsurge of evangelical Christianity in the US and Africa or for the upsurge in a politicized Islam. All are examples of faith institutions wanting more influence in public arenas and on social policy, sometimes aggressively so.

From the 1920s on social work was consistently secular in practice as it strove to establish credibility common to other well-regarded professions such as medicine and relied on approaches derived from psychology for its methods. It has, however, more recently become open to playing a more explicit faith-based role in work with clients. Arguments reflecting this turn (see **spirituality**) provide little analysis of secularization, yet the debate – for and against secularization – is by no means over.

Davie, G. (2004) *Religion in Britain since 1945: Believing without Belonging*. Oxford: Blackwell.

self-interest to act in one's own interest, to place one's needs foremost, ahead of others when seeking to maximize gains or to reduce losses. In the abstract, self-interest is the opposite of **altruism** and idealists are prone to equate it with selfishness, an isolating form of individualism. For realists, self-interest is clearly a prime motivator of human behaviour and pursuing it is regarded as in the natural order of things. However, just as altruism often incorporates elements of psychic or material rewards for the person undertaking the altruistic act for the sake of others, acting in one's self interest does not necessarily mean acting only selfishly but can include helping others.

Self-interest is the natural concern of a person for his or her survival and well-being and a priority, if not an exclusive one, in making decisions regarding not only basic needs and the necessities of life but also those regarding more complex needs and sense of fulfilment. Self-preservation, self-recognition, self-determination and self-respect can all be said to be components of self-interest. As such self-interest is one of the characteristics of personal integrity and wholeness.

Social theorists and political philosophers note that it is possible to interpret self-interest very narrowly, to the point where the self-interested individual excludes all consideration of others' needs and acts always and continuously in pursuit of his or her immediate benefit regardless of the consequences for others. At the same time they point out that acting in self-interest can be understood as including the needs of others. From this they argue that self-interest is not in essence something confined to the single individual body but exists within our relationships with others. Humans are interpersonal beings, fundamentally social and relational in nature; to live is to be among people and to realize one's interests in that context.

The concept of self-interest plays a central role in mainstream economic theory and in particular **rational choice theory**, both of which are based on the notion of the knowledgeable individual who is aware of her or his interests and is able to pursue them rationally and intelligently. But in economics, as in other contexts, self-interest is seen to be anchored by human reason enabling the development of moral codes that recognize the relational elements of self-interest and regulate the pursuit of self-interests in business and in social relations generally. As the classical economist and moral philosopher Adam Smith put it in his *Wealth of Nations* (1776): 'It is not from the benevolence of the butcher, the brewer, or the baker that we expect our dinner, but from their regard to their own self-interest. We address ourselves, not to their humanity but to their self-love, and never talk to them of *our* own necessities but of *their* advantages.'

Social scientists have also examined individual self-interest in relation to groups. Some have argued that individuals with common interests would voluntarily combine with others so as to try to further those interests. Others, chiefly Mancur Olson in *The Logic of Collective Action*, challenged the widely accepted premise that if members of a particular group have a common interest, and they would all be better off if those interests were achieved, they would act together to achieve those interests. Olson argued that unless the number of members was very small or a degree of coercion was exerted over members to make individuals act in the common interest, 'rational, self-interested individuals will not act to achieve their common or group interests'. This was because group members who could not be excluded from the benefits of a collective good have little incentive to be part of the effort to obtain that good. Olson's work subsequently stimulated a new and major field of research into what are called 'common pool problems' – how natural resources such as fisheries and water supply used by all can be shared without being destroyed by overuse.

sexuality the social construction of sexual identity as an expression of those qualities, desires, roles and identities that have to do with sexual behaviour in any society.

Populist notions of sexuality derive largely from the Freudian notion of libido (a biological impulse) and are commonly understood as an essential, natural and impulsive marker of sexual activity, desire and character present in all individuals. However, Freud also conceived of childhood as a period of *polymorphous perversity* where the child experiences the world in a holistic sensory manner and that the emergence of an individual's sexuality will reflect the norms and expectations of an immediate social environment and it is likely that there will be an element of *repression* in that process.

More recently, however, sociological and feminist theorists have pointed to the importance of recognizing the social significance of sexuality. A key figure in this area is Foucault, who examined sexuality in relation to **discourse**, concepts of **power** and the social construction of sexual practices. While Foucault's work is important, it has been criticized, especially by feminist sociologists, for underestimating the significance of gender relations and the unequal power between women and men. Debates within the feminist (especially radical feminist) and gay liberation movements have argued that dominant heterosexist discourses of sexuality are not in their interests and that such discourses distort and repress alternative and essentialist sexualities.

Social workers, counsellors and therapists do often become involved in a number of issues related to sexual behaviour and sexual identity including:

- *contraception* – especially in relation to children under the age of legal consent and children and young people in the care system, prisoners and people with learning disabilities;
- *sexual behavior and health risks* – particularly in relation to those with HIV/Aids and other sexually transmitted diseases;
- *pregnancy counselling* – especially if the pregnancy is unwanted and/or there is a health risk to the mother;
- *confronting unacceptable sexual activity* – direct work with sex offenders and with their victims, both children and adults;
- *counselling around problems of sexual identity* – work with children and young people in the care system who believe they might be gay or bisexual and issues around adoption and fostering if the adopters or would-be foster carers are homosexual or bisexual or a couple with children separate and one party is intending to live with another person of the same sex and there are custody issues to settle. (See also **gender**.)

Myers, S. and Milner, J. (2007) *Sexual Issues in Social Work*. London/Bristol: BASW/The Policy Press.

sick role a role that can be adopted by a sick individual, in which sickness becomes a special status, with potentially positive and/or negative implications for the individual concerned. The concept was first developed in the 1950s by the American sociologist Parsons, who suggested the following possible elements in the sick role:

(1) the sick person is exempted from many of the usual social and economic responsibilities (exemptions have to be endorsed by doctors or counsellors);

(2) it is accepted that the sick person may be unable to fend for herself or himself, or require a measure of support;

(3) the sick person is expected to actively strive for health; an integral part of this process would be that

(4) the sick person is expected to seek professional advice and treatment. The sickness role may sometimes be adopted or maintained by people who may wish to escape the burden of social and economic obligations. In these circumstances, professional agencies such as those of medicine and social work may be seen as performing a social control function in determining 'true' fitness and unfitness and thus the legitimacy of the adoption of the sick role. The concept of the 'sick role'

is central to the social and, often, political regulation of illness and impairment. Currently, there are major debates about the significant growth in the numbers of people claiming sickness/invalidity benefits in the UK. Successive governments have sometimes encouraged claims for such benefits, possibly to reduce the numbers of people deemed to be unemployed (only those fit for work can be registered as 'unemployed'), and sometimes, with the overall costs of such benefits in mind, seeking to require all those capable of some kind of employment to seek work. Social workers become involved in activities either to support individuals in their claim to be 'genuinely sick' with, for example, appeals to welfare tribunals or alternatively working with, say, depressed individuals or those lacking in confidence to help them regain 'employability' status. The dual aspects of both the care and control elements of the social work tasks are clearly evident here.

social capital elements of social organization that include trust, norms of reciprocity and networks that can facilitate co-ordinated actions within communities, neighbourhoods and the wider society.

Social capital has proved an adaptable and widely applied model of social organization across the developed and developing world, with theorists and researchers debating, defining, applying and criticizing its merits in equal measure. The concept has been highly influential within social theory from the early 1990s onwards because it highlights the kinds of social resource that communities and societies require to maintain social cohesion and solve social problems. These were precisely the kinds of resources that neo-liberalism, **rational choice theory** and theories supporting the free **market** were uninterested in. Social capital theorists argue that success in overcoming the dilemmas of *collective action* in resolving social problems depends on the broader social context in which those problems are tackled.

All forms of capital represent some kind of stored wealth or resources that have built up over time and can be drawn on when needed for specific purposes. The best way to think about social capital, then, is to see it as goods or resources stored within the social relations of a community, neighbourhood, or society. James Coleman, an American sociologist, was among the first to apply social capital in his study of young people (although he credited the African American economist Glenn Loury with first developing the concept). Coleman saw the development of young people as a product of the social relationships of the parents and the parents' relations with the community. Social capital he saw as the set of norms that develops in communities with a high degree of closure, that is communities based around relatively closed networks that informally enforce **norms** of behaviour, an interest in academic matters and avoidance of deviance. Lack of interaction between parents and children and between parents and other adults produces networks that do not enforce such norms or parental control.

Robert Putnam, in his study of Italian regional civic culture and subsequently of American civic culture in *Bowling Alone* (2000), widened the applicability of social capital in social analysis and enlarged the theory around it. In the first – based on many years of field research – he investigated how certain regions of Italy had become more prosperous while other regions were mired in poverty. He found that like financial capital for conventional borrowers, social capital served as a kind of collateral in which participants pledge their social connections to improve their efficiency. As with conventional capital, those who have social capital tend to accumulate more. Most forms of social capital – particularly trust – are the kind of resource that increase with use rather than decrease; conversely, they become depleted if not used. The more participants display trust towards one another, the greater their mutual confidence.

For Putnam, networks of civic engagement such as neighbourhood associations, choral societies, co-operatives, sports clubs, mass-based political parties, are the lifeblood of social capital. These are examples of *horizontal interaction* that foster robust norms of reciprocity, of acceptable behaviour, and convey their mutual expectations to one another. Such networks facilitate communication and improve the flow of information about the trustworthiness and reliability of others. Co-operation depends on reliable information about past behaviour and the interests of potential partners. By contrast hierarchical or *vertical interaction,* no matter how dense and/or how important it is to its participants, cannot sustain social trust and co-operation. Vertical flows of information are often less reliable because those in subordinate positions within the hierarchy hold on to information or shape it as a hedge against blame or exploitation from those elsewhere in the hierarchy.

In his later work, Putnam distinguished between 'bonding' social capital and 'bridging' social capital. *Bonding social capital* is based on close personal ties of family, kinship and immediate neighbourhood relationships. It is homogeneous and exclusive in nature, tightly knit and useful for everyday survival – a small loan, a car ride in an emergency, looking after a child at short notice – and may be thought of as 'networks for getting by'. *Bridging social capital* is based on connections with people from different areas, different occupations, different levels of income and educational background. It often spans geographical distance; its ties provide useful connections when, for example, looking for employment or to draw specific resources into a neighbourhood or community in which they are lacking. Bridging social capital may be understood as 'networks for getting ahead', for example, based on voluntary associations, links with educational institutions, religious institutions, employers' associations. Such ties are 'weaker' than those of bonding social capital in the sense that the personal relationships involved are not necessarily close or in frequent contact; they are utilized less frequently but nevertheless can deliver benefits, resources and connections that are unavailable to the denser but more inward looking solidarities of bonding social capital. Hence the well-known paradoxical phrase: 'the strength of weak ties'.

Putnam and others who explore social capital have generally argued that it is in relative decline in Western developed countries because individuals are less involved in voluntary associations and engage in activities in an individualized way. His book *Bowling Alone* does not argue that Americans literally go bowling on their own but do so now with friends and family and no longer join bowling clubs or leagues as they once did in large numbers.

Social capital has, as might be expected of such a prominent theory, attracted robust criticism. Some critics argue that it is imprecise in definition and difficult to measure in any objective way. Others argue that it implies that disadvantaged communities should develop their own social capital as a solution to the problems associated with poverty, to haul themselves up by their own bootstraps as it were without the need for government intervention. Still others have pointed out that some forms of social capital can be oppressive – enforcing informal norms by ostracism and veiled aggression in matters of sexual preference, for example. Putnam and others have rebutted such criticism and underscored that social capital does not replace government-brokered solutions to disadvantage. Rather there is a strong role for central and local government actively to encourage the formation of social capital.

Social capital is a real-world theory. It embraces characteristics of social behaviour that are highly relevant to social workers as they function in a rapidly changing environment. It is particularly relevant to community-oriented social work and outlines the kinds of co-operation local people and local organizations need to develop:

• putting in place the conditions in which local residents can gain some experience of wielding influence and power;

- developing leaders, running meetings, giving voice to community aspirations;
- equipping residents to contribute in an informed way to public discussions when and where important decisions are taken that affect their neighbourhood;
- raising the level of volunteering, bringing together peer mentors for younger pupils at risk of school exclusion, starting up a youth centre, convening a young persons' parish council.

Putnam, R. (2000). *Bowling Alone: The Collapse and Revival of American Community*. London: Simon & Schuster.

For a highly critical view, see Fine, B. (2010) *Social Capital: Researchers Behaving Badly*. London: Pluto Press.

social constructionism any theory that posits that social phenomena and social institutions are socially created rather than given, taken for granted or predetermined.

Social constructionism acknowledges that individuals are born into a particular social milieu but that they also have the capacity to interpret that world. In this respect, it is acknowledged that individuals have **agency** – in essence, that they have the capacity to act or function independently of the persuasive constraints or influences of social structures. Thus society needs to be seen as actively produced by its constituent members and, in this broad sense, is interpreted and created by them although 'agency' can be more or less encouraged or permitted (a liberal family as against a totalitarian regime suggest a range of possibilities) and societies can be more or less tolerant of differing social constructions of problems, social policies and beliefs. For example, some societies are tolerant of religious belief and others will punish denial of the religious 'truths'. Examples of the social construction of problems and behaviours are as follows:

(1) Behaviour thought appropriate to specific ages in relation to the 'life course' is shaped by presumptions that figure in any society at any point in history. Child labour, for example, featuring very young children of, say, age 5 or 6 has been a feature of many societies. An expectation that a child will earn its keep has characterized both Victorian England and, currently, many parts of Asia. In the UK, adulthood has been progressively postponed as the school-leaving age has consistently been raised and the prospect of a genuinely independent life made harder to achieve for the majority before the age of, say, 25 years of age or later. Old age has been similarly revised in response to increasing longevity, delaying the age at which the state pension might be accessed.

(2) Even death, at the physical level simply the cessation of life, is capable of subjective meanings that are clearly socially constructed. For some (for example, the atheist), death is the complete and final end of existence; for others (most Christians and Muslims, for example), death is a transitional event in a voyage to another world or state of being. In relation to other 'social constructions', suicide can be interpreted as a final act of despair for, say, the depressed individual or an act of altruism for the person who sacrifices himself or herself for the sake of the social group of which he or she is a committed member.

(3) The social construction of crime and of proportionate responses to crime can be illustrated in the proposal from some criminologists that drugs could usefully be decriminalized. At a stroke, a whole raft of offences, in the views of these advocates, could disappear to be replaced by some services run by health professionals working on issues framed by a paradigm that addictions were an illness needing treatment not punishment.

(4) The idea of 'race', of groups exhibiting different and discernible biological characteristics allegedly explaining distinct differences in behaviour and culture, has been wholly discredited as a scientific concept. However, sociologists are still interested in the use of the term 'race' and presumptions about different ethnic groups as social constructions because they continue to have resonance for 'racial discourses' often resulting in discriminatory behaviour on the part of racists.

It can be fruitful for social workers to 'deconstruct' any ideas, norms and behaviours that underpin negative behaviours and a willingness to go through a deconstruction process might well require the worker to identify 'alternative constructions' that might have improved outcomes for behaviour and for relationships. (See also **labelling**.)

Berger, P. and Luckmann, T. (1967) *The Social Construction of Reality*. London: Allen Lane.

social democracy see **left, left wing**

social distance a concept which attempts to describe degrees of tolerance or intolerance between different social groups and their willingness to have contact with other ethnic, religious or cultural groups or social strata. Social distance can be formal as with apartheid or caste systems or informal where the rules of social acceptability are more subtle and likely to be based upon fine distinctions of social status or reflections of different origins, as with 'outsiders' moving into a small rural community.

Bogardus devised a scale of responses which attempt to measure degrees of social distance between different groups. Decreasing degrees of acceptance of any group is thought to be demonstrated if any person is prepared to:

- have an individual become a relative through marriage (to have a daughter marry an 'outsider' is often thought to depict the virtual absence of social distance);
- become a close friend of a member of the other group;
- have someone from another group be a next door neighbour or, more distantly, just a neighbour;
- be a colleague;
- allow an immigrant to settle;
- allow an immigrant to have temporary residence rights;
- not to allow him/her into the country at all.

The concept of social distance is useful in describing relationships between groups and, over time, mapping any changes and trends. Thus, it is clearly evident that over the last 30 years or so people from ethnic minorities are to be seen in far greater numbers on television; that black footballers now figure prominently in professional football teams; and that there are now many more children of dual heritage. By these measures it would be reasonable to conclude that social distance in some respects had narrowed between white and ethnic minority people in the UK. Social workers might also use the concept to understand community relations in any neighbourhood or relationships between people in any social setting such as a school, workplace, a residential care home or in local political institutions. Social distance does not necessarily mean that there are problems, but the greater the social distance between groups the less likely it is that integration and a measure of power sharing has been achieved. (See also **white flight**.)

social exclusion a multidimensional conceptualization of poverty that acknowledges both monetary and non-monetary causes. Its first formulation in the mid-1970s in France was in essence symbolic, highlighting the fact that certain social groups had comprehensively failed to find their place in post-industrial capitalism and were cut off from the main institutions of society and state. As the concept was picked up by researchers and refined it reshaped policy development, particularly in Britain and the European Union. From the mid-1990s on it has provided a ready construct that both defines social problems and suggests policy responses to those problems.

From the beginning social exclusion has been a contested idea. Some critics have said it diverts attention from the fundamental issue of gross inequality in wealth and income while others have argued that it casts too wide a net, embracing more social problems than policy can possibly deal with. Yet the concept has also highlighted new kinds of deprivation and provided a platform for significant research and policy initiatives that address the many linked facets of disadvantage.

Social exclusion, as a concept, can best be understood as trying to bridge the gap between these two contrary approaches, at once able to shed light on *structural causes* of poverty – low wages, economic disorganization, racial discrimination – and on its *cultural, moral and behavioural sources.* Elasticity is built into the concept for this very reason; its objective is to define a number of factors, both individual and familial as well as social and economic, to account for the extent of poverty in a society *and* the psychological disengagement and aliena-tion that is its by-product. Fundamentally, the kinds of policy solution that emerge have not only to do with income support but also seek to change individual behaviour.

This elasticity arose in part from the different ideological strands that it embraced. In an influential text, Ruth Levitas uncovered three separate, conflicting discourses within discussions on social exclusion:

- a 'redistributionist' discourse concerned with the extreme inequal-ity of wealth which only redistribution of that wealth through taxa-tion, benefits and services can overcome;
- an 'underclass' discourse which concentrates on individual delin-quency and failure to uphold the norms of society particularly with regard to the work ethic. It pinpoints, for example, the behaviour of absentee fathers who evade child support responsibilities, young male offenders, and young teenage women who have children out-side a stable relationship. Proponents of this discourse argue that the excluded in effect exclude themselves by engaging in certain behaviours such as drug addiction, crime and having children out of wedlock;
- a 'social integrationist' discourse whose primary focus is on paid work and entrance into the labour market as a way of achieving a cohesive society. Levitas argues that this discourse remains upper-most in the policy and practice of the Labour government in the UK that came to power in 1997 (Levitas 2005).

Explorations of social exclusion have taught us a great deal about the effects of poverty in developed countries. As Danny Dorling argues in *Injustice* (2011), exclusion results now not from living in abject poverty but as the consequence of a new range of social assumptions based on the extraordinary disparity in incomes in the developed world, particularly in the US and Britain. That the incomes of the affluent are so much higher than the lower sixth has produced among policy elites the general assumption that poverty should no longer exist, that because the worst of twentieth-century poverty has been dealt with the poor have not done enough themselves to avoid being poor.

Pierson, J. (2010) *Tackling Social Exclusion*, 2nd edn. London: Routledge.

socialization the means by which the culture of any society, including language, norms, values, gender identities and social skills are transmitted to children and internalized by them and the principal means by which culture is passed from generation to generation, thus maintaining society although not necessarily replicating it.

Social scientists usually distinguish between *primary socialization* and *secondary socialization*; the first focuses upon childhood and adolescence in the 'journey' to become fully fledged adults; and the second on what is later learned through adult involvement in other institutions. Thus, it is accepted that socialization is a lifelong process with the possibility that major changes might well come about later in life. It is also accepted that individuals do not have to be passive recipients, but can play an active role in shaping their own identities especially if they live in an 'enabling' environment. In this regard, sociologists are now inclined to accept that in terms of the nature–nurture debate the importance of hereditary aspects of an individual as against the influence of environmental factors is a dynamic process where one or the other may be more or less influential at different times depending upon the circumstances.

Key dimensions of socialization include:

(1) the development of thinking skills (cognition) in children;
(2) the formation of identity including, crucially, gender identity;
(3) the development of a social identity including a moral framework underpinning how the child manages social relationships;
(4) the internalization of the values, norms and culture of the wider society.

Although it is helpful to understand the broad influence of structural factors upon socialization (see **life course**) in that childhood experience of, for example, **poverty** is likely to have profound effects upon a child, psychologists have been able to demonstrate that the individual experience of children can be very different even in the same family. An anxious parent, for example, might have relaxed a little by the time a second child has come along. The second child has a different experience because of having an older sibling. A child living in a family where there is an abusive relationship between his or her parents will have a profoundly different experience to the baby who has appeared shortly before the mother is able to get away from her abusive partner. Children's adaptability also varies and they can sometimes develop positively against the odds. (See also **acculturation, cognition, personality**.)

socialism see **left, left wing**

social mobility the upward or downward movement of individuals or groups, between different positions within a hierarchy of **social stratification** whether those positions are defined by social class, social status, income group or occupation. Sociologists have in general paid most attention to movement between social classes where they have examined the difference between the socio-economic origins and the later achieved class or status. While fiction generally dwells on the individuals who aspire to leave, for example, their working-class roots, sociology has historically looked at cohorts of working-class children who later entered the middle class and the mechanisms by which they were able to do so. Such movement within the lifetime of an individual is deemed *intragenerational* mobility. *Intergenerational* mobility has also been a focus of study – how the resources, attitudes and aspirations of parents prepare (or finance) the efforts of their offspring to seek higher status, higher paying occupations.

In many societies social mobility is virtually impossible – societies built on slavery, castes or clans permit no movement up or down the social ladder. In contemporary market democracies, however, the prospect of social mobility is there, even if it is not easily accomplished, and is often associated with the concept of *equality of opportunity*: ensuring that everyone has the same chance to make the most of their lives, whether in occupation, status or wealth. (Providing equal opportunity does not, of course, mean that all individual outcomes will be the same.)

Most politicians from across the political spectrum pay at least lip-service to the notion of social mobility and equal opportunity. The degree of social mobility that actually occurs within specific countries is, however, far from the ideal that politicians espouse. One way of measuring intergenerational social mobility is to track over time – at least 30 years – the income of parents and their offspring. High correlation between parents' income and that of their offspring suggests that affluent parents have affluent offspring and that low-income parents have offspring on low incomes. In that instance social mobility is low.

Such data are available for only a few developed countries but the findings are clear: the greater the level of inequality of a country the lower the social mobility. International research conducted at the London School of Economics that tracked father's income against the income of offspring established that highly unequal societies, the UK and the US among them, have the lowest levels of social mobility, while the more egalitarian countries, for example Norway, have the highest.

Recent research from the Pew Charitable Trusts in the US found that 42 percent of American men raised in the bottom fifth of incomes remain there as adults. That shows a level of persistent disadvantage much higher than in Denmark (25 percent) and Britain (30 percent) – a country famous for its class constraints. Meanwhile, just 8 percent of American men at the bottom rose to the top fifth. That compares with 12 percent of the British and 14 percent of the Danes. It also found that 62 percent of Americans (male and female) raised in the top fifth of incomes stay in the top two-fifths, while 65 percent born in the bottom fifth stay in the bottom two-fifths.

In this and other comparable studies Canada, Norway, Finland and Denmark emerge as the most mobile, with the United States and Britain roughly tied at the other extreme. Sweden, Germany, and France are scattered across the middle.

Economic Mobility Project (2011) *Does America Promote Mobility as Well as Other Nations?* Washington, DC: Pew Charitable Trust.

social network individuals connected through social relationships which can include face-to-face or electronic contact.

Social workers have been urged at least since the Barclay Report in 1982 to pay attention to users' social networks, to analyse them, to draw on their resources and do what they can to strengthen them if needed. Social workers have informally recognized the power of networks relying on instruments such as the eco-map to work out jointly with users what their individual connections are. Since the implementation of the Children Act 1989 they have preferred to place children with relatives and as near to home as possible rather than in a children's home or with distant foster parents, thus preserving the child's natural networks.

But in general, practitioner focus on networks has been intermittent and often of low priority. For instance, in social care for older people social workers have reduced their engagement with 'non-care' activities such as developing luncheon clubs, providing specialist transport services and befriending activities, which has undermined the network-enhancing role of social care practice. This is despite the clear evidence that networks and neighbourhood involvement are instrumental in underpinning older people's well-being.

Broad familiarity with how social networks function is an important element of the knowledge base:

• A person's social network tracks the individual life cycle to a degree, with weakening of social bonds from the death or movement of network members, loss of some social roles and tasks often related to retirement.

- A number of structural factors dramatically affect the kind and quality of networks that a person has. For example, income, educational background, age, gender, disability, ethnic origin and employment all shape the kinds of network available to people.
- Those who are older or in poor health tend to have less robust networks, with those age 85 and over having smaller networks than those who are younger. A decrease in the older person's capacity to undertake the social tasks required to maintain network links and a reduction in the opportunities for making new friends or new social ties also affect network ties. This trend can be offset by intensification of select friendships, the expansion of social tasks through volunteer work or reactivating family tasks.
- Those in higher income brackets, in employment and those who attended university tend to have more extended social networks.

As social workers we are vitally interested in how these networks are viewed by the people with whom we are working. They may be seen as affirmative, nurturing or accepting or as antagonistic and inaccessible. At their very worst they can be sources of heavy responsibility, aggression and scapegoating. Understanding how such networks function helps us to understand better the distinctive characteristics of socially excluded and isolated individuals and families. Demographic and social changes have weakened the capacity of networks that practitioners have been able to draw on to support users. More women working (and fewer seeing it as their job alone to care for an older person), fewer children, higher rates of divorce and greater geographical mobility have all made family networks more fragile. Not surprisingly, unmarried older people will have invested more in non-family supportive relationships and so may still have robust networks. For those over 85 the loss of same-generation relatives and friends and the tendency to put energy into only the closest relationships can undermine what a wider, more dispersed support network is capable of achieving.

Networks mixing both family and friends have the widest capacity to perform tasks and give substantial amounts of support. These may include emotional support tasks such as providing social interaction, reassurance, validation, cheering up and monitoring as well as material support such as household jobs like preparing meals, cleaning, shopping for food, providing transport, bill paying and banking money. The size of a social network, however, is not always a reliable predictor of support since any network may contain ties that have lost their friendship roles or have become impersonal. Support is more likely from those with continuing contact who form a smaller group (or 'subset') within the larger network. Such a subset might include immediate family, relatives or particular neighbours. But assumptions that older people who apparently have sufficient social ties will have the support they need are not always accurate. Support networks (with on average five to 10 people) are smaller than the personal social networks (on average 12 to 13) from which they come and are usually found among long-standing kinship and friendship ties with high expectations to provide reciprocal support.

In post-hospital care, social networks, to the extent that they are available, obviously become extremely important. Researchers have examined older service users' feedback and experiences in the wake of hospital discharge and confirmed the health benefits of practitioners facilitating access to social networks. By combining sensitive interpersonal interaction, advocacy and 'educational' assistance, social care workers supported older service users' re-engagement in a variety of networks. These included: friendship, recreational and family groups, health care treatment programmes, local contacts and organizations. Through these, material, interpersonal and health care resources are obtained which help sustain physical health and psychological well-being. Social support for example has been convincingly related to improved health outcomes – lowering blood pressure, maintaining cognitive functioning and greater psychological resilience.

social stratification different ways of conceiving of persistent and structured social inequality. Using a geological analogy of 'strata' (layers), society is conceived of as having discernible tiers with different characteristics. Membership of various social strata has been demonstrated to have profound implications for people's identity, the quality of their lives and their 'life chances' generally. Social stratification is probably *the* most important part of social structure.

Whereas psychologists have concentrated on individual differences arising out of innate characteristics and changes to personality as a result of interactions with an immediate environment, sociologists have sought to make sense of society by trying to identify structures. Structure can be captured by reference to the roles people adopt and enact (social institutions), but another kind of structure is discernible in social strata that tend to persist over time. Stratification has been debated primarily in terms of power, elites, social class, status, caste, age, gender and ethnicity.

Philosophers and political scientists, since Plato and Aristotle in the fourth century BC, have traditionally been concerned with the concept of **power**, acknowledging that power tends to persist in the hands of particular social groups over time. The preoccupation of these thinkers was with, first, how any society can secure the best and most able people to 'rule' or govern; second, the problem of legitimating power (for example the divine rights of kings, early forms of democracy, tradition); and, third, understanding how political masters might govern effectively. All these deliberations rest upon the notion that there are segments of society where power resides, and that the powerful are consistently marked out as a different group from the powerless. Later, Machiavelli in his book *The Prince* explored the more raw forms of political manoeuvring that identified the idea of political elites and of the attempts of aspiring people to displace them (a notion captured much later by the Italian sociologist Vilfredo Pareto in his concept of the 'circulation of elites'). Elites, for Pareto and another Italian conservative sociologist, Mosca, were the unavoidable consequences of people having different abilities, motivations and other psychological characteristics. Pareto took the view that elites would seek to defend their positions but would inevitably be displaced by ambitious and forceful others who would have to be accommodated into the elite. Later theorists argued that elites could be found in different sub-sections or even sub-cultures within any society. So, for example, it is possible that elites might emerge in religious institutions, the military, economic institutions, the professions, sport and politics. Others have questioned whether the elites are separate but perhaps interlocked and inter-related, recruiting new members from the same broad social group – and perhaps social class?

For Marx, social class was a reflection of a person's relationship to the means of production – a relationship that could be discerned most clearly in advanced capitalist societies. Here, if people only had their labour to sell then, for Marx, they were members of the proletariat (working class) and those who owned 'the means of production' (the factories, the companies, land and capital) were members of the bourgeoisie (the ruling class). He acknowledged that people often did not accept this way of looking at their society or themselves and he explained this problem with reference to the idea of 'false consciousness', which meant that people might be distracted by differences that made them feel inferior to some and superior to others – say a school teacher feeling inferior to the GP but superior to the caretaker. Marx argued that to be distracted by this kind of **status** distinction was to fail to understand one's objective class position – and such distractions were likely to inhibit involvement in the class struggle, a struggle that has the objective of establishing a 'classfree' society. In sum, Marx argued that all those who work for a wage or a salary are members of the proletariat regardless of how much they earn or their social status.

In addition to the proletariat and the bourgeoisie, Marx also identified other minor classes in the petit bourgeoisie and the lumpen proletariat. He thought of the petit bourgeoisie essentially as the owners of small businesses and the lumpen proletariat as those who are unemployed and not interested in seeking employment, those working illegally in 'black markets' and criminal sub-cultures. Some writers have relabelled the lumpen proletariat as the 'underclass'. Marx had a particular contempt for the lumpen proletariat because he thought they undermined working-class solidarity.

An alternative attempt to capture the concept of social class in the UK has been to associate occupational groups with social classes. The Registrar General's classification of occupations is widely used. These are:

- professional;
- managerial and technical;
- skilled occupations – both non-manual and manual;
- semi-skilled and partly skilled;
- unskilled.

This pragmatic approach excludes any notions of capitalists altogether and simply provides a kind of continuum of salaried/waged occupations from those that have high status and rewards (professional occupations) moving through intermediate groups to employment that has low status and rewards (unskilled occupations). Using this classification of occupations researchers have sought to map outcomes for families in relation to many areas of concern such as health inequalities (both morbidity and mortality), educational achievement, **social mobility**, social inclusion/exclusion, political behavior, income and wealth, housing, leisure and lifestyle choices. The evidence from many studies in the UK is that social class (measured by the occupation of, usually, a father) continues to be a powerful predictor of individual life chances generally. In the UK, social mobility is possible but intergenerational movements up or down the social class scale tend to be modest.

For Weber, social class, status and power were three aspects of stratification that could coincide for any individual but might also operate quite independently of each other. Thus a person might occupy a lowly position in class terms but have considerable social status because of a position he holds in a trade union perhaps or as a well-known sportswoman. Weber thought that traditional societies were more likely to have social strata where class position, status and power coincided for many people, but that in advanced industrial societies, especially in urban settings, it was more common for people to vary in their positions in relation to class, status or power.

Feminists have argued, mostly from the middle of the twentieth century onwards, that power, class, status and elites have consistently overlooked gender as an important form of stratification. Feminists have argued that much of the discourse about social stratification had been 'gender blind' and that the consistently disadvantaged position of women in all social institutions – especially in the economy, politics and religious institutions and their active mistreatment in relation to, for example, domestic violence – all testified to the importance of gender and patriarchy in social structure.

Yet other thinkers have argued that age is a key feature of stratification. In this context, older people are seen as occupying positions of power and influence over the young until such times as their economic position is reduced through withdrawal from the workplace, a contingent loss of income and, later, declining health, loss of social status and growing dependence. Disability and ageing can occupy some of the same territory, but disabled people of all ages are also arguing that they are often socially excluded and discriminated against and that they occupy a relatively powerless position in many societies.

For some, caste can be a critical social identifier and source of power or relative powerlessness. There is evidence of a weakening of the caste system in India, but it can still be hugely influential in some quarters in both south Asia and in the UK. Religious differences too can be sources of identity in societies where to belong to one religious group is to be relatively powerful and to belong to another is to lack power. The position of Catholics in Ireland pre-independence is illustrative of a group who experienced systematic discrimination. Finally, ethnicity is also clearly a major component to social structure and is often a key social identifier that will bring more or less power to the individual. African Americans in the US in the first half of the twentieth century experienced systematic discrimination and relative powerlessness until the civil rights movement gathered momentum. Ethnicity in the UK is also a factor clearly influencing **life chances**.

Social workers need to be able to locate service users and, where relevant, their families, in these broad social strata. To know that a person originates from the working classes, is female, is African Caribbean and a lesbian is to invite questions about differing sources of oppression and lack of access to opportunities that others have, with probable implications for constrained 'life chances'. (See **ageing and ageism**, **disability**, **gender**, **power** and **status**.)

Grusky, D. ed. (2008) *Social Stratification: Class, Race and Gender in Sociological Perspective* 3rd ed. London: Westview Press.

social structure any relatively enduring or recurring pattern of the elements/parts of a social system, group, organization or society.

Although the term is widely used there is no agreed definition or understanding of the concept of social structure among sociologists. Two major strands about 'structure' emerged in the nineteenth century with the work of Spencer and Marx. For Spencer, the organic analogy was influential in conceiving of society as a kind of biological organism with different but complementary parts each with its own function/purpose. Connected to this school of thought is the idea that *social institutions* can be understood as the key elements of a structure and as the way in which key roles in any society can be meaningfully grouped. Thus most societies have a major collection of roles concerning family and kin, economic activities, religious and/or cultural beliefs/activities, education, health, politics and leisure/community. Clearly different people will participate in some institutions and not others; children do not usually work, neither, by definition, do retired people. For others, participation in a religious institution will be all embracing – the nun or monk – for whom the role will encompass work, community and religious ritual; and for others, the atheist, there will be no involvement at all in these roles. Differential involvement in the full range of roles is to be expected but most members of any society will have some understanding of all social institutions, recognizing their relative domains.

For Marx, economic substructure (the organization of social relations around 'work') as against the superstructure (the ideological, cultural and political dimensions/aspects of society) were the key structural features of any society. Here Marx took the view that capitalist societies would inevitably feature just two classes – namely the bourgeoisie (ruling class) and the proletariat (working class) and that these two classes would absorb other classes that were primarily remnants of earlier historical stages – the aristocracy, the peasantry, the petit bourgeoisie and the lumpen proletariat (underclass). Marx fully understood that individuals' perceptions of their own class position did not necessarily accord with what he considered their true class position. This was an issue, for him, of *false consciousness* – in effect a preoccupation with personal *status*.

Other forms of social structure relate to alternative forms of **social stratification** based upon social status, power, elites, caste, cultural groups, religious affiliation, gender, ethnicity, disability and age. All of these ways of conceiving of structure invite different questions that should enable social scientists and social workers to understand the social forces shaping the position and social constraints affecting individual behaviour, affiliations and life chances.

social theory attempts to make sense of social phenomena in a systematic way to determine their nature, and how they function and change. Theorizing entails trying to identify the constituent 'parts' of any social phenomenon and understanding how the parts relate to each other, to enable explanations of the social behaviour of individuals affected by the social phenomenon and thus, finally, to be able to predict behaviour. The convention in sociology is to distinguish between *grand theories, middle-range theories* and, by implication, *micro-theories*. Each level of theory acknowledges that it has a relationship to other levels but the focus can be on the whole landscape (grand theories), the middle distance (middle-range theories) and the foreground (micro-theories).

Grand theories, such as **Marxism**, try to capture the essence of whole societies that are hard to subject to close empirical study; rather attempts are often made, first, to undertake historical analyses about particular societies to see whether their structures and cultures at any point accord with the grand theory and, second, whether the relationship between critical parts of this whole society or relationships between societies also seem to confirm the theory. Some researchers, for example, have offered detailed alternative accounts of the development of societies historically. One major focus has been upon whether the societies established in the Soviet Union and China, for example, accorded with Marx's predictions or whether they were aberrations throwing doubt on his whole historical conception of how societies develop.

Other studies have sought to challenge Marx's claim that dominant ideas and ideologies always reflect the interests of the ruling classes or that working-class conservatism is the result of false consciousness.

Middle-range theories are much more likely to be subject to rigorous empirical study simply because the scale of this kind of research makes empiricism practicable. Thus, using Weber's ideal type of *bureaucracy* (an *ideal type* is simply a construct of a social phenomenon containing key elements thought to typify the phenomenon), many researchers have used the device to compare real organizations as a way of developing a more accurate concept of bureaucracy and/or as a way of capturing the range of organizational forms that exist in reality. This kind of research has been very productive in generating understandings of many issues such as the nature of line or hierarchical management compared with 'staff functions' (such as human resources or research and development); whether roles are specific or diffuse (the latter would seem to be more amenable for creativity – the former perhaps clearer when consistency is required in the discharge of statutory duties); how organizations have formal structures as well as informal practices that can undermine the organization's mission; that the use of discretion can be a source of social justice as well as injustice; and other issues that may have repercussions for everyday operations.

Micro-theories are modest in scale, about smaller social entities with fewer **variables** to deal with. Whyte's study of gangs, *Street Corner Society* (1955), is indicative. Using participant observation, his study revealed that:

- gangs were relatively closed;
- positions and roles within the group, including leadership, were quite stable;
- gangs were often associated with particular, usually urban, areas;
- they were working class in origins;
- they quite often embraced deviant sub-cultures.

Titmuss's analysis of altruistic behaviour with regard to the behaviour of blood donors, in his book *The Gift Relationship* (1970), is another example of small-scale research with possibly profound implications for how a society might be structured in a more co-operative, humane fashion.

social work theory the different sets of ideas, principles and methods on which social work practice is based. Social work theory broadly embraces three groups: theories that seek to explain the activity of social work, theories derived from the social sciences that are used/applied by social workers and theories that have been developed by social workers or thinkers working in fields allied to social work such as counsellors. Inevitably, these different groups of theories have overlapped and influenced each other.

Theories that explain/critique the activity of social work. The fact that social work has always operated in a climate of ambiguity involves a central dilemma, because it has embraced the dual functions of 'care and control', often in the same job. There will be occasions where it can be argued, without ambiguity, that with someone so psychotic that they are intent on hurting someone else, care and control are the same thing. But much, if not most, social work practice is undertaken with the poorer sections of the population and the socially marginalized and, moreover, it is felt that it is this structural inequality which is the 'cause' of many of the difficulties faced by service users. In this context, it can be argued that practitioners are being asked to find technical solutions to what are essentially political problems. The radical social work 'movement' of the 1970s in the UK held that it was possible to:

- develop an 'emancipatory practice' by working *alongside* service users to campaign for improved social security and free welfare benefits;
- involve service users with community groups, pressure groups, trade unions and political parties to create progressive alliances so as to be able to challenge structural inequality;
- change the focus of social work practice so that the discourse of 'problem families' was replaced with another that involved 'working with families who had problems' (and minimizing 'casework' in favour of community development and community action); and finally;
- try to reposition social work within the trade union movement rather than aspiring to be a 'quasi-medical profession'.

In sum, theories about the activity of social work seek to ask crucial questions about both the intended and unintended effects of mainstream social work practice, especially in the statutory sector. Does social work effort result in a misplaced gratitude from the poor for the modest assistance practitioners have been able to offer, and does this gratitude inhibit a more forceful resistance that might otherwise emerge from disaffected service users?

Theories used or applied by social workers informed by the social sciences. At various points in the development of social work in the UK, social work has been influenced by a variety of theoretical perspectives including psychoanalysis, systems theory and behaviourism. Psychoanalysis was especially dominant in the 1950s where a casework approach utilized notions of unresolved problems rooted in negative childhood experiences. Social workers construed their tasks as trying to understand the origins of a service user's problems, helping them to express their feelings, and establishing a therapeutic relationship with service users, as a kind of model of how healthy relationships might work, to help overcome past negative experiences. Systems theory (which has its roots in the organic analogies of Durkheim, Spencer and Parsons) later relocated the focus of social work interventions in a nexus of systems in which both social workers and service users were part. Thus, in the hands of Pincus and Minahan (1973) the 'change agent system' relates to practitioners and the social work organization they represent, the 'client system' focuses upon service users and their social environment (system), the 'target system' relates to what service users would like to change and, finally, the 'action system' refers to the work that needs to be undertaken to address, hopefully, identified problems and the key players to be engaged in that process. It is understood that client, target and action systems might or might not be the same depending upon whether problems are located within, say, the immediate family and its problematic relationships or whether the problem is external as in a deprived neighbourhood and low expectations.

Behaviourism has also been very influential, for example with children's development in its emphasis upon programmes that identify desired goals, such as getting a child to bed on time, supporting a child to reduce the incidence of night enuresis and perhaps coming home at specified times. A planned programme of encouragement and rewards which chart, hopefully, progress towards the specified objective would underpin learned behaviour. Similar approaches have also been routinely applied in encouraging consistent parenting.

Theories that have been developed by social workers or allied professionals (practice theories). Task-centred working has been the dominant 'practice theory' in UK social work for several decades, although many would argue that it is essentially methodological rather than theoretical. The method emphasizes the importance of close and accurate assessments of problems (ideally using the exchange model of assessment), of identifying the tasks that can address the problems, of allocating tasks to appropriate players (the service user, the practitioner or some other agency/person), of prioritizing and sequencing problems/tasks, of setting time limits for tasks and finally of reviewing (and possibly revising) problems and tasks. A clutch of other theoretical perspectives including *motivational interviewing*, the *strengths perspective, solution-focused therapies, cycle of change* and *counselling theory* (e.g. the person-centred approach of Carl Rogers and cognitive behavioural therapy) have also been very influential. All of these theoretical contributions have some common themes in the stress they have placed upon:

- locating the 'humanity' to be found in all people and the necessity for 'respecting everyone';
- locating service users' own problem-solving skills;
- enabling service users to see their problems differently especially through the use of positive thinking and discouraging negative, 'trapped' thinking;
- mobilizing service users' capacity for change but only if they have recognized the need for change and they wish to change.

Payne, M. (2005) *Modern Social Work Theory*, 3rd edn. Chicago, IL: Lyceum Books.

Pincus, A. and Minahan, A. (1973) *Social Work Practice: Model and Method*. Itasca, IL: Peacock Publications.

spirituality the transcendent dimension in human experience: the sense of deepest meaning and purpose and of identification with the cosmos. It is used to embrace all forms of religiosity, organized faiths as well as 'new age' beliefs. It can further include personal observance and rituals and thoughts regarding matters of mortality, eternity, awe, beauty and grace. Spirituality has come to replace older terms such as 'mysticism' in discussions of the beliefs that matter to people that lie outside time and beyond science and everyday occurrence.

Those who use the term intend it to signify something broader than religion, to explore the degree to which people hold beliefs or practices in which they can lose themselves, find non-material meaning and a sense of the transcendent. The major sociological investigation of spirituality aims to find the degree to which people hold religious-like beliefs though they live in what are regarded as secular societies. Those addressing spirituality in social work argue that it allows practitioners to respond to ultimate questions concerning the meaning and purpose of life raised by service users without having to delve into the specific practices and organized doctrines of particular faiths. They argue that this is particularly relevant in work with children, older people and adults with mental health problems, and in general opens the profession toward working with people of faith more sympathetically at a time of religious revival. Canda and Furman (2010) offer the fullest template as to how social workers may cultivate 'spiritually sensitive relationships' with clients. For example, they propose questions for what they term an 'implicit spiritual assessment' including:

- What currently brings a sense of meaning and purpose to your life?
- What helps you feel more aware and centred?
- In what way is it important or meaningful for you to be in this world?
- When do you feel most fully alive? (Canda and Furman 2010: 266)

They define spirituality in the broadest conceivable way from organized, institutional religion to the barely perceptible new age yearning. In the course of this they advocate that social workers develop their own spirituality, to include mindfulness, relaxation and meditation and attention to the meanings of ritual and ceremony.

Canda, E. and Furman, L. (2010) *Spiritual Diversity in Social Work Practice: The Art of Helping*. New York: Oxford University Press.

status a concept used in the social sciences in two ways: first, to denote a position in any social system, bureaucracy or social group that carries with it specific roles, responsibilities and rights; and, second, to denote a measure of honour, prestige or social standing that may be negatively or positively expressed, articulated or viewed. Both meanings of status can be applied to individuals, groups, organizations and even ethnic or cultural groups.

In relation to the first version of status, the concept is relevant to the practice of social work because it invites analyses of social work agencies and their characteristic modes of operation. Statutory social work agencies are invariably hierarchical in nature, often with tightly prescribed roles related to each layer of local authority bureaucracies; thus frontline workers will be accountable to team managers, team managers to area managers, area managers to divisional directors, divisional directors to deputy directors or to directors of social services (children's or adults' services) and directors in their turn accountable to social services committees comprising elected councillors (who represent the public's interest and are accountable to them). There is a kind of assumption that each layer of the bureaucracy, at least theoretically, will be staffed by workers/managers who are more experienced and more knowledgeable than those in lower grades. In practice, this assumption can be questionable. Not all social workers wish to become managers, preferring instead to continue to work directly with service users. Yet salary scales usually reflect hierarchical position, a fact offset by just a few social work organizations that have created 'senior practitioner' posts – designed to keep experienced social workers in the front line with some recognition of their expertise through an enhanced salary. Another aspect of hierarchical status and contingent roles is the degree to which status/roles are, using Talcott Parsons' pattern variables, either 'functionally diffuse' or 'functionally specific'. 'Functionally specific' means tightly prescribed by rules with little or any room for discretion or creativity whereas 'functionally diffuse' offers the opportunity to rethink responses to problems, to use discretion and to be creative. These matters also relate closely to the opportunities to use professional expertise rather than bureaucratic prescriptions and legal/statutory directives.

The second meaning of the concept of status is conceived as a form of social stratification that may be closely related to social class and to the power that is associated with an individual's class position, or to be functionally independent of both social class and power. In some societies, class, status and power are likely to be fused in one social position. For example, an aristocrat in eighteenth-century England was likely to be a member of the ruling or upper class, enjoy immense social status and considerable power both formally (as a member of the House of Lords) and informally over the lives of many indentured labourers and tenants and through a generalized 'deference' on the part of people who were not members of the upper classes.

In contemporary Britain, deference has clearly less social influence (there are, after all, many people who count themselves as republicans, who would be happy to abolish the monarchy) and it is possible for an individual to be a member of the ruling class, yet have little or no social status because he or she is regarded as an exploitative employer or land-lord. Similarly, particular individuals might have considerable social status because of their sporting prowess or their position as a charismatic leader in a faith institution or religious sect, but not be a member of the ruling class nor able to wield political power. At a more mundane level social status can attach to many 'significant others' in any individual's social network: a teacher, a youth leader, a member of one's extended family, an employer or indeed a social worker without that 'significant other' having any economic or political power or influence. Yet in assessing both the life course of individual service users or the current influences on their lives and well-being, any analysis of these significant others' status and contingent influence can be revealing. Social workers, in their assessments, could usefully ask questions about who has status and power in any individual's life and how that status and power are legitimated. A useful example about the issue of the influence of status on behaviour can be seen in micro-social systems of small groups such as gangs. Whyte's classic study of *Street Corner Society* (1955) provides a compelling account of relative status within a group of young people and of how difficult it can be to alter perceived status in the light of improved performance of any individual member.

Finally, social status can be ascribed or achieved. Many traditional societies are more likely to have ascribed status and roles so that social change is likely to be slow or negligible; whereas more modern or post-industrial societies have witnessed greater levels of achieved status and thus more rapid rates of social change. These differences between different historical periods and differences within societies raise interesting issues about where the socially mobile originate from and questions about how social mobility can be encouraged. In this regard, research indicates that, to focus upon just two examples, looked after children and African Caribbean males are among the groups least likely to change their social status and the most likely to have severely 'limited life chances'. How to enhance the life chances of many different groups who experience oppression and thus have their social status altered positively is a key social work task.

stigma a personal or social attribute that is discrediting or devaluing for the individual, family or sub-group in the eyes of a society or group, so much so that an individual is socially marginalized and prevented, discouraged or disqualified from participating in social life.

The ancient Greeks used the word to signify a branding of a person who had done something regarded as morally indefensible such as being a traitor (the French shaved the heads of women who had, in their view, got too close to German soldiers in the Second World War).

Using this notion, Goffman distinguishes between stigmas that are bodily, moral and tribal. The concept lends itself to many scenarios including individuals with disfigurements and various impairments that may be visible or behavioural as well as hidden identifiers such as a criminal record or a visible identity that is communicated by clothing, jewellery or some other personal item (various religious groups/sects dress in particular ways or wear particular jewellery). Much will depend upon social context and the prevailing social tensions in any society. Thus it has been the case that inter-ethnic marriages have often led to stigmatizing responses by one or other community and perhaps both. To be a young, black African Caribbean or African American man in many urban settings has invited a stigmatized response from some representatives of law enforcement agencies in some countries where such young people are often demonized.

Key issues for social workers are, first, to deconstruct the stigmatizing responses of people who discriminate as a prelude to confronting them and, second, to support those experiencing discrimination to resist unmerited labels.

Goffman, E. (1968) *Notes on the Management of Spoiled Identity.* Harmondsworth: Penguin Books.

surveillance the close observation, monitoring and supervision of people by the state including, especially, electronic surveillance, the use of databases and policing. The modern state has rapidly developed many forms of surveillance in just a few decades enabling it to observe, record, store and transmit information rapidly about people, their circumstances, their behaviour and their geographical location. CCTV is now routinely a feature of shops and shopping malls, public transport, public places (both in general and with respect to public meetings including demonstrations) and locations such as sports events. In addition, it is possible for government to monitor telephone calls and emails if they so wish. Further, data about many aspects of social functioning are stored in government databases, often without the knowledge of people whose personal circumstances and histories are now routinely recorded.

Social workers have to use various databases in their everyday practice either because they concern service users or, on occasions, themselves. The key databases currently are:

- the Criminal Records Bureau;
- two databases kept by the Independent Safeguarding Authority about people thought to be unsuitable for direct work with either vulnerable adults or children;
- ONSET (a database kept by the Home Office about children thought likely to offend at some point in the future);

- the National Pupil Database (containing data on family background as well as pupil behaviour, performance and attendance);
- medical records databases;
- the DNA base.

Liberty and other civil rights organizations have identified a number of concerns about such databases including the appropriate protection of privacy (for someone with HIV/Aids, for example), the retention of information that is either inaccurate or lacks relevance, the security of sensitive personal data (given a number of well-publicized leaks or losses and issues around who should have access to data), whether they are 'fit for purpose' and, finally, whether they are legal with reference to the 1998 Data Protection and Human Rights Acts.

It is now accepted that surveillance is but one part of a broader picture about how policing is to be conducted in a modern state, whether policing broadly is undertaken with the consent of the communities being policed and whether the form of policing and the allocation of resources in policing are commensurate with problems of criminality and disorder. One well-researched aspect of these concerns has been in relation to the possible *amplification of deviance* and the notion of a *moral panic*. Where moral panics occur policing resources tend to follow and, of course, wherever the police are sent they will inevitably find crime. Many black activists would also argue that the policing of black communities is further evidence of such implied discriminatory behaviour.

Anderson, R., Brown, I., Dowty, T., Inglesant, P., Heath, W. and Sasse, A. (2009) *Database State*. York: Joseph Rowntree Reform Trust.

T t

tacit knowledge the implicit, uncodified knowledge that is embedded in the experiences and practices of an organization's employees. Such knowledge has been formulated as the accumulation of skills that result from 'learning through doing'. From an organization and management point of view the challenge is how to articulate and pin down tacit knowledge before it leaves the organization in the form of personnel either retiring or leaving, and to be able to utilize it and exercise control over it. This leads to the paradox that organizations seek to make its tacit knowledge explicit – separating it in some way from the practitioners who have developed it and carry it day-to-day in their practice. Other strategies focus not on the control of tacit knowledge but on mobilizing it, drawing on it and co-ordinating it when needed to apply to difficult problems facing the organization.

Tacit knowledge is a critical asset for social workers' practice and is acknowledged in the extent of supervision, team discussions and case conference discussion, all forms of informal practitioner-held knowledge obtained through dialogue and conversation. It is also captured in phrases such as 'practice wisdom' and 'practice theory' – the ways of working based on experiences that practitioners carry in their heads.

Polanyi, M. ([1967] 2009) *The Tacit Dimension*. Chicago, IL: University of Chicago Press.

tragedy of the commons the phrase given to the dilemma that emerges when pursuit of individual self-interest undermines and eventually destroys co-operative effort, even when that co-operative effort would have produced more of what those individuals wanted than relying on their own efforts.

The dilemma is often illustrated in the following way. Imagine that a pasture for grazing sheep is open to all – the village commons. It is in the interest of all the sheep owners to maximize their income by grazing as many sheep on the commons as they can. In the early days when the villagers were poor the total number of sheep remained small enough so that all sheep could feed as needed on the grass available.

But as the village expanded and grew more prosperous, the number of sheep put out to graze increased – slowly at first and then dramatically. The inherent logic of the situation then moves remorselessly toward tragedy.

Imagine the commons now functioning near the limit. The rational sheep owner wants to maximize his return and so decides to send one more animal out to the commons for grazing. As an individual he will receive all the proceeds from the eventual sale of the fattened sheep. Now he may be aware that overgrazing is a possibility but if he is he will realize that the effects of overgrazing are shared by all the sheep owners and will not fall to him alone. Hence the benefit (economists call it 'utility') of adding another sheep outweighs the negative consequence of overgrazing (not enough grass, sheep not fat enough for market, etc.). It is only rational for him to add another animal and another and another . . .

Tragedy arises because this is the same conclusion reached by every rational sheep owner who shares the commons. Each is driven by a logic that compels him or her to increase the herd as fast and by as much as they can – on a resource that is limited. Thus the freedom to use the commons brings ruin to all because the commons eventually is depleted completely of grass to the point that no sheep can survive on it, let alone fatten for market.

While the illustration is drawn from rural life and a simpler economy, the calculation of the individual and the patterns of behaviour that emerge is strikingly relevant to contemporary economic life; it can be applied widely to the use of environmental resources, fishing, managing rivers, tourism, or to more complex social choices such as parental choice in schools, or using health services. The dilemma it exposes is universal – how to achieve a necessary degree of co-operation when the individual's immediate self-interest drives a calculation that undermines co-operation. The way to prevent the tragedy from running its full course is through educating participants in the necessity of co-operation or, in some cases, enforcing particular policies limiting use of the resources – limiting fishing catches is one of several examples.

typification a process by which individuals organize their knowledge of the social world. This conceptual process involves identifying the 'typical' features of any social phenomenon. It is an intrinsic part of **social constructionism**.

Unlike stereotypes, typifications are much more flexible and amenable to change in the light of experience. In addition, they help individual social actors make sense of their social environment and, in this context, help them to be able to predict the behaviour of others with a measure of confidence. For example, typifications might be interpreted by an individual as a situation of some concern, say where a child is playing near a busy road, where an individual is effectively 'assessed' to be an unsuitable babysitter, or where the partner of an abused woman is in a bad mood and likely to be abusive. (See also **personal construct theory**.)

U u

underclass the largely pejorative term applied now by conservative commentators, to those they regard as dependent on welfare, tending to petty criminality and drug addiction and prone to poor moral choices such as bearing children outside marriage and forming single-parent households. In the US the term has also acquired racialized connotation, referring by code to African American ghettos.

The term is widely associated with the work of Charles Murray who examined his definition of the underclass in his book on the American welfare system *Losing Ground*, published in 1983. He visited Britain on more than one occasion in the 1990s and reached a similar conclusion – that welfare systems create dependency and thus trap people on low incomes who nevertheless remain outside the labour market. While many social scientists have taken issue with his empirical work – which he combines often with unsupported generalizations about underclass behaviour – his work, and the work of those with broadly similar perspectives, has been extremely influential. Much of the coalition government's argument about welfare comes straight from this perspective, albeit that the word 'underclass' is not actually used.

For a time in the 1980s the concept of the underclass had wider application, backed by significant urban research. The African American sociologist William Wilson, for example, used it in relation to his thorough examination of the black ghetto in Chicago, an analysis that pointed out how deindustrialization and the loss of steady employment have consequences for the way individuals and families are formed and behave. One of Wilson's conclusions was hotly debated at the time by liberal academics – that 'race' was less important than economic deindustrialization in the plight of African American ghettos. Ultimately, Wilson abandoned the term underclass in the mid-1990s, conceding that the term had become 'hopelessly polluted in meaning' and a way of denigrating urban African Americans' culture and family structure.

Lister, R. (ed.) (1996) *Charles Murray and the Underclass: The Developing Debate*. London: Institute of Economic Affairs.

Wilson, W.J. (1993) *The Ghetto Underclass: Social Science Perspectives*. London: Sage Publications.

urbanization see **rural–urban continuum**

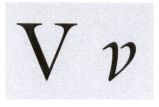

V v

validity see **research methods**

values moral standards or principles underpinning the beliefs and behaviour of individuals, families, groups, communities, cultural and ethnic groups, faith-based groups, political parties and social institutions including professions. Values are also, in a general sense, a statement of what is considered to be good or desirable.

Social work has had a sustained interest in values from several perspectives. As a profession it has sought to establish a code of practice to support the core objectives of social work as well as the behaviour of social workers in practice. Many of these guiding principles are to be found in different formulations in other professional codes for other occupational groups such as doctors or lawyers. The core ideas are to focus on the needs of the recipients of a service (patients, clients or service users), to do so in a way which promotes their interests and the interests of the wider society, and to be committed to improving practice so that the profession achieves wide public approval and support. These are admirable and widely understood values and principles, although there are sometimes problems associated with the public understanding of how social workers discharge these values, especially when trying to promote the interests of service users when their behaviour is a concern to carers, neighbours and the wider community. In such instances social workers operate in situations where their values come into conflict, for example, when they are required to protect vulnerable people and yet not be too intrusive in relation to family life and an individual's right to privacy.

Values also clearly underpin human rights although the implementation of human rights legislation is often contentious for the average citizen. The general principles on which, say, the 1998 Human Rights Act is founded are widely accepted, but people are then perplexed in its use for groups they find unsympathetic such as those imprisoned for acts of violence, or immigrants whose claims for asylum are hard to demonstrate because of a lack of supporting documentation or travellers camping in a local lay-by. The key aspect of the Act, as with other important international value statements such as the 1948 UN

Declaration of Human Rights or the 1959 UN Declaration of the Rights of the Child, is that human rights continue to be applied to everyone, although they may have committed an offence (that warrants some 'correction') or they are a marginalized group (and they are reacting negatively to being marginalized) or their legal status is not yet clear.

The value base of social work has also become distinctive because of its avowed commitment to anti-oppressive and anti-discriminatory practice. This humanitarian commitment of social work to solve problems and enhance **life chances** means that it has to engage with structures, cultures and individual beliefs and behaviours that oppress and discriminate against people often on grounds of 'race' and ethnicity, gender, disability, social class, age, sexual orientation and religious belief. Social workers are concerned to deliver services that are sensitive to the needs of diverse groups to ensure their inclusion, to routinely consult them on their needs and to ensure equal access to benefits and services based upon assessed needs.

Values often influence the way that social workers and service users interpret the world, formulate problems and potential solutions to problems. However, all this is contested territory, because many people take opposing or different views of key issues and often, by implication, the social worker's right to intervene. For example, what happens within the home is thought by many to be a private matter that should be of concern only to the people that live there. UK law takes the view that in matters of abuse the right to privacy is subordinate to the right to live free from ill treatment. Similarly the woman's right to choose whether to go through with a pregnancy or not is contested by those that argue the right of the unborn child to life. Others argue that 'mild' physical chastisement of children is reasonable whereas others regard such behaviour as assault because comparable behaviour between adults would constitute an offence. Social workers share some of these different beliefs and values; it is therefore important that they are conscious of these values and that they are prepared to continue to work with service users, and offer them the support they clearly need, even if the service user makes a decision that differs from the social worker's advice or convictions, so long as the resultant behaviour is within the law. A reflective social work practitioner will want to work in partnership with service users so far as is possible. Although there will be circumstances when legal authority will result in a social worker compelling a service user to do something, the aspiration is to minimize the occasions on which this is necessary and that, for the most part, it is possible to work with honesty on agreed agendas and goals even where there are differences of opinion and conviction. (See also **ideology**.)

Banks, S. (2006) *Ethics and Values in Social Work*, 3rd edn. Birmingham: British Association of Social Workers.

variable a social attribute, characteristic, quality or trait that can be measured and/or observed. The variable must be clearly definable and capable of being charted and recordable.

Key issues in relation to variables are as follows:

- The variable can be clearly operationalized, i.e. has clarity. Recording an individual's age, sex and social class is clearly easier than, say, their attractiveness to the opposite sex. Variables in this context need, first, to have *validity*: that the variable is an accurate or true representation of the social attribute. Second, variables need to be *reliable*: that is, that the measurement of the social attribute or characteristic is dependable and consistent.
- Some variables are *continuous*, which is that all measurements of a variable can be plotted on a continuum, for example age or income. *Nominal* variables refer to mutually exclusive categories such as marital status or ethnicity. Here variables are also construed as *discrete* because no individual can be in more than one category and the implication is that no category is to be regarded as 'better' than another. However, with *ordinal* variables such as income there is a clear implication that from highest to lowest positions are more or less favourable.
- Researchers usually think in terms of *independent, dependent* and *intervening variables*. For example, an experiment might be interested in the performance of girls compared with boys in a time-limited examination. The *independent variables* in this context would be the sex of the participants and the time allocated to the examination. The *dependent variable* would be the results of the examination in terms of the scores achieved by both the boys and the girls. An *intervening variable* might be whether students are allowed to take notes into the exam or not. The basic framework is one of trying to determine whether something *causes* something else; that the amount of time allocated to an exam has a bearing on the performance of boys and girls which may or may not be further influenced by having notes to hand or not. The possibility that, say, girls will out-perform boys, especially if notes are not allowed, might be explained by reference to existing knowledge about school performance and gender, but would still be formulated as a reasonable **hypothesis** to be tested. (See also **data, demography** and **hypothesis**.)

victim a person harmed, injured, killed or caused to suffer as a result of a criminal offence. Although the term victim is mostly used to refer to the individual immediately involved in the offence, it can also be more inclusive to refer to, say, wider kin related to a murder victim or those also affected as a consequence of a crime – say a family who lose a property because of arson.

Many commentators hold that the victim's perspective has only recently been recognized in the UK. The key dimensions to this recognition have been as follows:

- That victims can sometimes experience major psychological and emotional problems post-crime that can fundamentally affect social functioning and personal relationships. Post-traumatic stress disorder can be a reaction to crime for the victim, sometimes experienced immediately after the event but sometimes much later.
- That the victim's perspective can sometimes usefully be taken into account in pre-sentence discussions.
- That victims need to be kept informed about key developments – for example, the release of a sex offender back into the community in which the victim lives.
- That victims often need to be compensated for damage done to them and/or their property.
- That victims can sometimes usefully be involved in *restorative justice*, especially meetings involving perpetrator and victim or possibly the victim's family; meetings that would be orchestrated by a mediator. Such meetings can assist both perpetrators and victims if they work well, enabling perpetrators to begin the process of accepting the criminal nature of their behaviour and its impact on victims, and giving victims the possibility of beginning to understand the person within the criminal, a process that might make the thought of them less troubling.
- That victims need to be represented in any community safety forums (agencies that have a monitoring brief for the very particular patterns of criminal activity within a designated area) and working groups trying to address particular problems – such as domestic violence forums or race equality units monitoring racist crimes.

white flight the migration of white people as a result of a significant increase in the numbers of ethnic minorities in neighbourhoods, schools and other institutions.

Rapid changes in the ethnic composition of neighbourhoods can in fact result from multiple causes including changes in national immigration policies, the acceptance by any government of a substantial numbers of refugees and/or asylum seekers, the need for specialist workers because of skill shortages, free access to the UK from nationals newly admitted to the European Union and changes in the use of housing stock in urban areas.

The key areas of contention in the UK have been around education and the value of property. In relation to education, some white parents have become discomfited by a noticeable increase in the representation of ethnic minorities in the schools attended by their own children. Some have chosen to maintain social distance by moving to live in other areas or by moving their children to alternative schools. Reasons cited by parents for such moves have included a wish to have their child educated in a faith-based school based on Christianity. Others have expressed concerns about having a Christian-influenced education 'diluted' by a multi-faith curriculum. Where schools have had to accommodate a significant number of newly arrived immigrants, often refugees and/or asylum seekers, there can sometimes be issues about the resources needed to address the needs of children whose English-language skills are relatively poor and where these resources are perceived as being at the cost of pupils whose first language is English. In this context in the UK, the issue of education departments' requirement to support the notion of parental choice has seemingly been at odds with a local authority's duty to promote harmonious 'race relations' and to combat 'racial discrimination'.

In relation to property there is a belief among some white people in the UK that if an ethnic minority family move into a neighbourhood, the value of the white family's house will fall, and fall significantly if the newcomers move into the house next door. As an area becomes ethnically diverse this may become less of an issue following some kind of initial fall in property prices.

White flight can therefore be construed as arising out of concerns about 'cultural contamination' rooted perhaps in either prejudice or racist views and/or concerns about the economic costs of reducing social distance.

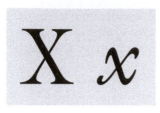

xenophobia a psychological condition or an ideology concerning a fear of 'outsiders' or strangers.

Politically, in Europe, such a fear has focused predominantly upon ethnic minorities, asylum seekers and refugees. Although xenophobia is regarded primarily as a fear of strangers and outsiders expressing cultural differences, racism expresses notions of biological inferiority in the outsider groups too. In practice, they often go hand in hand. The extreme discrimination currently being levelled at Roma communities in many countries in Europe, for example, appears to be an expression of both xenophobia and racist ideologies. And this is despite xenophobia being illegal in several formulations of social, economic and political rights in European Union legislation.

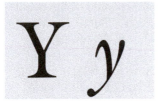

Y y

young offenders the broad term used to denote offenders who are generally between the ages of 10 and 18; the term may also refer to those who engage in delinquent acts but are under the age of criminal responsibility (which in the UK is 10).

The criminological literature has covered every conceivable theory as to why young people commit crimes. Offending has been attributed to: age and immaturity, a rational choice for monetary or short-term gain, lack of self-control, peer group influence and pressure, pursuit of excitement, pursuit of cultural or brand targets, lack of socialization in childhood, poor parenting, gang behaviour. (All such theorizing was on display following the riots in several English cities in the summer of 2011.) Conspicuously, such theories do not deal with cultural change or with the changing nature of institutions within which young people grow up. Neither does such theorizing come to grips with young women offenders who are far less numerous, are older when they do offend and in general express a greater wish to conform to social norms.

The problem of young offenders has been a long term concern to the public and government with an astounding degree of consistency in reactions that embrace both punitive and welfare perspectives. In general, there has been a slow recognition that children and young people should not be subject to the range of punishments that apply to adults. But the operative word here is *slow*: children under 18 were regularly sentenced to hang through the nineteenth century and while it is true that many sentences were commuted as the public grew increasingly uneasy with hanging children, many were not. The 1908 Children Act stipulated that a child had to be 16 years of age or older for the court to be able to sentence him or her to death. The last child to receive a death sentence was in 1932 although he was given a reprieve due to his age. The following year the 1933 Children and Young Persons Act raised the minimum age for a death sentence to 18. Across that same time span, however, there was recognition that work training in industrial schools and reformatories for delinquent youth was also necessary.

Offenders under 18 pose an age-old question: should children and young people who commit offences be treated as children in need or as criminals deserving punishment? The pendulum has swung first in one direction and then the other. Social policy of the late 1960s, for example, saw criminal behaviour as indicative of a child in trouble which could lead to the child being taken into the care of the local authority rather than punished explicitly. Even as late as the early 1990s, mainstream practice emphasized the importance of diverting young people away from the criminal justice system. Social workers were prepared to use multiple cautions for repeat offenders rather than recommend more serious punishments.

The murder of 2-year-old James Bulger in 1993 by two 10-year-old boys crystallized a swing of the pendulum in the other direction, a trend that was already under way among policy-makers and the public, to give young offenders a punishment proportionate to the crime they committed. Youth offending policy from the late 1990s onward not only presumed that from 10 years upward the delinquent youth was aware that she or he was committing a crime (reversing a century where the opposite was presumed) but also introduced social control functions in relation to young people that began to anticipate and prevent offending that authorities thought was likely to happen, rather than simply react to criminal behaviour by young people. Assessing risk factors within families – poor parental supervision, low feelings of guilt, unexplained school absences, association with peer delinquents – in the lives of cohorts of potential young offenders has become a major element in social science's approach to understanding youth crime.

Nowhere has the predictive and preventive approach been more apparent than in the expanding concept of anti-social behaviour – the acts of vandalism, rowdyism, fighting, graffiti and harassment which had become associated with young people in the public mind. There are competing perspectives concerning anti-social behaviour. One locates it as a function of community, pointing to the lack of informal social controls in a neighbourhood. This lack of capacity to uphold **norms** of behaviour produces a social vacuum that gives prominence to groups of young people – primarily but not exclusively young men – who in turn encounter no countervailing authority on the streets. A second perspective views anti-social behaviour as arising from particular family dynamics: the lack of parental supervision, parental rejection, erratic and harsh discipline, marital conflict, parental criminality and weak attachment are all significant predictors of anti-social behaviours, including drug use and offending.

Each approach has provided the rationale for numerous programmes that attempt to reduce anti-social behaviour. The first utilizes punitive responses such as anti-social behaviour orders (ASBOs), dispersal orders, or imprisoning parents for allowing their children to truant. The second develops intensive family interventions such as parenting programmes and programmes for intensive multi-systemic therapy. In the middle are mentoring schemes, car repair schools, community sports programmes and other efforts to engage and inspire young people in order to lead them to pro-social behaviour.

In a different account of youth offending, Monica Barry has linked it to the search for recognition, chiefly among peer groups, as young people negotiate the different and difficult phases of transition to adulthood (see **adolescence**). She rejects the notion of a 'trajectory' or 'career' in crime – terminology that implies a progression that may or may not burn itself out. Rather she adopts the French sociologist Pierre Bourdieu's concept of capital – social, economic, cultural and symbolic – and links offending to the need of young people to obtain durable and legitimate accumulation of symbolic and reputational capital. In the course of doing so, and on the basis of her interviews with serious young offenders, she looks again at how the peer relationship, far from simply one of adverse influences, is itself a source of capital. She cites earlier sociologists on reputation and identity, suggesting that disempowered individuals and groups are likely to focus on their immediate group for the development of identity and reputation, as an effective buffer against a hostile majority (Barry 2006: 2). While law-abiding behaviour only offers a reputation by default, display of deviance has a more profound and immediate effect on reputation.

For all this effect on reputation, however, it is important to bear in mind that young people are going through several stages of transition to adulthood, more prolonged and more difficult than in the past. While reputations are likely to be deliberately and rapidly cultivated, it is also likely that they are not sustainable as they negotiate their way: many young people will consciously discard deviant reputations in favour of more durable reputations associated with adulthood. Barry calls this *desistance* – the process in which offending as a course of behaviour is left behind. In this unfolding of behavioural choices, however, they are thwarted and thrown off course regularly by the extent of social inequalities, the youth justice system and perception of youth within the media and among policy-makers. Her basic argument is that young offenders, as all young people, aspire to social integration with positions of responsibility and trust. Offending is not a lifelong habit and investigating why and how they stop is as important a social science task as why they start. From this knowledge, a reciprocal and constructive approach – what society owes to young people as much as the other way around – to youth offending is possible.

Barry, M. (2006) *Youth Offending: The Search for Social Recognition.* London: Routledge.

Z z

zero-sum game see game theory

zero tolerance the notion that there should always be a firm response
to minor offending in order to prevent its leading to more serious
offences.

The theory was originally developed by American criminologists James
Q. Wilson and George Kelling in their article 'Broken windows' (1982),
referring to the idea that broken windows and graffiti in a neighbourhood – if not swiftly fixed and removed – convey a signal that public
authority and social norms no longer prevail in the area, leading to
further vandalism and an influx of criminal behaviour. By extension it is
argued that the police should bear down on minor crime and 'incivili-
ties' to prevent the development of criminal neighbourhoods.

This belief that even minor rule-breaking, if not challenged, is likely
to lead on to more serious offending has been highly influential in a
number of spheres. It has been a significant feature of policies to combat anti-social behaviour that favour firm early intervention in response
to minor offending by young people. This is the opposite of an
approach built on minimum intervention and the diversion of young
people *away* from the criminal justice system. This approach contends
that criminalizing anti-social behaviour too early is likely to provoke
worse deviant behaviour later on by labelling young people who may
only be going through a temporary and self-limiting phase of minor
misbehaviour which they will grow out of if left alone. However, in
certain types of offending, such as paedophilia and domestic violence,
there is wide recognition that zero tolerance is effective and necessary.

Kelling, G. and Wilson, J. (1982) Broken windows: the police and
neighbourhood safety, *The Atlantic*, March.

**AN INTRODUCTION TO SOCIAL WORK
PRACTICE**
A Practical Handbook

Melanie Parris

9780335238408 (Paperback)
2012

eBook also available

This practical workbook is written for social work students and includes both
theory and a range of exercises, providing a good foundation for the knowledge
and skills you will need for successful practice learning.

A variety of active learning features are integrated throughout the book. These
are designed to be worked through in sequence, so that the knowledge and skills
gained are steadily developed and consolidated.

Key features:

- Full of exercises, activities and case studies
- Unique in offering a balance of theory and practical exercises
- Can be used both in private study as an open learning pack and in
  classroom settings for small or large group work

www.openup.co.uk

OPEN UNIVERSITY PRESS
McGraw · Hill Education

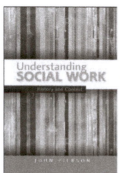

UNDERSTANDING SOCIAL WORK

John Pierson

9780335237951 (Paperback)
2011

eBook also available

The evolution of social work across the twentieth century offers a rich source of insight and inspiration for contemporary practice. It is essential that students new to social work understand how it has been shaped by past events and what this means for the future of social work and their roles as social workers.

This volume draws on archival material, social policy, normative theory and human rights doctrines to dissolve the border between past and present. Focused specifically on the UK, each chapter explains concisely how current practice was shaped by, and developed from efforts to build the 'decent society'.

Key features:

- Written in an accessible style and format that stimulates discussion
- Features case studies demonstrating specific approaches and styles of decision-making
- Contains exercises and extracts from the writings of prominent experts

www.openup.co.uk

OPEN UNIVERSITY PRESS
McGraw - Hill Education

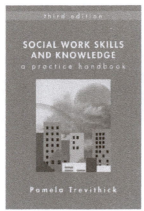

SOCIAL WORK SKILLS AND KNOWLEDGE
A Practice Handbook
Third Edition

Pamela Trevithick

9780335238071 (Paperback)
February 2012

eBook also available

Since its first publication in 2000, this best-selling text has been an invaluable resource for thousands of social workers preparing for life in practice. Written by an influential academic-practitioner, it is widely regarded as the leading book in its field.

Key features:

- 4 new chapters that integrate theory and practice in a Knowledge and Skills Framework
- 80 social work skills and interventions
- 12 appendices describing a range of different social work approaches

www.openup.co.uk   **OPEN UNIVERSITY PRESS**
McGraw - Hill Education